WORLD
PIECE

ALSO BY BETH M. HOWARD

Making Piece: A Memoir of Love, Loss, and Pie

*Ms. American Pie: Buttery Good Pie Recipes and
Bold Tales from the American Gothic House*

*Hausfrau Honeymoon: Love, Language, and
Other Misadventures in Germany*

WORLD
PIECE

A Pie Baker's Global Quest
for Peace, Love,
and Understanding

BETH M. HOWARD

MARGRETTA
PRESS

First edition
Published by Margretta Press
www.margrettapress.com

Cover design by Michelle Fairbanks

This is a work of creative nonfiction. While all the stories in this book are true, some names and identifying details have been changed to protect the privacy of the people involved.

Printed in the United States of America

For Doug

For those who will always live in my heart:
Tom Howard, Marcus Iken, Jack and Daisy,
Don Eakins, and Liselotte Kamer

For my hosts, friends, family, and followers
who supported me during my journey

For all immigrants seeking safety

And for all those who contribute to
making this a more peaceful world

AUTHOR'S NOTE

This is a memoir, which means the story is based on my personal experiences, perceptions, and opinions. For those of you mentioned in the story, forgive me if I didn't capture the events or conversations exactly as they happened—or as you recall. I have a terrible memory, which is why I have to write things down—and write memoirs. I referenced the journal, blog posts, emails, social media pages, and the photos I took throughout my journey, but I didn't have the time or energy to write down *everything*. Conversely, many stories and people got left out as I didn't have the space to include them (like the inspiring young architect in Mumbai, the friendly man at the Beirut shoe-repair who fixed the zipper of my carry-on at no charge, and the free-spirited archaeologist in Athens). I changed a few names in the book to protect privacy, but I did not change the chronological order of events to craft a more dramatic—or, dare I say, more optimistic—story (as some of my early readers suggested). The book has been vetted by a lawyer and several fact checkers, but world history—and world peace—is not an exact science. I just ask that you read this in the spirit intended: to educate, inform, entertain, and inspire—and to encourage generosity, openness, empathy, unity, and kindness.

The plain fact is that the planet does not need more successful people. But it does desperately need more peacemakers, healers, restorers, storytellers, and lovers of every kind. It needs people who live well in their places. It needs people of moral courage willing to join the fight to make the world habitable and humane. And these qualities have little to do with success as we have defined it.

—DAVID ORR, AUTHOR

Change is scary for many of us, yet it truly is, as the Buddhists say, the only constant. The better we get at facing and shifting with it, the more we free our minds and hearts for other things, like fun, love, and saving the world.

—MOLLY FISK, POET

If you don't know the guy on the other side of the world, love him anyway because he's just like you. He has the same dreams, the same hopes and fears. It's one world, pal. We're all neighbors.

—FRANK SINATRA

CONTENTS

INTRODUCTION

How to Make an Apple Pie and Change the World

I n the Before Times, in 2015, before COVID-19 when it was safe to travel—when it was safe to *breathe*—I packed up my rolling pin, a paring knife, two plastic mixing bowls, and the bare minimum of clothes for both summer and winter climates, and set off on a three-month, round-the-world journey in an altruistic, though possibly misguided effort to make pie in nine countries. Pie, I believed, could be a Trojan Horse for peace.

I had wanted to circumnavigate the globe since childhood. I don't know why. Where do anyone's dreams and desires come from? A mosquito of an idea enters your being, propagates in your cells, buzzes around in your brain with willful distraction, and no matter how much you try to swat it away it won't leave you alone until you take action—satisfy the itch, so to speak. Flying around the world in one go, hopping from one continent to the next, decorating my passport with a jumble of exotic stamps, living the pages of *National Geographic* instead of just looking at them, was something that had always intrigued me—before I worried about things like melting ice caps and carbon footprints. A few fellow travelers I met had done it. Books had been written about it, including one by an environmental journalist friend who, after a divorce, took his kids out of school to visit the earth's most endangered habitats; another by a guy declaring himself a grump searching for bliss. And, of course, there's the Jules Verne novel, *Around the World in Eighty Days.*

Verne's story was inspired by the first circumnavigation travel package for tourists organized by the Thomas Cook company in 1872, but that was more than three hundred years after the first person, Spanish explorer Juan Sebastián Elcano, made the full circle by sea in 1522, completing an expedition initially launched by Ferdinand Magellan in 1519. Magellan's motivation was to collect spices—pie spices like cinnamon, clove, nutmeg—and black pepper. In a time before refrigerators, these spices were as valuable as crude oil because they preserved food and masked the taste of spoiled meat.

Magellan's expedition was the first of many firsts. The first airplane flight around the world was in 1924, by eight U.S. Army pilots, and the first helicopter flight to circumnavigate the globe was flown by Ross Perot Jr. in 1982 at the age of 23. In 2002, Steve Fossett was the first to circle the planet in a hot air balloon, a feat he accomplished in only fifteen days—after six attempts. Others have traveled by bicycle, by sailboat, by rowboat, by foot, and by myriad other means. In 2004, British actors Ewan McGregor and Charley Boorman rode the "long way round" on all-terrain BMW motorcycles. In 2015, I merely aspired to strap myself into a coach-class seat on a commercial jet with my pie-making tools stowed in the cargo hold.

I wasn't vying for some unique travel hook or attempting to set an unclaimed record—this wasn't *Around the World in Eighty Pies*. I simply didn't want to travel as a tourist, touching down just to tick off an entry in *1,000 Places to See Before You Die*. I wanted a full-on immersion, to go places guidebooks couldn't take you, to learn about the people in each destination on a more personal level, and to give back in some meaningful way, more than by contributing a few American dollars.

Adding to the inspiration for turning my journey into a pie-making venture was an illustrated children's book called *How to Make an Apple Pie and See the World,* by Marjorie Priceman. A geography lesson in the guise of a search for pie ingredients, a young girl gathers eggs in France, flour in Italy, milk in England, cinnamon in Sri Lanka, sugar in Jamaica, and apples in Vermont. I had already been to all those places, except for Sri Lanka, but not for pie-related reasons. My search had been for language lessons in France, leather shoes in

Italy, afternoon tea in England, things-I-cannot-mention in Jamaica, and a ski weekend in Vermont.

I bought a copy of the kids' book just for its title, thinking it should be *my* title. For starters, I was a pie baker, predestined to be one even, as I was born because of pie. It was the banana cream pie my mom made for my dad that prompted him to propose to her. She knew it was his favorite and it worked, consequently embedding the pie gene into my DNA. I didn't learn how to make pie from my mom, however. She was too busy raising five kids, shuttling us to swimming, piano, ballet, tennis, cello lessons, and other activities. It was at the age of 17, while on a bicycle trip in Washington State, that I got my first pie lesson—when I got caught stealing apples from the tree of an old man who happened to be a retired pastry chef. I honed my skills over the years, graduating from a part-time pie-making job at a Malibu café, to running my own pie business in Iowa, to teaching pie classes whenever I got the chance. It's also worth noting that, like my mom, I baked pies for prospective husbands. I made so many, many pies whereas my mom had only needed to make one. Finally, right before I turned 40, I made a lattice-topped apple pie that led to marriage.

Besides being a pie baker, I was also a traveler and had been all over the world, but not around it, and not in one go. *One day*, I promised myself, *I will make it happen. And I will steal that book title the way I stole those apples from that old man's tree.*

A paperback edition of *How to Make an Apple Pie and See the World* sat on my shelf for a decade, collecting dust on its skinny spine, all the while taunting me, reminding me of my dream. *Come on*, its seductive combination of words called every time I browsed through my library. *Do it*, it urged as my hand brushed past it to pick out some other volume. *Go.*

But I didn't just want to make pie and *see* the world; I wanted to make pie and *change* the world.

My goal didn't seem far-fetched, because pie had changed me. Pie had saved my life—twice. The process of making pie—from mixing the dough with my bare hands, to rolling it flat and smooth, peeling the apples, and crimping the crust—was a moving meditation, a way to engage all of the senses, an activity that grounded me in the present. My first experience with this was when I left a grueling job as a web producer that drained my soul. I walked away from a six-figure salary to work as pie baker for minimum wage. The baking job drained my savings account, but its curative benefits were worth millions. Eight years later, pie brought me back from the brink after my husband died. Grief (complicated grief was the clinical term) had fought like hell to take me down, but pie helped me win the battle. I made pie for friends, for family, for fundraisers, I even handed out free slices of it on the streets of Los Angeles. By taking the focus off myself to bake for others, pie introduced me to people whose grief was greater than mine and the revelation that anyone could be suffering more than me shook me out of my self-pity. Pie was my therapist, my suicide prevention, my survival. I am not exaggerating when I say that butter, flour, sugar, and apples, along with the act of doing something nice for others, restored my will to live.

I had already tested pie's world-changing abilities in several countries. In South Africa, I taught pie making in a township to a hundred kids who lived in houses with no electricity. In Tokyo, I rounded up local ingredients like Fuji apples and rice flour, and baked with a group of Japanese business people who spoke no English. From Germany to Mexico, pie found its way into my travels, giving me an entrée into people's homes, cafés, kitchens, and conference rooms.

Pie, I had observed again and again, knows no cultural boundaries or language barriers. No matter where I went, no matter the age, nationality, or language spoken, making a homemade pie and then sharing it with others had the same results: the bakers beamed when their finished pies came out of the oven; they smiled for the camera as they posed for pictures with their pies; and they couldn't wait to take their pies home to share with their friends, families, and coworkers. I had seen the power of what a simple homemade pastry could do. Spending those few hours baking together, putting down phones and rolling up sleeves, setting differences aside and working together with a common purpose, not only creates something delicious, something tangible, it creates community. Internationally speaking, it's like the Olympic Games minus the competition with everyone on the same team. Pie unites people. Pie makes people happy. Give a man a pie, you feed him for a day, but teach a man to make pie, just think of the possibilities! If everyone, everywhere, were making and sharing pie, the world could be—*would be*—an exponentially happier place.

In my round-the-world trip, I would travel like a missionary, preaching the gospel of pie, spreading the religion of kindness, generosity, and goodwill. By representing America's wholesome and earnest qualities through comfort food, I also hoped I could give our eroding reputation abroad a positive boost. But in my role as pie evangelist, I wouldn't be imposing my cultural biases on anyone. I wouldn't claim that my pie is the best pie, the only pie, and that no other pie could lead to salvation, because pie is agnostic, non-partisan, and pie cannot be claimed by any single country or culture.

This may come as a surprise to some, but pie is not American. It's an immigrant whose origins can be traced to ancient Egypt, all the way back to 6000 BC, the New Stone Age, and has remained an integral part of human evolution ever since, proliferating in parallel with mankind. In the beginning, pie dough was made of a flour and water paste to preserve and transport meat—it was the Tupperware of its time—a trend the Romans expanded along with their empire.

Over the centuries, millennia really, pie evolved. Rather than being treated like cling wrap, the crust became edible, buttery, and filled with available foodstuffs like berries, nuts, vegetables, and eggs. The first recorded pie recipe was for a honey goat cheese pie and is said to be written on a stone tablet in Greece. Pie was embraced in France, where they preferred the single-crust tart style, before moving on to England, where apples first found their way into the dish. The English cookbook, *A Proper newe Booke of Cokerye*, written in 1545, described how to make pie dough by taking "fyne floure and a cursey of fayre water and a dysche of swete butter and a lyttel saffron, and the yolckes of two egges and make it thynne and as tender as ye maye."

The Pilgrims imported the recipes, along with smallpox, when they came to America in 1620. Pie, given its hearty nourishment, flexibility of ingredients, and ease of transport, endured with the pioneers, fanning out across the country by way of wagon trains, to become the iconic American symbol it is today.

During my three months of travel, I would not only teach pie-making classes but also explore the pies of other regions: Mexicans have empanadas; Italians, pizza and calzones; British and Australians, pasties; Indians, samosas; Greeks, spanakopita. If you go by the loose definition of pie—anything that consists of a filling encased in a crust, whether baked or fried, open-faced or folded over—every country in the world has some form of it.

I would sample as many as I could, learn how to make them, and listen to people's stories about baking and about life. Through this exchange of ideas, recipes, and food, we would forge new friendships, bridge cultural divides, and end up with, yes, world peace. I would call my mission "World Piece"—as in slice—and appoint myself as a pie ambassador. I was no social justice warrior. I'm not schooled in international affairs or politics or world history. Nor am I a trained pastry chef or culinary professional. I was just a bleeding-heart idealist with a nagging desire to travel with a purpose and give back to society in whatever small way I could. Making pie to promote peace and kindness would be that purpose. Bringing people together through pie would be that small thing I could contribute.

I kept stumbling upon films that fueled my world-travel fantasy. In *The Secret Life of Walter Mitty*, Ben Stiller's character travels his way out of his stale life. The Icelandic, soul-awakening skateboarding scene alone makes the movie worth watching. In *Hector and the Search for Happiness*, a therapist struggles to understand his patients until he confronts his own self-awareness by venturing to faraway lands and experiencing other cultures. Good-hearted to the point of naiveté, Hector inadvertently tries to date a prostitute, counsels a drug lord, and gets thrown into prison along the way. Quirky but inspiring. And in the documentary *Maidentrip*, a sixteen-year-old Dutch girl sails solo—solo, at sixteen!—around the world. I remembered being brave when I was sixteen, not nearly as brave as that Dutch girl, but I had been fierce, determined, and hungry for adventure, giving little thought to the things that could go wrong—like dying.

In spite of my desire, along with the proof that many others had circled the planet without falling off its flat edge, I had a long list of excuses for why I couldn't—or wouldn't—be able to take this trip.

For starters, I wasn't sixteen anymore. I was fifty-two, young and fit enough to get around, but old enough for the hard knocks of life to add up—and for fear to take hold. I had vowed I wouldn't become one of those people who grows more fearful as they age, but when your husband dies unexpectedly at the age of forty-three, as mine had six years prior, your worry quotient shoots way up. I had become afraid in ways I'd never expected from my previously strong self.

Marcus was traveling when he died, when his aorta ruptured without warning. What if someone else I loved died while I was on the other side of the globe? My parents were approaching eighty and I worried about them. They both had suspicious moles growing on their skin and needed surgery to remove them. What would the doctors find, if and when their insurance finally approved their treatments? I also worried about my little terrier, Jack. Jack was not just my dog; he was Marcus's and my dog. An athletic and willful Jack Russell–Yorkie mix, we got him as a puppy when we lived in Germany, and when I couldn't get pregnant, our dog became the child we never had. Jack had just turned eleven. What if he died while I was gone? The thought of losing him, and losing the connection to Marcus he represented, kept me from venturing out too far or too often. It was hard enough for me to leave him for a trip to the grocery store, but to travel as far away as I could possibly go without leaving the planet? And for three months? That was an Ice Bucket Challenge to my inner fire.

And what if I made another bad decision? My track record of recent choices was dismal. Eight months earlier I had moved out of my home, the American Gothic House (the little white farmhouse from Grant Wood's masterpiece painting) in Eldon, Iowa, where I spent the past four years rebuilding my life after Marcus's death. Still struggling with grief when I moved in, I elevated the healing power of pie to a whole new level by opening the Pitchfork Pie Stand, a little summer pie stand that grew into a big pie stand. In the off season, I held pie classes. I baked thousands of pies in the kitchen of that sweet old house. In the summers, I baked on the back porch, moving the oven outside like they did in the old days so I didn't melt the paint off the walls, or set off the smoke alarm as there was always something burning on the bottom of the oven. Between the quiet of country living, the charm of the historic house, and the massive amount of baking, I gradually worked my way back to well-being. But my success was also my demise. Some of the local residents were less than enthusiastic about the increased traffic my pie stand brought to the sleepy town. My pies had made countless tourists happy, but if I was out of pie or, god forbid, closed, they were quick to express their disappointment. The demands intensified after my cookbook was published. People could not get enough pie! Even with the extra help I hired and the generosity of volunteers, I could only make so many. I resorted to wearing a T-shirt that read "Make Your Own D*mn Pie," but that only made customers laugh and ask if they could buy a shirt along with a pie, so I had to make more T-shirts, too. I was so tired. But getting enough sleep was hard with travelers stopping at the tourist attraction in the middle of the night to take photos, their high beams pointed at the Gothic window—my bedroom window. And so, one August morning, four years after I moved in, I decided to move out.

I don't normally regret my decisions. Always look forward, not back, I say. Every life experience—good or bad—teaches you something in that "What doesn't kill you makes you stronger" kind of way. But my decision to move out of the American Gothic House resulted in a trifecta of loss of my home, my business, and my identity. And that was just the beginning of the hot mess I created.

I left Iowa to move back to Los Angeles, which was where I had been headed before taking what became a four-year detour in Iowa. En route to LA, Jack and my other dog Daisy, were attacked by a coyote outside of Dallas. Daisy, a street dog Marcus and I rescued while living in Mexico, was a white Jack Russell–poodle mix who looked like a sheep and possessed the street smarts of Oliver Twist with the docile demeanor of Winnie the Pooh. She was killed, and Jack almost died, escaping with puncture wounds encircling his neck like a ruby necklace. He recovered after spending a week—along with half my life savings—at an animal hospital. If I had lost them both, I'm not sure I'd have lived to tell this story.

Upon losing Daisy, my heart, having only just mended after Marcus's death, shattered all over again. I blamed myself for what happened to her and to Jack—and for every decision that led to it. How could I go around the world when I couldn't trust myself to make good choices anymore?

Even going back to Los Angeles had been a misstep. I was born in Iowa, but had spent the majority of my adult life either living in LA or using it as my base. I loved LA for its contrasts: its cosmopolitan lifestyle and proximity to nature; high-rises and hiking trails; martinis and surfing; platform sandals and flip flops. LA also fulfills my requirement to live near an international airport. So when I returned to LA after four years of rural living, I was surprised to find that my urban coping skills had been diminished. I could no longer shrug it off when a Prius with a "Save the Whales" license plate snagged my spot in the Whole Foods parking lot, or when my neighbor prattled on about her Botox injections. I couldn't live there again, but where would I go? Where was home?

I prided myself on being a free spirit and was normally comfortable with change. I had moved around so much my dad complained about my taking up too many pages in his address book, but this new wave of grief had dismantled my confidence. I would be leaving the country without a home to return to. And like Keiko (the orca in *Free Willy)* after being released back into the wild, I was ill-equipped to handle this new-found freedom. If I wasn't secure in my own skin, how could I feel safe out in the world?

There were also the concerns that accompany any big trip, compounded by being a woman traveling alone. Would I have enough money or energy? Would I be lonely? What if my plane crashed, or I had a car accident, or got sick, or mugged, or worse? How dangerous would it be? What if I got lost, more lost than I already was? These thoughts had me spinning on the wind like a fluff of dandelion seed.

There were plenty of reasons why I couldn't take this trip. Hell, just watching CNN would make even the most well-adjusted person want to stay home. But I had one big reason why I could: I had inherited Marcus's frequent flyer miles. All 420,000 of them. Marcus had racked them up traveling for his work as an automotive executive for Daimler, commuting between Europe, the U.S., and Mexico. For five years, I had been planning to use them for a round-the-world ticket, so I had been saving them. And saving them. But just like life, frequent flyer miles have an expiration date. I had to use them or lose them.

If I learned one thing from my husband's death it's that life is short. You can put things off until later, but there's no guarantee that later will come. I was sick of hearing myself talk about my dream—as was everyone else I had been telling about it over the years. It was time to make it happen. I was never going to have this kind of opportunity for free airline travel again, so with less than forty-eight hours before the miles expired, I booked my round-the-world itinerary—scheduling the maximum-allowed seven stops moving in one direction—all in a one-hour phone call.

But what happens when dreams become reality? Would my greatest fears be realized? Would everyone be okay while I was gone? Would I be okay? Would my efforts to promote peace have any impact? Would my faith in humanity be restored, along with faith in myself? Would I make it all the way around or give up along the way? And if I had known how it would all go—the illness, the missed flights, the monsoon, the meltdowns, the knife fight, the bombing, the pie thrown into the ditch—would I have ever boarded that first plane?

You can never foresee how things are going to go. No amount of planning, preparation, excessive worry, not even a travel insurance policy guarantees a smooth path. No matter how desperate you are for a clue, there is no shortcut to finding out what the future holds—no astrology chart or tarot-card reading can reveal what lies ahead. You can only take a deep breath and—*three, two, one, leap!*—trust that a net will appear out there somewhere.

CHAPTER 1

Ready for Takeoff

> All the art of living lies in a fine mingling
> of letting go and holding on.
> **—HAVELOCK ELLIS**

Things I do not recommend before starting a round-the-world trip:

1. Watching *Castaway*, especially when your first flight takes you over the same trans-Pacific route as Tom Hanks and you have no volleyball, only a rolling pin packed for company. Even if watching said movie offers an opportunity to spend time together with your dad the day before you leap into the unknown, you would be best advised to watch something else, anything that doesn't involve plane crashes.

2. Developing constipation. Stomach pain worse than a punch between the ribs from Oscar De La Hoya, and bowels seizing up to the point of shutting down—these are not ideal physical conditions under any circumstances, but to be in such ill health at the time of embarking on a three-month journey? That's bad luck and even worse timing. Make sure to pack plenty of stool softener and Pepto-Bismol tablets.

3. Eating wasabi peas to stay awake while driving from Los Angeles back to Iowa to drop off your dog at a friend's farm for the summer. These crunchy, spicy peas will indeed keep you alert, but one ill-timed bite will break a tooth and electrocute your brain with such an excruciating shock of

pain that you'll be forced to make an emergency stop at a rural Colorado dentist's office to extract the molar. This new gaping hole in your lower jaw means you can eat only scrambled eggs, bananas, and mashed avocado for the next few weeks and chew on one side of your mouth for the duration of your global culinary tour.

That is how my virtuous voyage of peace and pie began: newly toothless and scared shitless. This was going to be fun.

JUNE 1: LAX AIRPORT

"Couldn't you have worn something a little…nicer?" my mom said as she scanned the length of my body.

I looked down at my bib overalls, my cell phone, passport, and baggage claim stub filling the numerous pockets, the denim washed to a perfect softness, the pant legs comfortably loose for the fourteen-hour flight. "It saves space in my luggage. I'm wearing my boots, too," I said, pointing at my chunky-soled footwear.

"I think you look good, Boo," my dad said, nodding in approval.

"Thanks, Dad."

The international departures terminal at LAX was a beehive of activity with chatter and loudspeaker announcements droning, while travelers representing every inch of the globe swarmed the ticket counters. I wouldn't have had to travel farther than LA's airport to get an international experience. I could have just set up a pie-making work station next to the Lufthansa check-in. There were families speaking Spanish, surfers packing their boards into padded bags, school groups with matching T-shirts heading to Europe, couples leaving on honeymoons. And then there was me. In my overalls. With my rolling pin packed in my wheelie bag and my parents sending me off like a little girl going to summer camp. Except I was no longer young and not going to summer camp; I was a depressed, menopausal woman traveling to nine countries to make pie and promote world peace.

I'm the middle child of five kids, and along with the pie-making gene, I inherited more wanderlust than my four siblings combined. My parents had driven me to the airport for almost every major excursion I had ever taken: Hawaii when I was thirteen; Europe when I was twenty-two; Thailand at twenty-three; Kenya at twenty-four; and that was just the beginning. We'd had countless goodbyes when I flew back and forth to Germany during my marriage to Marcus. But this time felt different, heavier. We were all older now. My parents were in their late seventies. They were in relatively good health—unlike me, they still had all their teeth—but my dad had suffered a few mini strokes and was in a continual battle of Whac-A-Mole with the melanoma spots that kept cropping up on his bald head.

As for me, I was not traveling as light as I used to, carrying the weight of my grief, the load growing increasingly heavier with each loss. I was also burdened by baggage of the physical kind, packing far more than I normally—or sensibly—would. I had written a pie cookbook a year earlier and was bringing ten of the hardcover volumes to give as gifts, along with a dozen aprons printed with the World Piece logo an artist friend designed for me. The hand-drawn art—a blue and green earth with its round edge made to look like a fluted pie crust and a slice carved out of it, revealing a bright red cherry filling—was as whimsical as the notion of my trip. I had a box of business cards with the logo adding even more weight to my bag. As if hauling a rolling pin around the world wasn't enough.

My dad pushed my luggage cart forward, fighting its squirrelly wheels, playing bumper cars with the stanchions. He looked so cute in his signature seaman's cap, and his perpetual cheerful smile flashed at me whenever I looked over at him. My mom stood nearby in her matching shoes and purse, her silence no disguise for her maternal instinct to worry. We made small talk as we inched our way through the serpentine to the ticket counter, smothering the big feelings that big goodbyes invoke.

"Make sure you let us know when you get there," my mom said for the tenth time.

"I will. I'll Skype with you as soon as I get an internet connection," I assured her.

She nodded and was quiet a little longer. Then, to make conversation, she asked, "How's your stomach?"

"It's a little better," I said. "It still hurts, but I finally pooped." This was no joke. I had never had such a bad bellyache. For two weeks I had pain in the upper reaches of my stomach all the way into my throat, and my GI tract had shut down almost entirely. It had become the primary topic in recent text messages with my family, everyone invested in tracking my bowel movements, or lack thereof. "I left my bottle of MiraLAX for you, Dad."

He laughed his deep, playful laugh which made me laugh, grateful for the moment of levity, because I was scared as hell, more terrified than ever of leaving home. Home. Whatever that meant. With no idea where I would live when I returned, one of my personal missions for the trip was to look for the answer to the question, Where is home? I hung onto a fantasy of falling so deeply in love with a place—or a person—while traveling that I would stay. Though who was I kidding. As I had learned so many times before—in the way I met Marcus after taking a last-minute turn to Crater Lake National Park, and the way I discovered the American Gothic House was for rent by taking a six-mile detour—you can't find the answer by looking for it; you have to let *it* find *you*.

My mom may not have approved of my travel clothes, but she did not object to me taking this trip. I had expected her to be one of the first naysayers with objections like, "It's too dangerous," and had prepared myself for this reaction. But a few days after I broke the news, she emailed me on a Sunday morning after watching Joel Osteen's latest sermon. The television preacher was a new addition to my parents' lives and though my mother did not fully embrace Osteen's message of praying for profit, my dad watched faithfully and, I had to confess, some of the missives about overcoming loss and experiencing "explosive growth" had given me a boost.

In her email she wrote:

> *Joel talked about taking risks and not being afraid,*
> *just the things you've been aware of needing to do, too. Your*
> *change of 'energy' since making the decision makes it 'very*
> *apparent' that you are 'moving in the right direction,'*
> *though as we both know, there will be 'times' when you*
> *will wonder. Shake those 'feelings' off when they come and*
> *just stay focused on your 'plan,' and on the new people and*
> *opportunities that lie ahead. I'm off to noon mass soon so*
> *must get dressed. Enjoy your day. It's warming up outside*
> *after a very cool and overcast start here.*
>
> *Love, Mom*

I had smiled at her frequent use of single quotation marks for emphasis and how she included the weather report, given I was staying in a guesthouse only six miles away. My eyes welled up as I read her loving message, and I was encouraged by her show of support. I certainly needed it, because after the euphoria of booking my itinerary receded, the tsunami of self-doubt—and stomach cramps—came rushing in to take its place.

It was finally our turn at the ticket counter and my dad heaved my bag onto the scale. This is the part of check-in I was dreading. I watched the digital readout as the numbers flashed; I knew it would be close. "You're ten pounds over the limit," the agent scolded.

"I'll take some things out," I said, already unzipping my bag. With the agent peering at me over the top of her glasses, I moved my pie cookbooks into my carry-on, one at a time, watching the numbers on the scale creep down until my beast of a suitcase—a sports-gear bag on wheels—weighed in at 49.9 pounds, one ounce under the limit. No matter that my carry-on was now heavy enough to dislocate a shoulder; I just hoped they wouldn't weigh it as there was a limit for that, too.

We proceeded to the next line, the one that separates those leaving from the ones left behind. As other travelers eagerly passed by, boarding passes in hand, we stalled for time, lingering by the sign that warned, "Ticketed passengers only beyond this point."

Why was it so hard to say goodbye?

"Okay, well, I guess this is it," I said.

My mom hugged me first. I felt her slight, bony frame in my embrace. Even without the added height of my motorcycle boots, she was shorter than me by several inches, shrinking more with each passing year. I pressed my face against her cropped, brownish gray hair, breathing in her scent—Dial soap mixed with Windsong. Holding onto her longer than I normally would, the thought that had plagued me ever since I booked my ticket raced through my mind: *Please don't die while I'm gone.* That she had just purchased her crypt at the Cathedral of the Lady of Angels did not make me feel any better.

My mom fought back her tears, but mine flowed freely. "Your Grandma Ida had a hard time with goodbyes, too," she said, as if to make an excuse for my public display of emotion.

I didn't need an excuse. I had every reason to bawl my fucking eyes out. I was heading out into the world, an increasingly unstable place filled with weapons of mass destruction and people eager to use them. Where young schoolgirls were getting kidnapped by the hundreds. Where explosive vests were the fashion of the day. And where thousands of people were piling into leaky boats to escape one continent in hopes of finding a better life on another, many of them drowning on the way. But at that very moment I wasn't thinking about the perils that might await me. I was only thinking of how hard it was to leave the people I cared about most, the people who raised me and gave me the wings to fly.

"Onward and forward, Boo," my dad said, drawing me into his bear hug, the shoulder of his shirt turning dark from my tears. "We'll have a hot fudge sundae when you get back." He celebrated everything with either a three-olive martini or a hot fudge sundae, his favorite dessert after banana cream pie.

I waved to my parents as I rode the escalator up one flight to security. Locking my eyes onto them with laser-beam focus, I looked down at the cute, long-married couple who smiled and waved back at me as my body traveled upward on the moving stairs. The pull to them stretched like a rubber band, resisting the growing distance, straining to return to its safe resting state, tugging and stretching until—SNAP!—they disappeared from view.

The second they were out of sight I snapped, too, my Hoover Dam collapsing to spill a Lake Mead of tears. I cried as I plodded through the long line at TSA. I was still crying when I held my arms up in the body scanner. Tears blurred my vision as I made my way into the terminal, passing the overpriced fast-food restaurants, designer boutiques, and magazine stands. To keep myself from turning around and running back into my parents' arms, I gave myself a pep talk. *You are so brave. You are the bravest person I know. You are Xena the Princess Warrior. Or is it Xena the Warrior Princess. Why can't I remember that? Whatever. You are strong and brave.*

I kept the positive self-talk going until, somewhere in between the coffee kiosks, the drinking fountains, and my gate at the farthest end of the terminal, my tears stopped. With each step forward, the anxiety and my morbid imaginings were nudged out, replaced by a hint of excitement for what—and who—I might find.

Once I boarded my flight—the first of many over the coming months—I buckled myself into my seat and guzzled half the water from my bottle. *This was always your dream. You can do this.* We taxied to the end of the runway, the engines revving in sync with my anticipation, and then we were moving. The palm trees, framed by my window, whizzed by in an animated film strip, the speed growing faster and faster and faster until we untethered from the earth and launched into the sky. *Here we go. You're committed now.*

CHAPTER 2

New Zealand

> Grant that I may not so much seek to be
> consoled as to console, to be understood as
> to understand, to be loved, as to love.
> —ST. FRANCIS OF ASSISI

I planned my trip in a westward direction. This was based on the advice of a well-traveled friend. I don't remember his reason for suggesting that way; I only remember that I was seeking guidance in the early stages of planning. But it made sense. I would do the easy stuff first—start with the English-speaking countries of New Zealand and Australia. Sandwich the more exotic, more daunting ones like Thailand, India, and Lebanon in the middle. And end in Europe, going to Greece, Switzerland, Hungary, and, saving the hardest one for last, Germany. Hardest, because Germany is where my late husband Marcus was from, where we had lived for the first three years of our marriage, and where his ashes are buried. I would go to his grave, thank him for making my trip possible, and say a final goodbye so that I could move forward with my life. Because for as much as I had worked on letting him go, I was still holding on. I had finally put our wedding rings away, but I was still wearing his chunky silver ring, still carrying his picture in my wallet, and still keeping boxes of his belongings in my closet. He took up space in every relationship I had attempted since his death. Which is why there was another personal pursuit I hoped to achieve on my journey, the thing that the sudden and unexpected death of a loved one doesn't give you: closure.

I had been to New Zealand once, nineteen years earlier, and I am one of the few people in the universe who wasn't smitten with it. Probably because it rained the whole time. Wet clothes and constant shivering make it hard to appreciate even the most awe-inspiring beauty. The country, made up of two main islands and hundreds of smaller ones, is mostly wilderness and farmland, and can be described in precisely three shades: green, with its well-nourished grasses and orchards; blue, with its pristine lakes and sea; and white, with its icy glaciers and sheep. I have never been to a place other than the Sahara Desert that is so sparsely populated, though southeast Iowa could rival it for its dearth of humans. Nor have I ever experienced a place so rugged and remote. Even the Sahara, with its camel caravans hauling salt, bustles with more activity. If Australia is considered Down Under, then New Zealand is so much farther down it no longer feels attached to the earth. It's the reason tech billionaires are buying up land (though New Zealand is proposing changes to stop this), because not even fallout from nuclear war can reach it. The absence of people had unsettled me, tapping a vein of deep-seated loneliness, the existential despairing kind that makes you feel like you're the last human alive. I'd had that feeling once before, when winter camping in the Wind River Range of Wyoming, a frozen world of nothing but stillness, silence, and snow. It was not a feeling I ever wanted to have again.

So why the hell was I going there? Because I had established a few rules for my trip. The first was that my journey would not be about the places; it was about the people. Charity Nelson was the reason I was heading to New Zealand.

Charity knits prayer shawls the way I make pies, weaving loving thoughts into her work "to transfer positive energy," she says, and then sending her finished pieces to people to comfort them. She found me on Facebook after reading my memoir about how making and sharing pie helped me heal from the grief of losing my husband, and mailed me one of her shawls. "It's pie colors," she wrote in her note. After reading this, I looked more closely at the rows of yarn, examining the combination with a more open mind. "The tan color represents the crust," she said, "and the purples, light greens, blues, and magenta are the hues of berry pie." Yes, I guess it was like a pie, if you stretched your imagination. I wasn't sure what ingredient the purple fringe ends translated to, but still, there was magic woven into those wool threads because wrapping myself in the warmth of that shawl felt like a hug from Charity.

After she sent the prayer shawl—it had arrived in my American Gothic House mailbox two years before my trip—we talked on the phone several times, with some of our calls stretching two hours. I would sit on my front porch in Iowa with Jack and Daisy, a cup of coffee in hand, charmed by Charity's thick New Zealand accent, listening on my cell phone a hemisphere away as she talked, and talked, and talked. Charity is well read, and as she described books like Patti Digh's *The Geography of Loss*, it was clear she appreciated themes with a spiritual bent. "Patti writes about Kintsugi, the Japanese art form of repairing a broken vase. The cracks are filled with gold, making the piece more beautiful than before it was broken," she explained. Charity's oratories about Japanese wabi-sabi philosophy and everything else, were always delivered in a rapid-fire high pitch oozing with enthusiasm, and were as well-meaning as her knitted shawls. Which is why I didn't feel like I was flying fourteen hours to meet a stranger; she was already a friend.

I would have skipped New Zealand, not just because of my previous lonely and near-hypothermic experience there, but because this country had little need for my peace mission. Meager as my efforts were, I genuinely hoped I could make a difference. But New Zealand? It's one of the top five most peaceful countries in the world according to the Global Peace Index.

The Global Peace Index is an annual report produced by the Institute for Economics and Peace that uses data-driven research to rank 163 independent states and territories according to their level of peacefulness influenced by cultural, economic, and political factors. It measures "negative peace," which is the absence of violence and the absence of the fear of violence," not just the absence of war. Ultimately, though, the goal of the GPI is to promote "positive peace" by determining what institutions, attitudes, and structures we should be investing in to strengthen or maintain world peace.

In spite of New Zealand already ranking second as the most peaceful country in the world (Iceland is always number one), when Charity offered to host me after seeing a social media post about my trip, I said yes without hesitation. I would give it another chance. In New Zealand, I rationalized, I could learn about their meat pies and get an education in pie ingredients, like apples. If I was going to "make an apple pie and see the world," I would go to the country where Granny Smith apples originated. (It wouldn't be until I got there that I'd learn their true origin.) A variety well-suited to pie due to its tartness and firmness, I always used Granny Smiths for my pie stand. By sticking to one type of apple, I could assure the consistency and quality of my pies—that is when I wasn't forgetting to add sugar or burning them.

My flight touched down in Auckland at 6 a.m. The sky, a watercolor smeared with dark patches of rain, was so gray I could barely make out the city from my window seat. But before my seasonal affective disorder had a chance to set in, the Maori gods offered their immediate reassurance, throwing spears of sunbeams through the cloud cover to greet me with a rainbow. The first stop on my three-month trip and I was already landing on the pot of gold? Maybe it was a sign. Maybe New Zealand would feel different this time.

I pushed my luggage trolley out from customs and scanned the crowd for Charity. I had never met her, but I knew roughly what she looked like from her Facebook pictures: seventy years old and plump in a comforting mama-bear way, with gray hair bluntly cut in a page-boy style that framed her round, freckled face. She would have been easy enough to spot given the small number of people waiting—Auckland's airport was a fraction of the size of LAX—but I saw no one who even closely resembled her, no matter how much I squinted and projected my wishful thinking onto them.

I changed money at an exchange desk and stumbled in my jet-lagged stupor over to the nearest coffee kiosk, where I was faced with the first of the many perplexing questions I would encounter in my travels: What is the difference between a café latte and a flat white? The answer, the barista told me, is that when espresso drinks like the cappuccino were introduced to New Zealand, people didn't like all the foam on top; they liked the milk, but preferred it, as the name suggests, flat.

Apart from the English accent that was stronger than my latte, the pastel-colored currency, and the headache reminding me of my jet lag, it didn't yet feel as if I had left the U.S. In the sci-fi novel *Pattern Recognition*, William Gibson writes, "Souls can't move that quickly, and are left behind, and must be awaited, upon arrival, like lost luggage." It wasn't science fiction, it was true—my soul was still bouncing around in the late-night turbulence we encountered somewhere over the Pacific.

An hour passed. The coffee offered no help in fighting my fatigue, and my stomach ached worse than before I left. I wanted to flop face down on my pile of luggage and sleep, but since the flight announcements blaring over the loudspeakers ensured I wouldn't doze off, I sat on top of my wheelie bag parked next to McDonald's and watched families and businessmen wolf down Big Macs and French fries for breakfast. Ah, McDonald's. If I ever missed the U.S. during my travels, I would always be just one Egg McMuffin away from a taste of home.

There weren't enough people milling around the airport at this early morning hour to satisfy my voyeurism, so to pass the time and fend off the worry that Charity might not arrive (had we forgotten about crossing the International Date Line and confused the dates?), I scrolled through pictures of Jack on my phone.

Leaving my parents was hard, but leaving Jack was almost harder. If my soul had not yet caught up to my body, then my heart was even farther behind; so far back it never got on the plane. Jack, however, would not be pining for me. A thousand-acre farm is a dream for a fifteen-pound terrier who thinks he's a Lab. Even better when that farm comes with a farmer named Doug who can spare a few hours for a daily game of fetch, a leash-free walk through the cow pastures, and a swim in the pond. One hundred percent male terrier, Jack was a handful. He liked to chase things—squirrels, bunnies, cats, deer, motorcycles. He liked to bark. A lot. For hours. Especially at night, loud enough and long enough to wake an entire neighborhood. Fortunately, the closest house to Doug's was a mile down the gravel road. It took a certain kind of person who could handle Jack, tolerate him, and maybe even enjoy having him around for three whole months. Doug was that person. So while I was hauling myself across twenty-four time zones, disturbing my rhythms, Circadian and otherwise, Jack would spend his summer at "Camp Doug." I spent a week on the farm before starting my round-the-world trip from LA and had seen how visibly happy Jack was, happier than he had been since Daisy died. I could take solace in that.

Doug had been sending me pictures and videos of Jack every day since I left him in Iowa, which had been . . . was it only three days earlier? It felt like three weeks. I replayed his first video, watching Jack stick his head out the truck window, his long black and brown hair blowing straight back, his nose twitching to better savor the pungent scents of country life, predominantly pig manure—a smell so strong you can taste it in your mouth. In the next video, Jack was chasing Doug's dog, Mali, a white and red spaniel mix, a veteran farm dog who would teach Jack where to find rotten skunk carcasses to roll on and what to do if he actually ever caught a squirrel. They were doing high-speed laps around the lilac bushes, and Jack, in spite of being half Mali's size, was outmaneuvering her with the quick turns of a Chicago Bears running back.

I put my phone away to keep my battery from dying and pulled out my journal. In between the pages was the card Doug handed me as I was leaving. On the front, a dog gazed out over the Grand Canyon as if contemplating the wonder of such an expanse. I was impressed that Doug had found a card so fitting for me, especially impressive considering the only place to buy a greeting card in his corner of rural Iowa was the gas station. I read it again for the fourth or fifth time. "I will take good care of Jack," he wrote. "You have confidence and wisdom. Go share that with others, and come back safely so you can tell your stories."

Along with the card he had handed me a stack of crisp one-hundred-dollar bills.

"A thousand dollars?" I had gasped. "Are you crazy? Doug, this is—"

"I will never be going around the world," he interrupted, "and I'll probably never know anyone else who does. You're not going on vacation. You have a purpose and I want to support you in your travels."

Doug. A third-generation farmer with hair as red as copper, muscles as hard as iron, nerves as unbendable as steel, and values as solid as granite. He has the innocence of Opie Taylor, the manners of Mr. Rogers, and the brains to offset his brawn. He chairs an education foundation granting college scholarships to local high school students, subscribes to *The Economist* and *The New Yorker*, and donates regularly to public radio. We had had a short romance a year earlier. I stayed with him for two months after moving out of the American Gothic House, but I was convinced that my nomadic, city-girl ways could not mesh with those of a man married to the land. I disappointed him deeply when I left for California. And yet, when I called to ask if he would take care of Jack for three months, he readily and graciously said yes. That was Doug.

I tucked the card back in the envelope and rubbed the spot between my ribs where the pain persisted. I looked up just as a large woman came barreling toward me, her arms outstretched, and before I could say a word, she grabbed me in a welcoming embrace.

"I'm sorry I'm late I had a flat tire and I called the tow truck but they didn't come and a man stopped and helped me but then the spare tire was flat and finally the tow truck came and we got it fixed but it took longer than we thought I'm so glad you made it now let's get your things oh I see you're wearing your prayer shawl I'm making one for a woman in Canada who has cancer I'll take you on a tour of Auckland and show you the sites before we head to my house that's an hour to the north and we can get fish and chips on the way but we can also get pie we have good pie here like mince pie and lamb pie but we'll have time to try plenty of different kinds come my car is just outside let's go."

I wiped the tears that had spouted from my eyes. Tears of relief that I had arrived safely. Relief that Charity had shown up to rescue me. Relief that this journey I had been dreaming about for years, and planning for the past two months, was finally beginning.

Orewa (pronounced "Oh-ray-wa") is a small seaside town about an hour north of Auckland with a population of ten thousand. It's close enough to the city that it's considered a suburb, but far enough—and beautiful enough with its three-kilometer-long sandy beach—to also be a vacation destination. But no one vacations here in June. In the southern hemisphere June is winter, which would require me to wear every single item of clothing I brought, all at the same time. I couldn't wait to tell my mom how glad I was that I'd worn my bib overalls since I could fit my tights *and* yoga pants underneath them, though I would leave out the part about the buttons and clasps setting off TSA's metal detector. I would also let her know how much I appreciated the new hooded raincoat she bought me for the trip, as I would rarely take it off for the next ten days.

Charity lives a few more miles—er, kilometers—north of Orewa. Just two blocks inland from the beach, her village is nestled in a valley surrounded by an everything-bagel forest—a mix of tropical, coniferous, and deciduous trees, with a few palm trees sprinkled in. Rain clouds hung in ragged patches over the clusters of modest houses, muting what should have been vibrant hues of greens and blues into fifty shades of gray.

As we pulled into her steep driveway, she pointed up at her wooden house and said, "Welcome to the Christmas Cottage."

I dragged my suitcase along the wet sidewalk leading to a side door, and up the steps of a narrow stairwell crowded with household objects from watering cans, to empty jars, to rain boots. Inside the living room, floor-to-ceiling shelves sagged under the weight of all her books. It was Charity's voracious appetite for reading that brought us together, and as I cocked my head to read all the titles on the spines, I wondered how many other authors she corresponded with.

"I've been working for a week to tidy up for you, but I ran out of time," she offered as explanation for the mound in the middle of the room covered with a white sheet. "I'm not used to having guests."

"No worries, Charity. I'm just grateful to be here."

"And this is where you can sleep," she said, pointing to a corner nook where a single bed was wedged between a bookshelf and a sky-filled window.

Just off the kitchen was a sunroom with a well-worn armchair surrounded by stacks of more books, reading glasses, empty tea cups, and baskets of knitting. "Let me show you what I'm making now," she said darting over to pick up a fuzzy cascade of black, red, yellow, and orange stripes hanging from her needles. "It's for a woman in Canada who has cancer. The colors represent . . ." I didn't hear the rest because I was distracted by the piñata explosion of objects that filled the room—teddy bears, angel ornaments, collectible trinkets, plastic tchotchkes, and shopping bags overflowing with even more stuff. "I like to give gifts," she said. This must have been why she called her house Christmas Cottage: She was Mrs. Claus.

Cluttered and crowded as it may be, her house was cozy. It was also cold. In New Zealand older homes like this one are not insulated. Even with a space heater, warmth didn't stand a chance of winning the war against winter's dampness.

"Now then, are you hungry? Let's go get some fish and chips in town. We'll have a picnic at the beach."

A picnic? What? It was raining. I was jet-lagged and too tired to go out, but I was also hungry and my stomach was making a racket loud enough for Charity to hear. In spite of not being able to poop anything out, I could still take food in. "Fish and chips sounds great," I said.

"First I have to show you something!"

I wanted to protest and ask if it could wait, but she had already hurried over to the nook by my bed. "It's here somewhere. I'll find it." She rummaged around for several minutes, tossing books and dog-eared magazines aside. "Oh yes, this is it," she announced and pushed a cassette into the VCR.

On the screen appeared a nun in full habit and thick glasses, though distracting from everything else were her teeth. "She's got a class II malocclusion," my dad, a dentist, would say of the overbite. He was always diagnosing cases when we watched TV and would add, "I could easily fix that."

"I'm Sister Wendy," she said, introducing herself in a British accent, "and I'm here at the Art Institute of Chicago where we are going to look at Grant Wood's masterpiece." And there it was, in the background of the painting, the American Gothic House.

The pangs in my stomach were no longer about hunger or constipation. That painting portrayed what I had left behind, my old life in Iowa. My life before I made all those bad decisions, took all those wrong turns. *If I hadn't moved out of that house . . .*

A wave of pain surged between my ribs. But before I let myself dwell on the things that couldn't be changed, I quickly reminded myself that if not for those decisions, good or bad, I would not be here. And *here* was a whole world ahead of me offering new territory to explore, new possibilities, a new life. As much as I missed that little white farmhouse, wishing things had gone differently, wishing Daisy were still alive, I could not go back. Forward was the only direction—if for no other reason than it's the only option a round-the-world ticket gives you.

"I found it while I was cleaning," Charity said. "I thought it might be some kind of divine message."

What message would that be? That you can never outrun your past? That I still have unresolved grief? I didn't need a divine message to be reminded of that. No, Sister Wendy was merely highlighting *American Gothic* in her art history program because it's the second most famous painting in the world after the Mona Lisa, and the number one most parodied.

"That's very cool," I said. "But could we watch the rest of it later? I might pass out if I don't get something to eat."

"Yes, yes, of course. Now let me just find my keys."

The fish and chips café, tucked in between a cluster of buildings near the Orewa waterfront, was carryout only—*take-away*, in the local vernacular. It wasn't busy, probably because of the rain, even though a scissor blade of sunlight had just cut through the gray and black patchwork quilt overhead.

While waiting for our meal, I studied the map of New Zealand on the café wall. I had pored over maps during my planning stage, which was as effective as identifying craters on the moon without a telescope. Now that I was traveling, boots and rolling pin on the ground, all those squiggly lines and random dots—rivers and roads, small towns, and tiny outer islands—came into focus. I found the places I had visited nineteen years ago when I was on the South Island: Queenstown, the Milford Sound, and the Southern Alps. That part of New Zealand was an outdoor adventurer's holy grail, if you didn't mind sleeping on the ground in a bivy sack in the rain as I had done. This time I was on the more populous North Island, and according to the map, Charity and I would be covering two-thirds of it to get to the apple-growing region, but not reaching its southernmost point where the capital city of Wellington sits.

How would this leg of the journey go? I wanted to hurry up and find out, not just in New Zealand, but in every country on my itinerary. A burning sensation rippled through my chest at the reality that this was only day one out of ninety. If I looked at it in terms of months, it was only three, a much more digestible number. Still, the magnitude of what I had committed to nearly made me collapse right there under the florescent lights. I hoped it was just hunger and jet lag causing my panic attack and that I would feel better after eating, and sleeping. Inhaling deeply to steady myself, only to be overcome by the greasy fumes of frying fish, I recited my mantra: *Stay open.*

Stay in the present. Don't judge. Along with prioritizing people over places those were the three other rules I had set for my trip—and I had broken all three of them within the first few hours of arriving. *Stay open. Stay in the present. Don't judge.* I repeated it over and over, willing the words to sink in, until I was suddenly interrupted.

"All right then. Let's go have a picnic!" Charity announced as she carried our order out to the car. We drove to the park across the street where a handful of picnic tables sat like islands in a sea of puddles.

"Um, isn't it too wet to eat outside?" I asked as another rain shower erupted. New Zealand in winter: It's sunny for five minutes, then it rains like hell, then it's sunny again, then another rain shower. Sun. Rain. Sun. Rain. Sun. Rain. But Kiwis (nicknamed thus for the nocturnal flightless bird native to their country, not the green fruit with hairy brown skin, which they call Chinese gooseberry) are a tough bunch, immune to hypothermia. As if to validate my theory, a couple of young girls walked past wearing shorts, while I sat inside the car clenching my teeth to keep them from chattering. Even with the heater running, I couldn't get warm.

Charity handed me my meal: a thick hunk of white fish covered in a crispy batter, and a serving of chips (a.k.a. French fries) wrapped together in white paper. No plastic bags or Styrofoam here. Bonus points to New Zealand for its environmentally friendly packaging.

"Traditionally these are wrapped in newspaper, but now they use clean paper," Charity explained. "First you tear a hole in the top here." She demonstrated, ripping the paper. "It lets the steam out so the food doesn't get soggy."

Without waiting for it to cool, we dug in to eat, the crunching sounds of each bite drowned out by the rain hammering on the roof. I chewed carefully—on the good side of my mouth. We ate in silence, watching the waves as if we were at a drive-in theater. One after another after another, they rose up, unfurled, and slammed down on the beach before crumbling into a trail of foam that blew across the sand—a sequence that could describe my state of mind.

Our view looked east, toward Los Angeles, where I had just come from. Less than twenty-four hours earlier I had been at my parents' beachfront apartment looking west over the same ocean, toward this spot where I was now sitting. Eating fish and chips. In the rain. I have never been homesick, not even when going to summer camp for the first time at the age of eight, but sitting here by the sea on the bottom half of the world, I had only one thought: *I want to go home.* No matter that I didn't actually have a home to go back to.

I hoped I was just tired and that this trip wasn't another bad decision.

My dad had given me some advice before I left, telling me, "When you get down, remember what you are doing is helping other people." Right. I was here on a pie mission, because pie makes people happy—including me. I would focus on the purpose of my trip.

For most of my stops I had a calendar full of confirmed activities, classes, and events. For New Zealand, however, the plans were a bit, shall we say, loose. We had discussed in advance that Charity would arrange for me to teach a pie class to a widows' group, learn to make meat-filled hand pies from her local chef friend, and drive down to Napier to visit some orchards near her daughter's house.

"Charity, can we talk about the schedule for the week?" I asked. I wadded up my greasy paper and rolled it between my palms as I waited for her answer. *Why wasn't she answering?*

"I was so busy getting my house ready for you, I didn't have time to arrange anything," she finally said.

As I took in this bit of information, I kept my eyes pointed straight ahead, out the rain-blurred window, across the ocean, where LA suddenly felt even farther away.

"I thought you had everything lined up. I . . ." I stopped in midsentence. "It's just that I'm not here that long and I'm anxious to get started."

"I thought you could take a few days to rest up first."

I had spent the past six months in LA doing nothing but resting. I had whiled away my days lying in bed reading travel guides, international-cuisine cookbooks, and self-help books. Though my library checkout history revealed the truth: most of the books were self-help. I had slept, walked Jack, slept, ate dinner with my parents almost every night, slept, planned my trip, slept, and finally, with great effort, I had launched myself into the world. This was no time to rest! I needed to make pie! Pie had helped me heal after losing my husband. Pie had given me direction when I was lost. I already felt lost in New Zealand. I needed pie, not rest. *Stay open. Stay in the present. Don't judge.* I drew in the words like a puff of albuterol to keep from hyperventilating.

I chose my words carefully. "I only have ten days here—nine now—and I want to get my World Piece mission started. What about heading down to Napier tomorrow?"

I could tell from the way her smile faded that this was not what she was expecting. Maybe she hoped we would just hang out in her Christmas Cottage, talking over cups of tea while she knitted prayer shawls, whereas I wanted to hit the ground running, meeting as many people and covering as many miles as possible. Our difference in expectations damaged our new friendship, but I wouldn't find out until later just how badly, and how permanently. So much for world peace. I totally sucked at this. And I was only eight hours in.

Halfway to Napier is Rotorua, a popular tourist town known for its hot springs, mud pools, and sulfur smell that has prompted some to call it "Rotten-rua." It's built around a lake that boils, bubbles, and hisses like a witch's cauldron, and sits in a valley filled with steam vents that shoot out tall columns of smoke. *The Hobbit* was filmed nearby in the bucolic countryside, but the town? It could be the set of a sci-fi disaster movie the way it leaves you in constant suspense as to when the planet is going to let loose and blow itself up. All it would take is one little bump of the two tectonic plates beneath the surface to set off a disaster of cataclysmic proportions. While the plates jockey for position, the molten magma underneath churns in fiery fits, heating up any water that dares to seep down into the belly of the beast, and when it does, it shoots it back up to the surface in a roiling rage. The Maori people of earlier times used this boiling water as a stovetop for cooking, and in the areas where it wasn't as hot, they used it for bathing, finding that its mineral properties cured their aches and pains.

Dear, sweet Charity. She was living up to her name doing all the driving and navigating, figuring out the logistics, and in spite of my panic and pushiness, still acting as a most gracious host. It was her suggestion that we stop for a night in Rotorua and visit one of its spas on our way south. Maybe she thought a soak in the hot springs would calm me down. That or she secretly hoped I would boil to death.

Boiling water isn't the only hazard in Rotorua. There's boiling mud, too. The earth is very much alive here with its above-average geothermal and volcanic activity, holding the potential for hydrothermal eruptions, ash deposits, and, here's a good one, the collapse of unstable hot ground. Of all the risks I had imagined and feared on this trip, I had not factored in getting swallowed up into a pit of molten lava as one of them.

"Did you bring your togs?" Charity asked.

"My what?"

"Your togs, your bathing costume."

"Oh, my swimsuit. Yes, I did," I replied.

We paid the entrance fee at the Polynesian Spa and spent several hours soaking, separately making our way from pool to pool, trying each one like Goldilocks searching for the temperatures we liked best. We gave each other space, allowing me a break from her constant chatter and her, a respite from my anxiety. Charity had made a good call. I really did need to calm the fuck down. And warm the fuck up. If these waters were believed to cure arthritis, they could certainly cure the chill that was growing like cancer in my bones.

The spa was nice but not the ultra-sanitized resort kind. This was more natural and rustic, but not so wild as to be unsafe—a Jurassic Park for wellness without the dinosaurs. Wooden walkways wound through the boulder fields that surrounded the various pools whose water temperatures were regulated. There would be no death-by-boiling here. Built along the lakeshore, you could look out over the carpet of steam (apparently there was a lake under there somewhere) toward the mountains (allegedly in the distance beyond the heavy clouds) while immersed in a hot pool as volcanic gases pumped their plumes sky-high and cold rain splashed on your head. I always talk about how making dough by hand is a tactile experience that engages all your senses. Soaking in New Zealand's hot springs was that tenfold. Adding to the list of sensory stimuli was the pervasive scent of sulfur. The rotten-egg smell had seemed repulsive at first. When we arrived at the spa I had wanted to cover my mouth and nose with my turtleneck, but in the same way the initial sting of hot water wears off after a few minutes of soaking, I didn't notice it anymore.

Exposure over time to something unfamiliar or new—be it a country, culture, language, religion, or even odorous gasses— eventually leads to conditioning. By dipping a toe in and gradually immersing yourself fully, you gain understanding, and eventually acceptance. I could accept, even come to love, the smell of hydrogen sulphide if it meant getting to soak in these hot, healing waters, because it meant that I was finally warm, and, to both my benefit and Charity's, more relaxed. If only I could have stayed in those hot pools for the next eight days.

I spotted Charity—or some apparition of Charity as her body was shrouded in steam—walking toward the pool I was in. "Charity! I'm over here!" I called, happy to see her after a few hours apart. "This pool is a good one. Come try it."

The next day we continued south toward Napier, driving through the towns of Rangitaiki, Wairakei, Te Haroto, and Te Pohue, mouthfuls of letters as thick as the gravy in a meat pie. I had learned just how thick that gravy was the day before when Charity and I stopped for gas—er, petrol. The meat pie, New Zealand's most popular snack food, is to Australasia what the pizza slice is to Americans. Whether miniature and round or turnover style, Kiwis consider it a staple and often eat it for tea, which is dinner (or supper if you live in Iowa).

Some say pie is what you eat when you're coming home from the bar. Regardless of when and where you eat it, the hand pie is such a big part of New Zealand's culinary culture it should be the emblem on the country's flag. The history of their meat pies, like so many pies in the world, hearkens back to another time and place. British settlers of the mid-1800s brought them from England, but British meat pies can be traced back to Spain, and Spanish meat pies can be traced all the way back to Romans and Egyptian pharaohs. So not only is pie an immigrant, it represents the original globalization of fast food, even though McDonald's always gets the blame. Here, meat pies can be found in any direction you look: in stand-alone pie shops, grocery stores, bakeries, restaurants, food carts, food trucks, and, as I quickly learned, gas station kiosks. Even McDonald's has assimilated the local fare and features meat pies on its New Zealand menu.

The pie assortment at the BP station included steak and cheese; beef and bacon; sausage, potato, and onion; Thai chicken; Indian butter chicken; and lasagna, to name a few flavors that the Kiwis created, expanding beyond the original beef and potato British recipe. The pies are served warm, making the crust flaky, albeit a little greasy, and the fillings are generous, gooey, and just spicy enough not to be bland. That first one I ate—a butter chicken pie served in a small brown paper sack—would not be my favorite of the many pies I ate during my stay; the crust was a little too mealy and the gravy a little too processed tasting. But it was good enough to satisfy the belly and quiet the mind of a jet-lagged, American woman on the verge of a nervous breakdown.

As we continued south in Charity's Toyota station wagon, the terrain grew more mountainous, the forest thicker and darker, the roads steeper and windier, the blind curves tighter and more dangerous. That they drive on the left side of the road added to the tension of this stomach-dropping amusement park ride. Charity proved to be a conscientious and safe driver, even when it seemed her talking would distract her, but on a mountain road this wild, a leap of faith was required to trust the *other* drivers sharing it. We were heading uphill, going around yet another sharp bend, when coming downhill, toward us, going waaaaay above the speed limit, was a house. A house! In our lane! No, in both lanes! The driver of the wide load was passing another car and coming straight toward us. *Death by mobile home.* Add that to the list of Things I Didn't Think of That Might Kill Me. Any bit of relaxation from the hot springs came undone in an instant. We were about to die in a gruesome wreck. With nowhere to go, no shoulder, no extra lane space, Charity held tight to the wheel as we braced for impact. The truck driver swerved back into his lane at the last possible second, missing us by a hair. This was the second time in forty-eight hours that I thought I might die—the trampoline bounce of turbulence during my flight over the Pacific Ocean being the first. At this rate how would I manage to stay alive for three whole months?

"Bugger, that was close!" Charity said. "That bloke shouldn't have been going that fast."

"No kidding. And did you see his face? He acted like it was nothing."

Hawke's Bay is a photographer's dream, especially from the top of Te Mata Peak where you can see the whole panorama of the region. It's one big travel brochure of grassy fields, shimmering ocean, and pristine beaches as far as the eye can see. If world peace were defined in visual terms, it would be Hawke's Bay. A balm for the eyes and for the soul, the open, untrammeled terrain did not evoke the deep loneliness I feared, because it was—halle-fucking-lujah—sunny! The mineral-rich, volcanic soil isn't the only reason this region is ideal for growing grapes and apples; it is also one of the sunniest places in New Zealand.

Charity told her daughter, Annette, that the "American pie lady" was coming to visit and, because Annette lives in Hawke's Bay, asked if she could help organize an orchard tour. A few days before my arrival, Annette was grocery shopping and in the supermarket parking lot saw a truck with the words "Johnny Appleseed" painted on its door. Johnny Appleseed is a brand name used by the Yummy Fruit Company, the largest and oldest fruit producer in the area. In serendipitous timing, a man stepped out of the truck just as Annette passed by. His name was Terrence, and he was the operations manager of the fruit company. He gave Annette his card, and after Annette passed his info on to me, I emailed him.

After the initial exchange I got an email from the company CEO, Paul Paynter, who offered to conduct an orchard tour himself. He wrote, "We are completely snowed right now, so I don't have a lot of time, but you are mad enough that I want to meet you. The world needs more mad people." Mad as in crazy. Yes, I suppose I might seem that way to some people.

Ushered into the boardroom of The Yummy Fruit Company, Charity, Annette, and I were greeted by a man with dark, curly hair in a plaid shirt and down vest wielding a red knife. Meet company chief, Paul Paynter. And he was calling *me* the mad one? I liked him immediately.

After introductions, we sat down at a long table filled with apples and bottles of apple cider to begin our tasting. Paul randomly chose an apple from the assortment of red, yellow, and green ones and cut it with surgical precision, proving just how sharp his knife was. In a ninja move, he lifted the blade and brought it down hard, stabbing into a slice like he was going to slaughter it. Just as quickly and unexpectedly he thrust the tip of his dagger in my face. *Death by apple slice.* Jesus. Just how mad was he?

Very cautiously, I slid the slice off the would-be murder weapon and put it in my mouth. Paul had seen the shock in my face and laughed. He got the reaction he wanted. "This is how my grandfather did it. I learned the knife trick from him." He puffed out his chest knowing his grandfather would be proud. He continued to dole out slices in this same swashbuckling manner and as he worked his way through each apple variety, his theatrics never ceased to amuse. His grandfather must have been a real character.

"I'm a fifth-generation apple grower," he explained. "My family came here in 1862 and we've been on this property since 1904.

This room was the dining room when my great-grandparents lived here." It still resembled a family home with all the old photos and paintings of apples hanging on the walls, though the flat-screen TV was something his ancestors would not have had.

"Seventy percent of New Zealand's apples are grown in Hawke's Bay," Paul told us, launching into more specifics than I could hold in my head. I took notes: Ballarat is good for cooking and for cider; it stays on the palate but needs a lot of sugar. Ambrosia is sweet; it's popular in Asia. Lemonade is a cross between Braeburn and Gala. Sweet Tango was developed by the University of Minnesota and has large cells so it breaks down when cooking. Apple quality is based on an acoustic response; when you tap them you want loud apples, not hard apples. There are two hundred fifty acres of Smitten apples growing in the state of Washington. Pacific Queen is a rose-colored apple that has nice aromatics. Granny Smith apples originated in Australia . . .

Wait, what? After all these years, having made thousands of pies with them, I had always thought Granny Smith apples were from New Zealand. Only now did I learn the hard truth—I could have avoided New Zealand's cold and rainy weather and gone straight to Australia.

When he started talking about high levels of polyphenols, astringency, and other chemical terms, my mind wandered elsewhere, like when I would get to eat my next meat pie. My stomach, befuddled by the nineteen-hour time difference, was growling again. I would be changing time zones every ten days. Did that mean I would live in a constant state of jet lag-induced hunger for the duration of my trip?

After our sampling of apples and hard cider, our brains numbed by the alcohol and the overload of scientific information, the four of us piled into Paul's SUV for a tour of his orchards. "We have seventeen hundred acres," he said as we drove down the dirt lanes in between the rows of fruit trees. "I'm sorry there isn't much to see. Harvest was several months ago, and now it's winter so there aren't any apples on the trees." Apart from the few stragglers unwilling to let go, he was right, the branches were almost entirely bare.

"Here's the Granny Smith section," he said, pointing to the naked trees. Their discarded leaves covered the ground, where a flock of fluffy white sheep grazed on them. I grabbed my camera to take pictures of this ridiculously quaint setting, teasing Paul, "Did you bring in those sheep as a prop to make the place look more New Zealand-ish for us?"

"No," he laughed, "they serve a purpose. They eat leftover apples off the ground and they stomp the leaves with their feet, turning them to mulch."

Driving on to another section of the farm, he continued, "This is my test plot where I'm experimenting. I try to create and grow new varieties." We got out of the car and he walked us through the orchard, grabbing stray apples as he went, picking one, taking a bite, and spitting it out the way wine tasters do. "Do you see the pink spot on the trunk of this tree? It's marked to be cut down. They don't all measure up, so we make room for new and different trees until we come up with a variety and taste that we like and think we can market."

Everyone knows apples are healthy: they contain fiber, vitamin C, antioxidants, and potassium, and can reduce the risk of obesity, heart disease, diabetes, and cancer. But not everyone eats them, or not enough of them, so the Yummy Fruit Company came up with a program to encourage school kids to eat more apples by getting them to collect the stickers that come on each one. Yes, those tiny stickers, the ones that are hard to pick off without gouging the skin, printed with the name of the apple, the place it comes from, and a bar code or number for the cashier to ring it up. Once the kids fill up a collection sheet with the stickers, their participating school will get a share of $200,000 worth of sports equipment. But Paul really is onto something, because healthy eating and physical activity don't just fend off disease, they contribute to world peace. According to London-based peace organization International Alert, "A physically and psychologically healthy person has more options: they can attend more school, earn more, save more, and have more control of their life. They are less susceptible to being manipulated into violence, to being a victim of violence, and more likely to be in a position to stand up for peace and against violence and war."

An apple a day indeed!

"You're teaching a pie class tomorrow, right?" Paul asked, as we got ready to leave. "Let me give you some apples." Terry, the operations manager Annette met in the grocery store parking lot, loaded three cases of apples—one each of Lemonade, Ballarat, and, my standard, Granny Smith—onto a dolly and wheeled them out to Charity's car.

It was Annette who also arranged the pie class. Her friend, Brett Zimmerman, a.k.a. Mr. Z, teaches culinary arts and nutrition at the William Colenso College in Napier. It is not a college as the name implies to an American; rather a secondary school, or high school. Brett offered the use of his classroom—a pie teacher's dream with six long stainless-steel tables and seven ovens. To think what I could have done with seven ovens when running my pie stand in the American Gothic House! He rounded up participants by sending out email invitations to the school administrators, his cooking students, his catering business helpers, and a few local Hawke's Bay friends.

Brett, a tall, strapping blond in his thirties dressed in track pants, appeared more suited to the sports field than the kitchen. This impression was not wrong, as he is also the school's rugby coach.

"I couldn't get proper pie plates," he apologized in our planning meeting. "But I got these at the restaurant supply warehouse. I hope they'll be okay."

The aluminum tins, round and deep, were meant for cake. "These are perfectly fine," I said. And they were. Pie is versatile and can be made in myriad shapes and forms, with or without a dish. Hand pies, freeform pies, slab pies on cookie sheets, miniature pies made in muffin tins or ramekins, canning jars, spring-form pans, casserole dishes, the possibilities are endless and creative improvisation is part of the fun of baking. "We have plenty of apples to fill them," I continued. "Besides, my pie mentor, Mary Spellman in California, taught me to make pie with generous portions. She was always telling me, 'Don't be stingy,' if I put too little filling in a pie dish."

"Americans like to do things big," Charity added.

We all nodded.

"I couldn't find shortening either," Brett continued. "But a vendor donated a case of pastry gems. Will that work?"

"Pastry what?" I asked.

He brought out the box containing six-inch-long rods that looked like breadsticks made of grease. I picked one up to examine it. Hard but breakable, white with hints of yellow, its resemblance to shortening or lard was close enough for me. "Sure, we can use them," I said. It wasn't until after the class that I learned that pastry gems are made of "edible tallow" (a rendered form of beef or mutton fat) and "vegetable fat pastry compound." Any food product given an intentionally vague name should be cause for suspicion—or avoidance. And yet I had already been consuming my share of it, as it's the same fat used for the puff pastry of meat pies. My preferred crust recipe calls for half vegetable shortening and half butter. Either one on its own makes a flaky crust, but I like the combo because shortening gives the crust lightness while butter gives it flavor. In hindsight, I should have skipped the pastry gems and gone with an all-butter crust, but at the time it hadn't occurred to me that one of New Zealand's most prized food products is butter. I don't know how I missed this fact as Charity and I had even stopped at the original headquarters for Anchor Butter in Waikato on our way south. Our tour there included The Reynolds' Woodland House—the dairy farmers' home-turned-museum—that, with its gabled roof and arched windows, looked like a bigger, more elegant, American Gothic House. Right after the tour, we stopped for coffee at the nearby Cambridge Country Store, where sun streamed through Gothic windows identical to the ones in my old house. Was this another divine message or was it just that Carpenter Gothic architecture happens to be popular in New Zealand? I was beginning to wonder. But in the industrial kitchen of William Colenso College, there was nothing other than pie to remind me of my past.

Brett brought out the butter supply for our class and there, printed on the boxes, was the Anchor logo, so even if the pastry gems were a bust, the high-quality butter would make up for it.

Before the class started, Brett opened the cartons of Paul's apples and took out a Granny Smith, perfectly formed, light green, blemish free, and so polished you could use it for a lipstick mirror. He reached for a knife and said, "Before I started teaching at the college, I worked at a five-star restaurant." He sliced the apple in half and with the reverence of a sushi chef carved wafer thin slices from one of the halves. At odds with his manly, athletic hands, he gently pulled at the delicate slices as if unfolding a fan. He cut a thick slice from the other half of the apple, and tucked the half-moon piece in between the accordion slits.

"It's a swan!" I said, as his artwork took shape.

Still concentrating, he took two apple seeds and poked them into either side of the swan's head for eyes. Fascinating, but I was more enamored with him than the swan, his cheekbones and jaw as chiseled as a Michelangelo sculpture, his muscular forearms covered in blond hair, his friendly blue eyes focused intently on his art. If I were one of Mr. Z's students I would be hanging out in his classroom all the time.

"We used to make these as a garnish, not to eat," he said. "We worked fourteen-hour days at that job."

"All that for a garnish? Whoa. I take it you're happier with what you're doing now."

"Oh, yes."

Around 7 p.m. the students started arriving for the four-hour class. The first arrival was a guy—a bloke—in his late twenties with a soul patch below his lips. His hair was neatly trimmed, but his fashion sense treaded a fine line between hippie and homeless in his pair of frayed patchwork pants, each square of fabric a drug trip of psychedelic colors and patterns.

"Oh my god, look at those pants! I have never seen anything like them," I couldn't help but blurt out.

"They're twenty years old," he said, as we both looked down at his legs.

"They're very flash," I said, showing off that I had picked up some local lingo. "Can I take a picture? I know a lot of quilters back in Iowa who might get some inspiration from these."

He stood back with his hands on his hips, grinning so big his eyes scrunched shut.

"I'm Beth, by the way."

"I'm Neil."

The rest of the participants had filed in by then: a florist, a school nurse, a librarian, a businessman, several of Brett's students dressed in starched, white chef's jackets, and a food judge. Charity and Annette were also taking the class. Their ages were as diverse as their livelihoods, ranging from seventeen to seventy.

"I count eighteen people," Charity announced.

A woman named Sam showed up with her hair in braids and I heard one of Brett's students ask her if she was the pie lady. She laughed and said, "No, that's her," pointing to me, my hair also in braids.

No matter where in the world I teach a pie class, it is pretty much always the same format: I start by introducing myself, talk a little about my pie background, and then give an overview of what we're going to do.

"We are each going to make our own apple pie," I began. "I'm going to stay one step ahead of you as we go, demonstrating each stage and then you'll do it. I will come around the room and keep checking on everyone and answer any questions."

The class format was the same, but I did have to make one adjustment. "Bear with me, as I'm not used to the metric system. We were supposed to switch over to it in the U.S. when I was in third grade. I don't know why it never happened. We do have measuring cups to use, so that will help with the way my recipe is written, but Mr. Z also translated everything into grams for you."

I knew from living in Germany that Europeans measure by weight, not volume, and while, to the uninitiated, it seems like a hassle to rely on a scale, it's a more precise way to measure. As for me, I always tell first-time bakers, "Pie is not about precision and it's not about perfection. The pilgrims made pies traveling in wagon trains, and they didn't have refrigerators and gourmet food stores." This simple fact eases their fear of doing something wrong.

With that we were off and running, in my case, literally. When teaching in large classroom settings, it's a workout to move between the tables, rushing to the aid of people, dodging rolling pins, and trying not to slip on the flour and pie dough dropped on the floor.

"This is the most important stage of making dough," I instructed. "It should be chunky. Your butter should be no smaller than the size of almonds and peas. Pie dough is very forgiving, but if you overwork it in this stage there is no going back. This part is faster than you'd expect, so once you get your dough mixed, leave it alone. If I see you overworking your dough, I will come around with my rolling pin!" I made a lap around the room, and when I finished my inspections, continued to the next stage.

"Now we add the ice water. Most pie recipes say you should only add five tablespoons. You use tablespoons here, right? But there are many variables that affect how much water you need. The brand of flour or butter or, ahem, pastry gems you use can make a difference. So can the weather. Your damp climate here might mean there's more moisture in your flour so you'll need less water. You'll know how much to use by feel. That's why I like to make dough with my hands. Just pay attention to what is happening in front of you. Drizzle the water in and mix it like you're tossing a salad. Work lightly! As you add more water, you'll see your dough start holding together; you'll feel it start to get heavier. When the dough can be picked up without crumbling, form it into two discs. If it's sticking to your hands, coat your hands with flour, like flour mittens, and it will take the stickiness right out of it."

I ran another lap, moving as quickly as I could to make sure everyone's water content was sufficient before it was too late, before they kneaded their dough into stone. If you added too much water, you could at least add flour to compensate. "I see a lot of you trying to force the dough to hold together instead of adding more water. Let the water do the work. Think of it as the glue." I jogged back to my work station to demonstrate the next step.

"Okay, now we're going to roll the dough. Rolling dough is like horseback riding: you have to take control of the reins. If you don't show that dough who's in charge it will take off on you and instead of staying round it will look like a map of Africa." They laughed. That line always got a laugh.

We peeled the apples—the Lemonades, the Ballarats, and the Granny Smiths—emptying all three cases. We laid our crusts in the deep aluminum pans and filled them with apple slices, cinnamon, sugar, and a little flour for thickening. We crimped our edges and brushed the tops of our pies with egg wash. We cut out shapes of dough—flowers, hearts, and letters—to decorate the tops. We offered our eighteen pies to the oven gods. And then we waited for them to bake.

"I'm so sorry, I have to leave early," Neil Patchwork Pants announced.

"You can take your pie with you and bake it at home," I assured him, offering some rudimentary instructions. "Start with a hot oven to set the crust. After the crust starts to brown—that can take anywhere from ten to twenty minutes—turn the temperature down. It will take at least another thirty minutes for the filling to bake, depending on your oven. Make sure the filling is thickened and bubbling, and poke it with a knife to make sure the apples have softened. And that's it. Good luck!"

I didn't realize his mode of transport was a bicycle and, curious how he was going to manage, I followed him outside watching as he mounted his steed, balancing the pie on the palm of one hand while holding the handlebars with the other. He pedaled off into the dark while I shook my head and laughed, marveling at his adventurous, can-do Kiwi spirit. I never did hear if the pie made it home intact.

I went back to attending to the pies in the ovens. I couldn't read the dials, not just because the numbers were in Celsius—the numbers were completely worn off. I sprinted from oven to oven, doing squats in front of them to peer inside, occasionally opening the doors to rotate the pies. I was sweating more than I do in power yoga. I didn't need the hot springs to get warm, I just needed to make pie. "Hey Brett," I said, "this could be a new workout for your rugby players."

"Nah yeah. Want to try out for the team?"

Browned to a golden sheen and still bubbling, we lined up the finished pies like beauty pageant contestants on one of the stainless-steel tables to end the class with a victory shot. "I know you're tempted, Mona," I teased the food judge, "but this is not a competition. Every one of these is a winner. Okay, everybody, let's take some pictures."

In a world that's become increasingly focused on seeking attention for one's self, and where posting selfies on social media has turned into a paid profession, the group photo serves as an antidote. Everyone squeezed in behind the pie table for the shot, smiling broadly and proudly, not just because of the pies but because of an overall enjoyable evening spent together. Pie really does make the world a better place, even if just for those few people, for those few hours. The class reminded me of what I was setting out to accomplish on my journey. I wished Paul Paynter had been at the class. He could have seen I wasn't so crazy after all.

After four days in Napier, Charity and I drove back to Orewa without incident—without getting run over by a house or buried by a volcanic eruption or stabbed by an orchard-owner's knife.

During the last days of my stay, Charity took me to her local library to show me where she had discovered my memoir that led her to finding me, and introduced me to the librarian. After that, Charity drove me into Auckland to bring a pie to a health-food-restaurant owner who she thought would be interested in my pie journey. (He wasn't. Oh well.) Then she volunteered me to give her sister-in-law and niece a pie class, which I happily did.

On my last night, we settled into the homey chairs in Charity's sunroom wrapped in her prayer shawls, sipping tea and watching Anderson Cooper on CNN. Charity was uncharacteristically quiet and I felt the tension growing, becoming so uncomfortable I could have popped the air with one of her knitting needles. "What's wrong, Charity?" I ventured.

She didn't answer right away, hesitating the way she did when we sat in her car eating fish and chips nine days earlier. "You were in such a hurry to get to Napier," she said. "You pushed me too hard."

"I know. And I'm so sorry," I replied. She was right. I hadn't taken into account her needs, her energy levels, or her expectations, maybe because I didn't know her well enough and hadn't taken the time—didn't feel like I had the time—to. And yet for two strong women who had just met, spending almost ten days together 24/7, I thought we had managed incredibly well. I usually have a good sensitivity radar. I had no idea she had been harboring resentment from the get-go.

She didn't respond to my apology, so I continued, "This is my first stop and I haven't figured out how to pace myself. But it went well, don't you think? We had a successful adventure. And your excellent driving skills got us to Napier and back safely."

Her normally cheerful, open face was harder than a Maori whakairo carving. I didn't know how to make amends, but I knew it would take more than pie to fix this problem—worse, a problem of my own making. I took a sip of tea. I had left my tea bag soaking in it so long my drink had turned as dark and bitter as the mood. Sitting with Charity in her unhappy state evoked more loneliness, isolation, and cold than New Zealand's location and weather ever had. We went back to watching TV, looking to Anderson Cooper for comfort, his American accent only making me more homesick. I had two and a half months and eight more countries to go. I could only hope that I would do better, be more patient, and be a more diplomatic and sensitive representative of my country. Because if I couldn't, then I'd have to do something I promised myself I wouldn't do: quit.

CHAPTER 3

Australia

Until he extends the circle of his compassion to all
living things, man will not himself find peace.
—**ALBERT SCHWEITZER**

After clearing customs in Sydney, I entered the arrivals hall and was greeted by three television cameras pointed right at me, their spotlights glaring, their boom poles hovering. My friend and Australia host, Kate, told me she was going to try to get some publicity for my trip and when I saw the swarm of news crews, I thought, wow, she went way overboard. My World Piece project may have been a principled effort but it didn't warrant *this* kind of attention. Flattered, I braced myself and smiled as I walked toward the cameras. As I got closer, they rushed forward like a scrimmage line of defensive tackles, shoved me out of their way, and kept going, right past me. When I turned to look in their direction, they were already shouting questions and jutting their microphones into the face of the man directly behind me, a tan and burly guy in a tracksuit and mirrored shades.

"Beth!" Kate spotted me and made her way past the onlookers, flashing a huge welcoming smile as she approached.

"Kate!" I shouted back. We grabbed onto each other, hugging in the way that close friends who hadn't seen each other in twelve years do. We had met more than twenty years earlier, when we rented rooms in the same beach house in Venice, California. She had left an investment-banking job to start a tennis racquet company, promoting a wishbone-shaped racquet with two handles "so you never have to play backhand," but the concept didn't catch on. The last time we had seen each other was at my wedding, the casual outdoor American one in Seattle, as opposed to the elegant church one Marcus and I had two weeks later in the Black Forest of Germany. A full foot taller than me, Kate is long, lean, and still Australia's record holder in several track and field events. I was as dwarfed by her height as I was embarrassed by my mistake. "For a second, I thought those cameras were for me," I admitted.

This caused Kate to break into a fit of laughter, which made me laugh, too. "That's Jarryd Hayne," she said. "He's a rugby player. He plays football in the U.S. now." Hayne, of Fijian descent but born in Australia, had just flown in from California, where he was a running back for the San Francisco 49ers. Kate continued laughing, howling even, which kept making me laugh. That laughter did not stop for the next ten days.

Yes, thank god, I was feeling better already.

I dragged my fifty-pound wheelie bag down the hall of Kate's apartment building, noting the 1970s metallic wallpaper and white wrought-iron sconces. "My building is kind of boring," Kate said by way of apology. Then she opened the door to her apartment.

"Are you fucking kidding me? Kate, this is amazing!" I walked straight toward the wall of floor-to-ceiling windows overlooking all of Sydney Harbor. All of it. The turquoise body of water glistening in the sunlight, the cargo ships coming and going, the sailboats gliding across the bay with their colorful spinnakers cupping the wind, the seagulls hovering in midair, the ferries shuttling passengers to the opposite shores, the waterfront cafés, the cluster of high-rises on the city skyline. In spite of her tennis racquet company being a bust, Kate had a knack for making money. She had gone back to investment banking, and now, instead of a moldy house share in Venice Beach, she had *this*.

"Forget pie, Kate. I'm going to spend the next ten days just looking at this view."

"Okay, Bethie Boo, let me show you your room."

"I own the apartment next door and I would have had you sleep there, but some other friends are using it," Kate said, apologizing again. "I'm giving you my office. I'm so sorry, it's just a mattress on the floor. I borrowed it from my mum."

I peeked into the room, immaculate and sparse with white carpet, her office files stacked straight, her stapler and pens in a perfect row. And a window—an airtight, insulated window with double-paned glass—that looked out into leafy trees, where a pair of long-beaked birds sat chirping in the sunshine. I wouldn't need to sleep with a hot water bottle like I did in New Zealand. And she was sorry? I already wanted to change my ticket and stay longer. Like six months, maybe a year.

I carried my laptop out to Kate's balcony to Skype with my parents and let them know I had arrived. The timing for my calls to them was hard to synchronize with the time difference (now seventeen hours instead of nineteen) and the international date line between us. We were both in daytime hours—it was 10 a.m. in Sydney and 5 p.m. in LA—but different days of the week.

"Happy birthday, Boo," my parents said simultaneously. I was so focused on getting out of Auckland I barely remembered it was my birthday. But I was also surprised they knew it was June 14 in Australia, when it was still June 13 in California.

"Fifty-three years ago, you finally arrived. You were two weeks late."

"I know, Mom. You tell me that every year."

"It's cocktail hour here. I'm going to toast to you with a martini," my dad said. "What are you doing to celebrate?"

"For one, I'm enjoying this view. Can you believe this?" I spun in a slow circle, giving them a three-hundred-sixty-degree look at the harbor outside and at Kate's elegant living room, with her white sofas and evenly spaced accent pillows and her clean white walls that showcased a gallery's worth of original art. There was no mountain in the middle of this room. No teddy bears or angel ornaments or abandoned tea cups. "Kate and I are about to go out for a power walk and tonight we're making dinner here at her apartment."

"Those birds are so loud," my mom said, though my dad, who is hard of hearing, didn't notice them.

I swung my laptop around to the balcony railing where three green birds strutted along the edge as if they owned the place. With blue heads, orange beaks, lime-green neck rings, and a tricolored breast of red, yellow, and orange, they were a flock of flying rainbows. "I have no idea what they are, maybe some kind of parrot," I said of the growing number of visitors that now totaled six. "All I know is that I am so grateful to be here."

"Before you hang up, I have a question," my dad said. "Have you pooped?"

I laughed. "Yes, Dad, I'm back on track. Thanks for asking."

Kate's walking route took us through parks and soccer fields, past the rowing club, along the waterfront path, straight to a pie shop called Harry's Café de Wheels. Identified by the neon sign reflecting off the shiny, silver trailer surrounded by a counter and bar stools, Harry's is a Sydney institution that opened in 1945. Probably one of Australia's first food carts, it's strategically located at the entrance to the wharf where military ships dock. Besides the prime real estate, its success can also be attributed to what they serve: warm comfort food.

"You have to try the Tiger Pie; it's the house specialty," Kate insisted. "It's quite something."

Harry's Tiger Pie was indeed "quite something." A small, round meat pie filled with spiced beef, chicken, veggie, or curry—all normal meat pie ingredients—was the foundation. The pie is then covered by a mound of mashed potatoes and a generous heap of mashed peas on top of that, with gravy poured over the whole lot. It must be five thousand calories, an indulgence surely welcomed by hungry sailors, though celebrities like Sir Elton John and Frank Sinatra have also sampled the goods, as evidenced by their autographed headshots covering the trailer's walls. Another celebrity pictured on the Wall of Fame was Barbra Streisand. I knew firsthand that she likes pie because I made a lemon meringue pie for her once, when I had my pie-making job in Malibu. I didn't get to meet her—she sent her driver to pick it up—but I got word the next day that he had driven over Malibu Colony's speed bumps too fast causing the meringue to stick to the lid of the box, so the pie never made it to her dinner table.

Standing at the counter to eat, Kate and I shared a Tiger Pie filled with chicken, taking turns digging into the pile of mush with our plastic forks. It was perfectly . . . mushy. Salty. Warm. Filling. Now I could say I had eaten at the famous landmark. But I would have to be a drunken sailor to eat there again.

Kate had to work the next day so I joined her on her morning commute, taking the ferry across the harbor—or harbour as the British spelling goes—to Circular Quay, passing the iconic Sydney Opera House en route. A collection of arched-roof buildings arranged like nesting dolls, the architecture conjures the impression of giant, half-sunk rowboats standing on end. A UNESCO World Heritage site and an iconic symbol, if not *the* iconic symbol for Australia, it towered overhead, casting a shadow over us as we sailed past. I've always declared myself a traveler, not a tourist, but upon seeing the Opera House so close up, I fished out my camera from my bag for a selfie. While I snapped a few shots, my eyes wide with awe, the business commuters on board didn't bother to look up from their newspapers or phones.

I left Kate at her office and walked a few blocks over for a meeting with Sam Cawthorn, an author and motivational speaker whose work is based on his experiences as an amputee. While I was in New Zealand, Charity insisted, "You have to meet him. He's so inspirational." Given my world peace theme, I wanted to meet all the do-gooder people I could, so I contacted him and, given my pie theme, asked him if he'd like to meet for pie. That way, no matter what transpired with him, there was a 50 percent chance that the time spent would be worthwhile.

We met at a pie shop called Pie Face. I first heard about this chain of pie shops when its New York City location, next door to the

Ed Sullivan Theater on Broadway, was featured on *The Late Show with David Letterman*. Letterman ordered a dozen of the Australian hand pies and had them delivered to his talk-show desk while live on the air. Ever since I watched him bite into one of those flaky little devils, decorated with a smiley face on top, I'd wanted to go to the shop. And now I was going, right to its Australian source, to have pie for breakfast.

Sam Cawthorn, walking with a slight limp, approached the outdoor café table where I was already sitting. A handsome young man of Indian-Scottish descent, with black hair slicked back and a groomed beard, he was smiling in an easy gap-toothed grin that could convince anyone to follow his trademark motto to "bounce forward, not back." He was dressed in a wool blazer, so I couldn't see his right arm—a full metal jacket of bionics that included a mechanical five-fingered hand and a bendable elbow. Nine years earlier, when he was twenty-seven, he had been in a car accident that caused him to permanently injure his leg and lose his arm. But in turn, he gained a career in promoting a positive mental attitude, and just three years after his accident he was honored by the government as "Young Australian of the Year." He is one of the few above-the-elbow amputees in the world who can play the guitar, though he has not received an award for that—yet.

"Beth?"

"Sam?"

We got straight to business, ordering pie. This Pie Face location was more of a kiosk with a storefront of glass doors that slid open to a walk-up counter, making it easy for office workers in this busy downtown district to grab a quick bite. Focusing on the lit display in front of us, we perused the rows of miniature pies, the tops of the golden-brown pastries decorated with the signature happy face logo in icing. "Look at all these! They are so cute," I said. "Australia is such a happy place, even the pie is smiling."

"I'll have the steak and mushroom," Sam told the cashier.

"I'll have the same," I said, even though it didn't sound very breakfasty.

I reached for my wallet to pay, but Sam quickly waved me away and said, "No. This is on me."

"Thank you, Sam. I really appreciate it." I zipped my purse closed and thought of how I had split everything fifty-fifty with Charity. It was, and will always be, my biggest regret about my time in New Zealand. I should have been more generous. I should have paid for her share of everything. But just like I didn't know how to pace my travel speed for fear of running out of time, I was equally worried about running out of money.

We sat down at a café table on the sidewalk, ignoring the noise of the buses delivering their passengers to the high-rise office buildings that blocked the morning sun. Sam talked about his work, but mostly about his busy schedule. "I just flew back from speaking in Melbourne and I'm flying out to Perth tonight," he said as if to underscore his importance. "I love my work. I'm absolutely passionate about it." I expected him to say more, but he changed the subject. "Tell me about World Piece."

I explained my mission, about wanting to facilitate cultural understanding and spread kindness, but according to him I was downplaying it. Of course I was downplaying it. I was just one person, traveling alone, filled with self-doubt and fear, and making a few pies. I wanted to make an impact, but I was in no position to be overconfident or cocky. I hadn't forgotten the cameras at the airport, and I was still subdued after leaving New Zealand on bad terms with Charity.

Without warning, he pounded his fist on his chest and, in a voice so booming it frightened the birds that were pecking the crumbs at our feet, he launched into a speech.

"Our deepest fear is not that we are inadequate. Our deepest fear is that we are powerful beyond measure. It is our light, not our darkness, that most frightens us."

I recognized the quote by Marianne Williamson.

"We ask ourselves, who am I to be brilliant, gorgeous, talented, fabulous? Actually, who are you not to be? You are a child of God. Your playing small doesn't serve the world. There's nothing enlightened about shrinking so that other people won't feel insecure around you."

Oh my god, he has this whole thing memorized? I had read the passage from Williamson's book, *A Return to Love*, but I certainly didn't know it by heart. I pressed myself back against the chair trying to create more space between his intensity and me, while at the same time nodding to demonstrate my polite active-listening skills as he continued.

"We are all meant to shine, as children do. We were born to make manifest the glory of God that is within us. It's not just in some of us; it's in everyone. And as we let our own light shine, we unconsciously give other people permission to do the same. As we're liberated from our own fear, our presence automatically liberates others."

The two businessmen at the next table looked over at us, as Sam gestured wildly with his arms and accentuated his words as if performing on Broadway. Unfazed, he recited the entire passage without pause.

Sam, who is also a success coach, hurled his next piece of advice at me. "You need to shoot more video," he commanded, "for your social media sites."

"I don't feel comfortable doing that," I told him. "It feels too unnatural, too much like self-promotion."

"No!" he barked. "The video is how your message will reach more people, and it will make you more successful. Promise me that you'll do it, that you'll shoot one video a day."

I thought about the Australian guy I met right before leaving LA. He was on the first mile of his yearlong bike ride around the U.S. when I encountered him on the bike path just south of LAX. Riding alongside him for a few miles, I asked him, "Do you have a website? A Facebook page? Somewhere people can follow your progress?"

His name was Rob, he had just quit his job as a naval engineer in Melbourne, and, no, he didn't have a website or a Facebook page. "I barely had time to get all my gear organized, and any energy that would have gone toward social media was spent trying to navigate the bureaucracy of getting a twelve-month U.S. visa," he said. "Besides, this trip is for me, to find the 'real' Rob."

I totally understood as I had the same sentiments about my own journey. When planning my trip, I had gotten overwhelmed trying to turn it into a project with sponsors and media. And while, unlike Rob, I was touting the public side of my journey on social media, I was aware that the personal side was equally, if not more, important. I needed to travel to get un-lost, to reconnect with that fearless and adventurous girl I used to be, and to make myself feel better by making others feel better—by giving of myself through the making and sharing of pie. Hearing about Rob's lack of need or desire for publicly sharing his bicycle tour, let alone his inner transformation, affirmed my own thoughts: *Personal journeys require some privacy.* I found it refreshing that Rob had opted to travel so humbly and quietly. Meanwhile, I had already come to my own conclusion that a big, life-altering trip did not need to go viral to be valid. I was going to continue blogging and posting about my travels on social media—I'm a writer; telling stories, ideally inspirational ones, is what I do. But make videos of myself every day? I don't think so.

"Yes, okay," I told Sam. "I will do that."

"Promise?"

"Yes," I lied again.

"Let's do one together. Right now."

I smiled into my iPhone with the Pie Face logo behind me smiling back. I should have pursued acting; I was pretty good at it. "I'm Beth Howard and I'm here in Sydney with Sam Cawthorn . . ."

That was the first and last selfie-video I would shoot.

I thanked Sam for his time, then rushed off to join Kate and her parents, Bill and Ali, for lunch. It was a ticketed affair at a luxury hotel next to the Royal Botanical Gardens. I had met Bill and Ali before, when they visited Kate in the U.S. All three of them slender and tall, they were a trio of palm trees, their attitudes perennially sunny, and it was pleasant to stand in their shade. Bill had been the headmaster at a private school and though he was retired he was still invited to highbrow events, which he often attended—even the ones, like this one, that didn't align with his politics.

The ballroom was filled with well-heeled, gray-haired guests seated around tables covered in white linen. We found our seats, each place set with a confounding assortment of fine china, crystal glasses, and silver cutlery. On the dinner plate sat a booklet listing the lunch menu, the speakers and sponsors, and the title of the event: "The English-Speaking Union and Australians for Constitutional Monarchy Joint Luncheon to celebrate the 800th Anniversary of the Sealing of the Magna Carta."

"Kate," I whispered, "I have to confess, I don't know what the Magna Carta is."

Kate laughed in her loud, infectious way and said, "I didn't know either! I had to look it up before I got here. It was the first charter to declare that no one in society is above the law, not even a king or a queen."

I looked it up later and its history confused me as much as the layout of the luncheon cutlery. In the simplest of terms, when British settlers came to America, along with pie they brought the Magna Carta. Later on, when the colonies fought for independence from Britain, they looked to the charter as a symbol of liberty and based the American Constitution on some of its principles.

That's why it's good to travel: it fills in the missing pieces of your education.

We dined on grilled salmon, carrots, and white wine. The speeches would require at least two glasses, as the speakers, including former Prime Minister John Howard, did not possess the lively, attention-grabbing theatrics of Sam Cawthorn. How quickly this new perspective made me appreciate Sam's thunderous speaking style. And how were all these gray-haired guests not slumping over in their chairs?

In spite of the tranquilizer-pill talks, I marveled at being there. I had wanted an immersive cultural experience and I was getting one—though I had been thinking more along the lines of making pie with First Nations Peoples (a.k.a. Aboriginal peoples), not eating pie with members of an octogenarian underworld dedicated to saving the monarchy. Which is not to say the lemon pie served for dessert wasn't delicious. It was simultaneously sweet and tart with a delicate shortbread crust and topped with a touch of whipped cream. The contrast of eating a slice of pie with a silver fork while sitting beneath twinkling chandeliers, instead of devouring a messy meat pie with a plastic spoon while standing outside in the winter chill, underscored the opposing entities of life.

Once the presentations ended and we were no longer held hostage in our chairs, the guests scurried between tables to greet their friends and former colleagues. Amidst the mingling, we found ourselves in the vicinity of the former Prime Minister and Bill introduced me.

"She's American, traveling around the world promoting peace," Bill told John Howard.

"Oh?" he said blandly.

I reached out my hand to shake his. "My name is Beth Howard and my dad's name is John. I wonder if we're related." I laughed.

"Nice to meet you," is all he said with a slight nod of his shiny head. He did not possess the broad and welcoming Australian smile I'd seen from just about everyone else since my arrival in the country. He was the same height as me, but not of the same disposition. In fact, his politics were the antithesis of the cultural acceptance I was promoting.

In 1999, when the majority of Australians wanted to become a republic, he used a referendum to retain the constitutional monarchy—perhaps a reason why he was the keynote speaker at the luncheon. During his four-term tenure, he touted a "One Australia" campaign that was anti-multiculturalism, anti-immigration, and anti-Aboriginal land rights. In one of his most notorious actions— or, more accurately, inactions—he refused to make an official apology to Indigenous Australians. He used terms like "social cohesion" to defend his ultra conservative stance. And they call his The *Liberal* Party? He said things like, "I don't think it is wrong, racist, immoral, or anything for a country to say '*We* will decide what the cultural identity and the cultural destiny of this country will be and nobody else.'" Sorry, dude, but that is totally wrong, racist, and immoral. The voters thought so too, and that was the end of his reign.

However, he did make a significant contribution to an important aspect of peace in his first term as Prime Minister. In response to a mass shooting in Port Arthur, Tasmania, in 1996, in which thirty-five people were killed, he initiated a mandatory government gun-buyback program resulting in the collection and destruction of roughly a million firearms. The success of this effort makes a compelling case for gun regulations with the proof lying in Australia's ranking on the Global Peace Index as one of the top ten most peaceful countries in the world. And to think it was founded as a penal colony! Meanwhile, the U.S., with its proliferating gun ownership and growing appetite for semi-automatic weapons, keeps moving closer to the bottom of the Peace Index every year.

One of my scheduled pie endeavors was a presentation to the Sydney Women's International Club. This organization offers support, cultural exchange, and activities to help women of all nationalities, including Australians, feel more connected in Sydney. I always talk about how pie helps build community, but so do organizations like SWIC, whose only real mandate for membership, besides being female, is to respect all cultures, including the "Traditional Owners" of the land on which they meet. I was impressed that they included this in their mission statement, and even went a step further in their acknowledgment: "We recognise their connection to the land, waters, and culture. We pay our respects to their Elders past, present, and emerging." There would be no monarchy lunch ladies in this crowd.

My friend Foong is a member of SWIC and had arranged for me to give a talk, followed by a pie demo, at their monthly meeting. Foong is a friend I met in German class nine years earlier, when I lived in Stuttgart with Marcus. Foong is the definition of multicultural—she's Chinese, born in Malaysia, educated in Australia, and married to a German whom she met when working as a banker in Sydney. She and her husband, Karl, had moved to Hong Kong, then to Singapore, then to Stuttgart, where we met. She now divides her time between their house in Sydney, where her son goes to university, and their new apartment in Frankfurt, Germany, where Karl works. When I asked her about her splintered roots, she said without a hint of longing, "I'm a global citizen." Home to her is not a place but a feeling. "Home is where my friends are, where I can cook and paint and read and get involved in the community."

The morning before the event, Foong picked me up at Kate's. We hadn't seen each other since Marcus's funeral in Germany, making our greeting and hug all the more potent.

"You look amazing!" I told her. And she did—dressed in black jeans and a black wool coat, a silk scarf tied loosely around her neck, and her short black hair tucked behind her ears.

"You, too," she said. "I'm really happy you could make it to Sydney."

"This place is great! It's like London, but in the Pacific, as if it's a European gateway to Asia. I love how it feels like a blend of cultures. It reminds me of California, or how California must have been fifty years ago." I paused and added, "I don't know how you stayed in Stuttgart so long when you could have been here."

"Where Would You Rather Live" and "How Soon Before We Can Move Somewhere Else" were frequent topics of conversation during our time in Germany. We would sit in her living room for hours talking over lattes, while Oscar, her son who was eight at the time, stayed in the backyard kicking a soccer ball around to keep Jack, who was a puppy then, from barking. So much had happened since that period a decade earlier. Marcus was gone. Oscar was in college. Jack was on a farm in Iowa. And I was here with Foong in Australia. *Stay in the present*, my mantra warned as *Sehnsucht* flooded my heart. As impossible as I find the German language, it contains words that are so perfect they defy translation. *Sehnsucht*—a yearning, a desire for utopia in an imperfect world, a search for happiness while coming to terms with the fact that some desires are unattainable, a longing for a distant place that doesn't necessarily exist, or a nostalgia for home—is one of them.

Stay in the present, I reminded myself, more sternly this time.

Our first task was to buy pie ingredients for the evening's pie-baking session at Foong's house. Together, with the help of several other SWIC members, we would bake eight apple pies to be served at the group's event the next day, plus a few extra. We stocked up on flour, sugar, butter, and Australian-grown Granny Smith apples at the supermarket, and afterward we went out for a late breakfast.

Foong lives on the north side of Sydney Harbor, in an affluent area called Mosman. Just a few blocks from her house, on Balmoral Beach, is Bathers' Pavilion. Built a century ago as a swimmers' changing room, it has been revamped into a chic bistro with cabana-striped banquettes upon which Foong and I settled before placing our order for eggs, croissants, and lattes. Overlooking the Pacific Ocean, we talked nonstop for the next three hours about light, uplifting things, like how disillusioned we had become with the world, how prevailing attitudes have shifted toward selfishness where "it's all about me," how it's so competitive, so noisy, so greedy, and how people are killing in the name of religion.

"The Dalai Lama is in Australia right now," Foong said. "He is saying that it's not enough to teach religion; we need to teach ethics."

"How about teaching manners?" I suggested. "Peace could start with being more polite. There's a book called *Using Your Turn Signal Promotes World Peace.*" Foong raised an eyebrow. "I know it sounds like a joke, but it's true. We need to communicate better and be more considerate of others."

"You're doing that with your pies, getting people to think of others."

"I try. But it's not enough."

We talked about my time living in the American Gothic House and why I moved out.

"The media could not resist the story of a young widow baking pies in that famous farmhouse," I told her. "I got so much publicity that my Pitchfork Pie Stand kept growing."

"That must have been good for business."

"It was. But it got to the point where I couldn't manage it. Worse, the better my business did, the less privacy I had. The public attention became too much—it was like *I* had become the tourist attraction—so my only option was to move out."

"It was probably time to move on," Foong said. "You wouldn't have been able to stay there forever."

"But I loved that house so much, Foong. It's almost like it was alive, like it had a soul. It sat empty for two years and I nurtured it back into good condition, and it gave me the sanctuary I needed to heal from my grief. And then I kind of ruined it for myself."

She laughed a little, but then shook her head, not playing into my drama. Foong was too pragmatic to assign feelings to a house or to dwell on the past. And I hadn't really ruined anything, had I? I was here, on this journey, bringing a dream to fruition.

Finally, because it was inevitable, we talked about Marcus.

"I read your book," she said. "It brought tears seeing what you went through after the news. Nobody will ever know why he died when he did."

I scoffed. "You can't believe how many people said 'It was his time.'"

"With his precondition, it could have happened anyplace, or at any time, but that doesn't take the pain away. I know there's a big black hole that can't be filled, but hopefully with what you're doing, traveling and meeting new people, you'll find peace."

"I don't know," I said, fingering the handle of my coffee cup. "I felt like I had finally gotten my life back on track after he died, but since I moved out of the American Gothic House, I've been so lost, like I have no roots left to hold me to the earth."

"What about LA?"

"LA no longer feels like home."

"Your parents are still there, aren't they?"

"Yes. And I loved being near my parents for the past six months, but that's another thing; I'm already grieving the fact that they won't be around too many more years." The thought of losing my parents was my weak spot, the secret door to the dark places inside me. Just the mention of them created a salt shaker of tears that sprinkled down onto my scrambled eggs.

"No one knows how long they're going to be around. You know that from losing Marcus at such a young age."

"I know. That's what I'm talking about. Life is so precarious, so fleeting. I'm living in a constant state of paranoia that I'm going to lose more of the people I love at any second. Dogs, too. I just lost Daisy, and Jack is getting older. I can't take any more sadness, Foong." I began to cry harder than the rain beating down outside on the sandy beach.

The waiter, noticing we weren't eating our food, stopped by to ask, "Is everything all right?"

I looked up at him with my wet face and said, "Well, the food is," which I knew was true from the few bites I had managed to take before the onset of my grief burst.

He left and came back with a handful of tissues, silently and discreetly handing them to me under the table. After all our griping about how shitty the world seems, here was a stranger offering a gentle reminder that kindness is alive and well, and that faith in humanity can be restored with a gesture as simple as a well-timed tissue.

After breakfast we took a short walk on the beach to get some fresh air. The rain had stopped and so had my tears, leaving me feeling as cleansed as the air. I zipped up my down jacket and put my face into the wind, letting the sea salt scrub my skin. I was feeling thankful for my friendship with Foong and how, in the midst of her moving-target life as a global citizen, we had found each other again.

The next morning Foong had arranged for me to get picked up at Kate's by SWIC member Christine, a German woman who had lived in Sydney for forty years. She drove Kate and me to Foong's

Mosman neighborhood, to the house of Satya, another member who was hosting the meeting. Satya was from Fiji but of Indian descent. Her German-Italian husband was a developer and had built their house, a massive architectural showcase of white marble floors and giant windows that looked out onto their groomed lawn and private beach. Satya greeted us warmly and led us down to the lower level, next to the indoor swimming pool and sauna, where the meeting was being held. About thirty women had gathered to hear me talk about pie and my theory of how it can make the world a better place. Besides Christine from Germany and Foong from, well, all over the place, there were women from South Africa, Denmark, Greece, England, the Philippines, and Japan. While everyone in the room spoke at least some English, I made the effort to speak slower—not louder—and enunciate my words, but language mattered less when I had my rolling pin to do the talking.

I wasn't sure the women would care that much about the pie-making demonstration part of my talk, but it was only when I started mixing the dough and slicing the apples that their interest perked up. My speech couldn't possibly have been as dull as the monarchy speeches. Or was it? As I stepped through the process, several women put their heads together, murmuring, apparently commenting to one another about my technique. They were the first to ask questions during the Q&A after the demo, asking, "Why do you leave the chunks of butter so big? What kind of flour do you use? Why don't you roll your dough on wax paper?"

My answers: "Because the bigger chunks make the crust flakier. All-purpose, white flour. Because it wrinkles and wads up and makes it harder to roll; better to just roll on a washable mat or directly on a clean smooth surface." I've given dozens of talks and the questions are almost never about grief or ways to give back to the world or how to build community; they are always about the pie recipe. But, like in the way that using your turn signal promotes world peace, you have to start somewhere.

I couldn't stay with Kate for ten days and not offer to give her and her friends—her mates—a pie class. Kate was all for it and asked me to email her a list of what we needed. Sometimes I have people bring their own ingredients, but Kate insisted on buying everything for the group. I was quick to put up a fight. "No, Kate, let me do something for you for a change."

"No, Bethie Boo, I'm getting this. You just crack on here while I go to the store."

Instead of arguing, I took the path of least resistance and did as I was instructed. I "cracked on" and disrupted Kate's life in a whole new way by rearranging her furniture. I laid bed sheets on her white carpet before setting up the folding tables she had borrowed from her neighbor. The tables were too low to work comfortably, so with Kate's permission I borrowed some books from her shelf and raised the tables six inches by placing two volumes of the *Short Oxford English Dictionary* and two volumes of the thicker *Webster's New International Dictionary of the English Language: Second Edition* under the legs. I asked her later why she had four dictionaries and two copies of each, but she just shrugged. On a side table, I laid out dessert plates, forks, and two of the extra pies I had made at Foong's to serve during Kate's class.

Late in the afternoon, as the sailboats and ships crisscrossed the harbor, the kookaburras cackled and cooed in the trees off the balcony, and the Southern Hemisphere sun beamed its lightsaber rays into Kate's living room, seven women tied on aprons, rolled up their sleeves, and got to work baking. Kate had invited three friends from university, her Greek neighbor from upstairs, and Pip, her friend from France who was staying in Kate's apartment next door for several months with her husband, Chris, while he went through chemo. Kate had also invited her mom, Ali, to join us. Ali was eighty-seven, though she looked no more than seventy, and in the early stages of dementia.

Once the class got underway, I made the rounds in the room, taking care not to trip on the sheets, and checked everyone's work as they moved through the stages of measuring, mixing, rolling, peeling, slicing, filling, and crimping. Every time I came to Kate and Ali's workstation—they were making a pie together—Ali would look up and smile. She looked so serene, so regal, even with a pink gingham apron worn over her red cardigan. Her blue eyes radiated happiness, giving no indication of her age or condition. Only when she spoke was there a clue.

"Is this sugar or salt?" she asked Kate.

"It's sugar, Mum. Let's sprinkle it on top here."

"Now, what are we making again?"

"Pie, Mum. We're making apple pie."

Ali replied, "Well, this is fun. I'm really enjoying this."

Kate was so patient and tender with her mom. It broke my heart to know they wouldn't have too many more opportunities for lucid conversations, but when I reminded myself to stay in the present, I focused on the positive, overjoyed that they could share this experience. I would hold fast to this memory, and use it as a reference for the times I questioned the purpose of my trip, and the meaning of life itself. *Love*, I would remember. Love is always the answer.

As for me learning how to make the local kinds of pies—an Australian meat pie, or a New Zealand one for that matter—I wasn't doing so well with that part of my mission. As an alternative, Pip told me about a pie shop where you could watch them make the pies and took Kate and me there to check it out.

The first thing I learned at Cousin Jacks Cornish Pasty is that pasty is pronounced "pass-tee," not "paste-ee." It's different from a meat pie in that a pasty is folded like a turnover, whereas a meat pie, while also a hand-held size, is round with a top and bottom crust—though I rarely saw this distinction made in the display cases of other bakeries or pie shops.

The history of Cornish pasties dates back to the 1200s, when pasties were the food of tin miners in England, specifically the county of Cornwall that makes up England's southwest peninsula.

The sealed, crimped edge of the crust was used as a handle so their arsenic-covered fingers wouldn't touch their lips. When they were done, they threw the crust edge into the tunnels as an offering to the ghosts, reasoning that if the ghosts were happy they would leave them alone; maybe even protect them. Their wives sometimes put a dessert filling in one end of the pie and marked it with an initial so their men would not eat the dessert first. It is known that in 1787, twenty-two out of the fifteen hundred convicts that first came to Australia were from Cornwall; it is not known if they brought the first pasty recipes with them. It wasn't until the mid-1800s, when Australia saw a huge influx of Cornish miners seeking work, that the pasty proliferated in Oz. Cousin Jacks pie shop name is a nod to those migrating miners who were called Cousin Jacks and Cousin Jennys.

Today, you can find pasties with all kinds of combinations of ingredients, but a traditional Cornish pasty is made with seasoned chopped skirt steak, diced potatoes, turnip, swede (a.k.a. rutabaga), and onion. The recipe has "Protected Geographical Indication," similar to how you can't call sparkling wine champagne unless it's made from grapes in France's Champagne region.

I didn't get a hands-on lesson, but the baking at Cousin Jacks was done in the front of the shop, behind a glass partition, so I could observe the process. A young woman in a baseball cap fed dough into a sheeter, a machine that weighs, rolls, and shapes the dough. As the sheeter spit out uniformly sized circles onto the table, she lined them up in preparation for filling them. She had a tub of some pre-made green mash with bits of yellow in it, which, based on the menu, must have been for the spinach, cheese, and corn pasty. Using an ice cream scoop, she dropped a mound of filling on top of each circle, then, one by one, unhurried, relaxed, and confident, as if she had done it a million times, she folded the dough into a half moon and pinched the rounded edge to seal it, forming a spiral pattern as she went. She placed as many pasties as she could fit onto a cookie sheet before pushing the tray into the oven. I watched her for a good fifteen minutes, the rhythm of her peaceful work lulling me into a trance.

There, in the middle of bustling, cosmopolitan Sydney, watching the young woman working, I thought about my Pitchfork Pie Stand and all the things I missed about it. I had made pies in bulk for four years, in a makeshift assembly-line production, and always found satisfaction in touching the dough, molding its soft and supple texture with my fingertips. I took pride in creating so many works of edible art, knowing they would make people's faces light up when they saw them. I also missed how the pie stand created a hub of activity and built community in that tired rural town. How neighbors would bring me bags of rhubarb or baskets of pears, sometimes leaving them at the back door with no note. How customers would come for pie but end up staying for hours, volunteering to help fold pie boxes, hull strawberries, and peel apples, coming as strangers and always leaving as friends. How people from all over the world stumbled upon the house the same way I did, but with the added benefit of finding pie. However, all of that added up to the pressure of never being able to make enough pies, and expanding the business meant losing what made it so special. With the mounting demand for my pies, along with my own demand for quality control and no visible way out, I became so tired that I sometimes snapped at my employees. If I had had a sheeter and an ice cream scoop and made only these little pasties, maybe I wouldn't have burned out. Maybe I wouldn't have been such a bitch.

"Bethie," Kate interrupted me from my Dreamtime state. "What kind of pie do you want? Pip and I are getting the steak and onion. But they have sweet ones, too. How about if we get a few different ones to share?"

We sat outside at a table in the pedestrian zone, people darting in and out of stores all around us, and savored our pies. I ate every bite, including the edge of the crust, and licked the gravy and crumbs off my fingers—there was no arsenic on my hands. The pie was so good, one of the best I had had in this part of the world, that I wanted to lick the plate, too. But I didn't.

Kate's friends, Edgar and Lynne, invited us for lunch on their farm an hour south of Sydney near Camden. Using the leftover dough from Kate's class, I made a Shaker lemon pie (a lemon curd pie made with whole lemons, including the rind sliced paper thin), and we brought it along for dessert.

Kate drove us through Sydney's urban congestion, crawling along until, finally freed from the last tentacles of its suburban sprawl, we reached the Brownlow Hill farm; an undeveloped oasis that seemed to be surrounded by an invisible shield holding back the encroachment of civilization. We turned onto their long driveway, lined with olive and eucalyptus trees, climbing higher until we had a view of tall grasses and the silhouette of distant hills that could have passed for the Serengeti.

It was even more *Out of Africa* when Lynne and Edgar greeted us and ushered us over to a glass table and wicker chairs overlooking the valley. "Please sit. I'm just going to pour us a glass of champagne," Lynne said. "Please take a seat." Lynne and Edgar were both short but strong in stature, big on warmth and friendliness, each dressed in corduroys and wool sweaters, and about a decade older than Kate and me.

Just as I was about to sit, a chicken jumped up on the chair. "Oh, don't mind her. Just shoo her off," Edgar said. The chicken jumped down, but as soon as I was in the chair, a dog jumped into my lap. A terrier who, based on its confident attitude, had to be part Jack Russell.

"It's fine," I said before Edgar could grab him. "I need my dog fix." And I got it, as there were three more dogs who came sniffing around: a shaggy white terrier that reminded me of Daisy, a border collie mix, and an odd-shaped beagle mix with legs too short for its body.

"His name is Soup Spoon," Lynne said of the Jack Russell on my lap.

"He looks like trouble," I said, smiling as I stroked his back. When I stopped for the occasional sip of champagne, he nudged my hand to keep petting him, which I gladly did.

When we moved to the lunch table, set up on the veranda of the house, the dogs and the chicken followed us over. Lynne brought out a platter of grilled lamb chops, or choppies as they call them. I was noticing how Aussies liked to use the diminutive—Kate called me Bethie, breakfast was brekkie, chocolate was chockie, sunglasses were sunnies. The other dishes Lynne served were as colorful as her Provençal tablecloth: orange sweet potatoes, green and red Sicilian salad, white and yellow cheese, crusty golden-brown baguette, and a bottle of pink rosé. I couldn't concentrate on the food, let alone the conversation, with all the entertainment going on around us. Soup Spoon was humping the chicken and the chicken (or chookie) was flapping her wings to get rid of the pest. She finally shook him off, but Soup Spoon just followed her, sniffing her butt as she fled.

As much as I was enjoying myself, which is to say *very much*, I had a pang of guilt that I shouldn't be. When Foong dangled the idea of making pies with underprivileged, Indigenous kids at their school, I should have pushed for it. I should have insisted that I'd find a way to bake at the women's homeless shelter. I should have, could have, been focused on giving, not indulging. But I had to admit, the food, the wine, the whole afternoon on the farm was a little bit of heaven.

"There's a brown eagle," Edgar said, pointing to the sky. We all turned to look. "They're rare here, but there are two of them nesting on our property." The eagle soared above us, a drone on a surveillance mission, its impressive wingspan the avian equivalent of a 747.

"Where's Soup Spoon?" I asked. "And Yuri?" Yuri was their white cat who, not wanting to be left out, had also joined the lunch gathering. I had last seen them wandering across the open yard, directly below the eagle's flight path, and now they were nowhere to be seen. "I'm sorry," I said. "I'm just too worried. I'm going to look for them."

Edgar looked at me, puzzled. I didn't waste time explaining, but Doug had just posted on Facebook that morning asking if anyone had seen his cat Frankie who was missing. Frankie was a petite black cat with a deformed front leg, but her disability didn't stop her from claiming the pack-leader role among Doug's pets, including the current houseguest, Jack. Because he was a terrier, Jack was a born cat chaser and, as an only child, he was used to getting his way. But not with Frankie. When Jack pursued her, she would stop, turn to face him, and swat him with her good paw. She stayed outside most nights, but was always waiting for Doug at the door in the mornings. Until she wasn't. In rural Iowa, or rural anywhere, including Australia, cats and small dogs are easily scooped up in the talons of eagles, hawks, and owls. Doug was still hoping Frankie would show up, but based on the nightly chorus of hooting owls on his farm, the chances were slim, and I was praying that Jack wouldn't be next.

With my heart rate accelerating along with my fear, I jogged to the far side of the yard, scanning the surroundings as I went. I found Soup Spoon and Yuri just standing on the grass without a care in the world. I exhaled at the sight of them. They were safe. I returned to the table and downed a glass of wine.

After lunch, Edgar gave us a tour of the farm. He started with the dairy barn where his work crew was milking cows. "We have a hundred cows and they're milked once a day," he explained, as we watched a man affixing an old-fashioned sucking contraption to the cows' teats. "The operation isn't making any money," he added. "The milk prices are too low." But Edgar wasn't giving up. This had been his great-grandfather's property. Like Paul Paynter with his apples, Edgar was a fifth-generation farmer. These guys made Doug's third-generation farm in Iowa—more than a hundred years old—seem like an infant in comparison. "I'm working on ways to protect the land and make it a heritage site," Edgar continued. "The farms in this area are getting turned into subdivisions and they're building plain, ugly brick houses on small plots."

"Yes, we saw them when driving in," Kate said.

"I'm selling carbon tax credits to neighbors who are developing their land. This will help keep our farm going, and let us continue our conservation efforts. We have some protected Cumberland Plain forest on our property."

Colonialist white men had plundered Australia's land from the Aboriginal peoples, and this area was no exception. One of Australia's

most autocratic governors, Lachlan Macquarie, established the farm
in 1815 as a government cattle station. He was also responsible for
creating deadly conflict with the Aboriginal peoples after forcing
their children to go to European schools. Alexander Macleay, another
colonist, purchased the farm in 1829, and Edgar's family leased it
from him in 1859, eventually buying it. Two hundred years later, here
was Edgar, working hard to return the land to its rightful owner,
the Earth itself. We can't change past wrongdoings, but we can start
from where we are. And whether he realizes it or not, Edgar isn't just
preserving nature, he is doing his part to promote world peace.

How so? In an article for *Conservation International*, Sarah Hauck
writes, "The links between human conflicts and natural resources are
clear—and as populations grow and unsustainable development is
exacerbated by climate change impacts, tension over ever-scarcer
resources will only escalate." Nelson Mandela took this seriously and
co-founded Peace Parks, also known as "transfrontier conservation
areas," that bridge man-made borders of countries. Its mission is to
encourage communities of adjoining nations to work together to
protect ecosystems, the same biodiverse systems we rely on for food,
energy, medicines, clean water, and air—basically, everything we need
for life to survive on earth. To date, the landmass of Peace Parks in
Africa equals the size of France and Spain combined.

Edgar may not be saving the African continent or the Amazon
rainforest—and eventually humanity—from the consequences of
global warming, but he is saving his little garden patch of the planet.
If everyone followed suit, even by planting a tree here and there,
we could take "extinction" off our collective list of Things to Worry
About.

When we returned to the house, Lynne met us at the car and
said, "I have a surprise for you."

We followed her inside. The four dogs, draped across the sofa in
their family room, were piled on top of each other with their heads
on the pillows. I smiled at the sight of their audacious repose. "Oh,
look at them, they're so funny."

"No, no," Lynne said. "Over here."

There, standing by the refrigerator, was . . . a baby kangaroo!

"This is Skippy. He's a wallaby." A wallaby is essentially a small kangaroo, with shorter legs and a shorter lifespan, and, if you want to get technical, flat teeth, made for eating leaves, whereas a kangaroo's teeth are curved for eating grass. Any Australian could spot the difference immediately, but to me, this darling little thing still looked like a kangaroo. When kangaroos and wallabies overpopulate, they can be a nuisance and farmers can get a permit to kill them. "His mother was shot by a farmer and when they found him in her pouch, they called us to rescue him," Lynne explained. "We've been bottle feeding him."

Edgar added, "It's rare these rescues reach maturity, but he's a year old already."

With his huge feet protruding in front of him and his long heavy tail trailing behind as a counterbalance, the wallaby stood on his haunches and watched Lynne's every move as she got the milk bottle out of the fridge and heated it up. Even his name, Skippy, made him seem like a dog waiting for his breakfast, and yet this was no dog. This was a wallaby—in the kitchen! Meanwhile, the pack of real dogs remained in their napping positions, unmoved by the marsupial in their presence. "Mostly he stays outside grazing on leaves in the ravine next to the house," Lynne said. "But he likes to come inside in the mornings and sit next to the space heater when we're having tea in our sunroom off the bedroom. He comes every afternoon for his milk. It's lactose free. Here, do you want to feed him?"

"Really? Yes!"

"Sit on the stool," she said, handing me the bottle. It didn't take any coaxing to get Skippy to follow. As I settled into position, pointing the nipple toward the wallaby's mouth, he reached out with his little black hands. He wrapped them around the bottle in a very human-like grip and sucked down his milk without stopping. I tilted the bottle up as he emptied it and stroked his neck with my free hand, easy to do given his seated pose brought his head level with my knees. His fur, gray with streaks of dark brown, lighter in color on his chest, was like a deer's but longer. I rubbed his coat, its hint of coarseness a reminder that he was a wild animal. He took one of his hands off the bottle and put it on my knee.

"He wants to hold your hand," Lynne said, "so just put your finger in there and he'll be happy."

He clutched my index finger and kept sucking. "He's like a baby," I cooed as my maternal instincts surged; it was the closest I had ever come to breastfeeding since I had only been a mother to dogs, not humans. From my vantage point, I looked straight down the length of the plastic bottle into Skippy's face, past his round black nose and into his liquid black eyes, which were staring back at me. Not just back at me but *into* me. I swam in this moment of serenity, our connection of woman and beast causing the world around me to fall away and take me into another dimension. It sounds woo-woo—after all, it was "just" a young wallaby in Lynne and Edgar's kitchen—but I felt like I was communing with the universe; that I had arrived at, to put it in Joseph Campbell's words, my "bliss station."

"There should be at least a room or some corner where no one will find you and disturb you or notice you," Campbell wrote. "You should be able to untether yourself from the world and set yourself free, losing all the fine strings and strands of tension that bind you, by sight, by sound, by thought to the presence of other men."

Though Campbell might have used the words in a different context, the sentiment fit this moment. I found all that he prescribed, even if just for a few fleeting seconds, the utter freedom from all that worried me—the fear of losing Jack and my parents, the world's increasingly vicious politics, the threat of climate disaster, my loss of faith in humanity's goodness, all of it—in the eyes of a half-wild wallaby.

When his bottle was empty, I set it aside, but Skippy didn't leave. He started licking my hand.

"Are you wearing perfume?" Edgar asked.

"No, I didn't even shower today," I said.

"That must be it," he replied, making everyone laugh.

When Skippy tired of tasting my skin, he laid his head in my lap and stayed that way for several minutes.

"That is just amazing!" Lynne said, watching me stroke his head. "He is just loving you. I can't believe it. I've never seen him do that before."

"If you ever need a babysitter, I'll come back," I offered.

"You'll have to change your wardrobe to khaki," she teased.

"I brought my bib overalls, so I'm all set," I teased back.

When Skippy decided he was ready to take leave, Lynne held the door open for him and we watched as he transitioned from his domestic life back to his wild one in one easy leap. He hopped down the steps to where the chicken was poking the dirt between the paving stones. I couldn't take my eyes off the two of them as they hung out together for a few minutes. Civilization was pressing in on all sides of the farm, yet here remained a sanctuary where an improbable menagerie of species—animals and humans alike— peacefully coexisted. If world peace was indeed possible, it could be found right here on this Camden doorstep.

"Now then," Lynne said, breaking the silence. "I'm going to put the kettle on. Shall we go into the library and have some tea with our pie?"

CHAPTER 4

Thailand

> Independence is my happiness, and I view things as they are, without regard to place or person; my country is the world, and my religion is to do good.
> —**THOMAS PAINE**

Julia Gajcak is a vice president of marketing and public relations, a position she's held at several different luxury hotel and resort companies throughout the world. I met her twenty years earlier when I went on a press trip to Bali, where she was living at the time. The invitation was meant for another journalist named Beth Howard who wrote for the same health and fitness publications as me, which sometimes caused the magazines to get our paychecks mixed up. I always fessed up to the paychecks, even though hers were bigger than mine, but for the trip to Bali, I said nothing. Even though I admitted it to her years later, and Beth forgave me—laughing it off and insisting she probably couldn't have gone anyway—I still feel a little guilty. But if I hadn't gone to Bali, I wouldn't have met Julia, who had become a good friend. If I could trade lives with anyone it would be Julia. She's successful, but humble and down to earth; independent but with a tight-knit circle of family and friends; and worldly but with Midwestern roots (she's from Chicago). She has spent most of her career living in tropical locales like the Maldives, Mumbai, Bali, and, at the time I was making my way around the world, Bangkok. I was looking forward to staying with her, but a few days before I arrived, she emailed and said she was still in the States and wouldn't be back until the day after I left. "I'll leave the key with the concierge. Make yourself at home," she wrote. I would be alone in her apartment for my ten-day stay. While I was disappointed to miss her, it was good she was away, because the young girl who sat behind me on the flight from Sydney coughed the entire nine and a half hours without covering her mouth, thus passing her cold (and luckily nothing worse) on to me, which meant I spent my first three days in Thailand in bed.

Tucked in a quiet corner of central Bangkok—though "quiet" and "Bangkok" in the same sentence is an oxymoron—Julia's apartment was an oasis among the constant throng of traffic. To go from the street noise outside into the hushed, almost reverent ambiance of the residential grounds, was like stepping into a giant spa. Her two-bedroom condo was in a luxury apartment tower surrounded by a moat filled with lotus flowers, their white blossoms and green leaves resting on still waters. Pagodas and gold Buddha statues, almost as tall as the palm trees behind them, lined the portico. Illuminated displays of Asian fine art adorned the hallways leading to the lobby, where Thai women in long silk skirts and gold sashes staffed a twenty-four-hour concierge desk. It was so opulent I didn't feel like I belonged, couldn't belong, no matter how hard I tried. I thought of an old boss who, upon seeing me once dressed in my very best, said, "You still look like a granola cruncher," a comment I've never quite been able to shake off. I hadn't worn my bib overalls to Bangkok—I wore black linen pants and a white linen blazer, hand-me-downs from my sister—but I didn't have the designer clothes, let alone ironed clothes, or the stilettos and salon-styled hair to blend in. My pie supplies and the World Piece aprons and stack of pie cookbooks I brought as gifts took priority over clothes in the limited space of my suitcase, which itself was a beat-up sports-gear bag that I got from Costco ten years earlier. The only other footwear I brought was running shoes and a pair of flat sandals. But stilettos? I didn't own anything with a heel higher than the motorcycle boots I traveled in, wearing them to shave three pounds off my overweight baggage. As for styled hair, my blond mane was like my personality: it leaned toward the feral side. But, fuck it, I wasn't there to blend in; I was there to make pie.

When I first told Julia about my trip, in addition to offering her place to stay, she suggested I bake pies for the American Embassy's Fourth of July party. "You could recreate your Pitchfork Pie Stand," she said.

"That's a great idea," I told her. "It would be a fun twist to celebrate an American holiday on the other side of the world." I had envisioned U.S. diplomats and their families picnicking on the lawn of the American Embassy, but forty emails and one security clearance later, I learned that this was no picnic; it was a formal event in the ballroom of the Grand Hyatt Erawan Hotel.

"This year's theme is State Fair," the organizer Saul told me.

"Perfect! I will make sure to wear my bib overalls," I responded, thus the real reason I brought them on the trip. That they were ideal for piling layers underneath to stay warm in New Zealand—and that they riled up my mom—was a bonus.

"We're expecting a thousand, maybe twelve hundred people, dignitaries from all over Southeast Asia," he said.

"Oh, okay, that's great," I answered, as if it were no big deal, like I bake for twelve hundred dignitaries every day.

"We can provide ingredients," he continued. "And we've arranged for you to use the Grand Hyatt's kitchen. Their pastry chefs will help you with whatever you need."

Julia's apartment was on the eleventh floor and had a big balcony. I opened the sliding glass door and stepped outside, willing myself not to look down. Even when I was in my strongest, most stable frame of mind, I couldn't suppress the thought of what would happen if I fell—or jumped. "The Call of the Void" or High Place Phenomenon (HPP), as it's known, has been studied with results showing that the impulse to fling yourself off a ledge is not an indication of being suicidal, rather it affirms your desire to live, as your mind adjusts and your body backs away from the drop—hopefully. Still, I squeezed the railing with both hands to ensure I stayed put while I took an inventory of the city view. A jumble of skyscrapers dominated the horizon. Joggers and bikers crisscrossed a large, green open space, Lumphini Park, Bangkok's "green lung." An endless river of cars, trucks, and motorcycles inch-wormed their way along thoroughfares that extended as far as the eye could see. If Sydney was the London of the Pacific, then Bangkok was the New York City of Southeast Asia. Gripping the railing tighter, I looked down. I was glad I did, because right below me was an uncommonly long swimming pool, an alluring aquamarine stripe bordered by green grass.

The stomachache that had tortured me from LA to Auckland had dissipated, replaced by a headache from my cold. But it didn't ache badly enough to keep me from that giant swimming pool, so long it spanned the full length of the apartment complex. I was in the tropics at last. I could go outside without a coat and actually feel warm—even better, hot—and my body was begging to be outside in that heat.

If there was ever a good place to be sick with a cold it was Thailand. With street food vendors on almost every block, it was easy to eat well. I had already stocked Julia's fridge with spicy red and green curries, lemon grass soup, ramen noodles, fresh papaya, limes, and pineapple-banana smoothies. I bought whole coconuts out of the back of a farmer's pickup truck, and he whacked them open for me with his machete so I could drink the coconut water. Along with the health benefits of this Thai diet, sitting in the sun, I reasoned, would be the best way to sweat out the toxins and add "D" to the alphabet of vitamins I needed to recover. And it was urgent that I recover because I needed to start prepping for the seventy-five pies I was going to make for the Fourth of July. So I put on my swimsuit, grabbed a towel and a handkerchief, and dragged my congested ass down to the pool.

I lowered my achy body into the water. It was no Rotorua hot spring, but it was warm and sure to be healing. Doing a very slow breaststroke, I swam two laps, which left me exhausted, though in fairness it was more like four laps given the pool was double the length of an Olympic-size one. To catch my breath, I sat on the pool's edge, dangling my legs in the water. Wheezing in and out, barely able to breathe through my nose and unable to fill my lungs fully, I tried to get into a rhythm. Inhale. Exhale. Inhale. Exhale. You couldn't really call it meditation, but I was doing my best to focus, to subdue my headache, which had gotten worse, and to quiet down the fountain of noise and sorrow that bubbled up to the surface during my swim. I had already tapped a well of self-loathing earlier, thanks to Julia's full-length mirror, where I stood naked when changing into my "togs." If I could go within—if I could sit still long enough— maybe I could turn down the volume in my mind. But I was joined by my worst enemy, my personal saboteur—me—and thus began the downward spiral of inner bullying.

I feel old. I don't have as much energy as I used to. I feel fat and flabby. My body has changed. My skin is dimpled and I have a muffin top. I can't sleep. My body temperature is all over the place. My sex drive is in the toilet. I'm always so sad and depressed. I don't like myself anymore.

Ensuring the circle of self-criticism be unbroken, I added, *I hate myself for hating myself.*

This is what happens when you are sick, jet lagged, menopausal, and nostalgic all at the same time. It's a perfect storm that hurtles you into that miserable, self-defeating, pointless territory of comparing your present self to the version you were thirty years earlier.

Thirty years prior I had been sitting by a pool, albeit a smaller one, in this same city. The year was 1984, I was twenty-two, and I was invited to Thailand by two new friends, sisters Uschi and Eve Kamer, who I had met during my first trip to Europe. How we met is a story in itself. It began with the question of where I should start my continental travels, prompting me to use one of my preferred methods of decision-making. No, not the coin toss, though it is often helpful for an indecisive Gemini. There were too many options for a simple yes-or-no answer, so I opted for another method. With a paper map of Europe laid out in front of me, I smoothed out its wrinkles, closed my eyes, and waved my hand in a circle above it. Wherever my finger landed would be the place I started: Bern, Switzerland. On my second day there I met the two sisters sunbathing topless in a park. "Don't stay in the youth hostel," they insisted. "Come stay with us. Our parents are out of the country so we have plenty of space." Their parents were living in Bangkok where their dad was the Swiss Ambassador to Thailand. Moving in with my duffel bag, the Kamer's apartment in Bern became the basecamp for my European travels, hitchhiking through Italy, studying French in Neuchâtel, and working on a boat in the South of France for the summer. When summer turned to fall and I was still there, they said, "Come to Thailand with us for Christmas." I had never spent Christmas away from my family, but for this once in a lifetime opportunity, my parents said, "You should go!"

I loved Thailand so much that when Uschi and Eve returned to Switzerland after the holidays, I stayed. For three months, I trekked among the poppy fields and Hill tribes in the north and camped in primitive beach huts in the south, hooking up (in both senses of the word) with fellow travelers along the way.

Thailand was my happy place, and after all those years I was finally back. So why was I feeling so sad? Because the looking glass of the swimming pool reflected the hard truth: I was not that free-spirited girl anymore. I had lost my husband, my hormones, and my muscle tone, along with the feeling of invincibility that comes with youth. All I had left were depression, fear, and a growing layer of belly fat.

My dad told me more than once, "The quickest way to be unhappy is to compare yourself to others." He should have added, "And don't compare your present-day self to who you were in the past."

Inhale. Exhale. *Stay open. Stay in the present. And for fuck's sake, stop judging yourself.*

But my physical state wasn't the only thing bringing me down. I had other reasons to feel like S-H-I-T. I was still fretting about wanting to make my World Piece project significant, to impact lives in a positive way, and make it worthy of the support people had given me. Doug wasn't the only one who had made a financial contribution. Others had chipped in, even if just twenty or fifty bucks, and I felt an obligation to them. Hell, I felt an obligation to all of humanity. And here I was, unintentional as it was, staying in yet another posh apartment, not exactly immersing myself in the Thai culture. Well, it was one part of the Thai culture, just not the making pies by a rice paddy, grass-roots level that seemed more . . . more what? Important? Necessary? Never mind that Thais don't have ovens for baking since their food is boiled in water or fried in woks. If I thought I had come here to help, the joke was on me. I needed this country—and the peace it already possessed—more than it needed me.

Another contributing factor to my malaise was that I had looked at Facebook that morning. When I traveled decades earlier, long before we were connected 24/7 by a world wide web, you wrote letters instead of emails and text messages—aerograms, they were called, delicate sheets of blue tissue paper and envelopes with red and blue striped borders. You would wait weeks to get a return correspondence. I thought that being able to stay connected so easily and instantly with video calls and social media during my pie journey would erase any FOMO, guaranteeing I'd have no fear of missing out, but scrolling through my Facebook newsfeed had had the opposite effect. In America, my friends were all celebrating the U.S. Supreme Court's decision to allow same-sex marriage in all fifty states. Everyone had changed their profile picture turning the site into an endless column of rainbows. Friends were also mourning the nine Black people a white supremacist had gunned down in a Charleston church. President Obama was giving a eulogy for them that day, while the state of South Carolina was finally taking down the Confederate flag still flying over their capitol building. *Why was that even still up? Anyone with a grade-school education should know that flag stands for racism.*

I kept scrolling. My friend Stacy, who loves dogs even more than I do, had just put down her fifteen-year-old cocker spaniel. Doug had posted pictures of Jack, whom he had taken to the groomer for a full-body buzz cut—without consulting me. Alongside it was a photo of himself with his own hair buzzed off. The caption read, "I got my annual hay-baling haircut, so Jack got one, too." He also posted several videos of Jack who, apparently liking his newly shorn hair, was barking at the cows in the pasture, swimming with a stick in the pond, and running after a Frisbee. I should have been grateful they were bonding, but it made me feel left out. And there was Julia, who I had been so looking forward to seeing in person, surrounded by her family on a Nantucket beach, arms around each other and smiling radiantly. It should have made me feel connected to home, but it just made me lonely.

The worst thing on my Debbie-downer checklist was the text exchange I'd had that morning with my sister, Anne. "Dad hasn't gotten approved by his insurance company yet for his melanoma surgery," she wrote.

"WTF???? IT'S BEEN OVER A MONTH AND A HALF. CANCER SPREADS QUICKLY!!!!" I shouted in all caps with ten steaming-orange-face emojis.

"They can't do anything. They just have to wait," Anne wrote back.

"NO, THEY CAN'T WAIT!!!!! They have to be their own advocates. Why aren't Mom and Dad being more assertive? They need to get this taken care of. If I were there, I would get the phone numbers and call the insurance company and the doctors myself."

But I wasn't there. I was fourteen time zones away.

"They are on their own journey," Anne replied with her gentle wisdom. She was one of the few who knew which of my levers to pull to wind me up, but also the ways to calm me down. "You can only help so much. You have to let them live their own lives. Just like they let you live yours."

She was right. We are all on our own individual journeys. As much as I wanted to offer advice or take charge, the only person's life I could meddle in, the only path I could alter, was my own. And given that that path was at present taking me in the opposite direction of enlightenment, I needed to focus on getting myself turned around. Or, as my sister would tell me, "Turn that frown upside down."

Sitting there sweating under the Southeast Asian sun, I kept my eyes closed and continued wheezing. *You're going to be okay. You're just exhausted and not feeling well and that's making you vulnerable. Your coping mechanism always fails when you're tired or sick. You just need to get rid of this cold.*

For as much as I longed to feel better, a cold can't be rushed. You can't will it to leave your body. It doesn't clear up in an instant. It has to move through its paces, through the throat, the sinuses, the glands, the lymph nodes, and the lungs—the place, according to Traditional Chinese Medicine, where grief is held. My lung energy, my *qi* (pronounced "chee"), was definitely taking a hit, making me wonder, *Could it be my lingering grief, and not that young girl on the airplane, that made me sick?*

It was in this meditative, mucous-altered, borderline-mental state that I had a vision of Marcus. He appeared to me as clear as the chlorinated pool water, his dark hair swept back off his forehead, his green eyes, high cheekbones, and soft breathy voice in that sexy German-British accent. "My love," he said. "You need to let me go. It's time to move on. Let go of the sadness. I realize I should have been a better husband. I was so focused on my work I didn't make our marriage a priority. I'm sorry." And then, like a ripple moving across the water, he was gone.

I opened my eyes and looked around. I was still here, at the Sukhothai Residence, with only a few other people standing in the shallow end of the pool. Marcus was nowhere in sight. I shut my eyes again, not wanting to miss him in case he came back.

It wasn't Marcus, but Daisy who appeared this time. Again, the vision was clear—her coarse and curly white hair, her pear-shaped body, and the deep brown eyes of her angelic soul. "You need to let me go," she said, her English surprisingly clear considering she was from Mexico. "You got me off the streets and gave me a better life. There are so many dogs and other animals who need rescuing, and you have so much love to give. Adopt another one."

When she disappeared, I didn't open my eyes. I was too curious to see who else might show up.

And there it was: the American Gothic House.

More dollhouse than farmhouse, I had fallen in love with it at first sight, with its front porch and slamming screen doors. And the way, in spite of its Lilliputian size, it stood so strong, having staked its claim one hundred and fifty years earlier, before the arrival next door of the double-wide trailers, the modern visitor center, and the city's unsightly maintenance shed. "You need to let go," it whispered in the same way it did when we first met, when it had said, "You need to live here. We need each other." I had heard it speak to me that first day, like a spiritual calling, a *knowing* that it was the right place to be at that time. And I had listened. I followed my own gut and not the opinions of others, like my mother who wanted me to live by her in LA and not by a cornfield in rural Iowa. The house had been vacant for two years before I moved in and I had brought it back to life after its neglect. I cleared away the cobwebs and dead flies—along with the long, dried snakeskin I found in the heat register—and scrubbed it all the way down to its square-headed nails. I filled it with furniture, with friends, with strangers who became friends, with dogs, and with pie. So. Much. Pie. For four years, the house had anchored me, protected me, and brought me back from the brink. I was finally thriving, not quite like my old self—I would never be the same after the trauma of losing Marcus so suddenly—but like that snake who had left its skin behind in the heat register, I had shed a layer of grief. I had learned to accept that transformation is a natural, ongoing cycle of renewal, and that, for as much as I hated to leave my beloved house, it was time to begin anew. "Let go," it whispered again. "Find a new house."

I had already found a potential new house—in Australia. When Edgar gave Kate and me the farm tour, we stopped at one of the buildings on the property. It was his mother's old house. She had been gone for several years and, apart from her antique furniture that still filled the rooms, the house was empty. It had the same curb appeal as the American Gothic House—the front porch, the pitched roof but made of corrugated tin—and it was small enough for one person to live in without feeling overwhelmed by too much space. It was charming. And it was available. Even more incredible, when we peeked inside the first thing I saw, propped up next to the kitchen door, was a pitchfork! I didn't need Sister Wendy—or Charity—to interpret this as a divine message. Its providential point was as sharp as the three tines of the farm tool.

I had wanted this trip in part to help determine where I would live next and I was open to finding a new house. And while the opportunity was tempting—at Edgar and Lynne's I'd be able to commune with Skippy every day—could it be that *it* had found *me* too soon? I still had two and a half months and seven countries to go, and I had my parents and my dog waiting for me back in the U.S., which was awfully far from Australia. I had to leave the house—and Skippy—behind.

"Onward and forward," my dad had said as I boarded that first flight from LA. I had moved forward—all the way to this swimming pool in Thailand, where I was in the throes of a head cold and hallucinations. I took one last dip in the water, diving down to wash away the ghosts, and went back up to bed.

The Grand Hyatt Erawan Hotel is a stately monument of a building, its white exterior punctuated by a colorful row of international flags flapping in the warm breeze. To get inside you pass under the *porte cochère* where Thai doormen in formal white jackets and black trousers open the doors of Jaguars and Mercedes for hotel guests, bowing to them as they step out.

Inside, the lobby is like a palace, an airy atrium with columns, three stories high, that hold up the sky, visible through the glass ceiling. One floor higher, ornate balustrades are lined up like wooden soldiers to create a barrier on the wraparound balcony, from which a wide waterfall of a staircase cascades down. Leafy, thick-trunked trees grow tall in stone pots, positioned for show rather than shade. This was a place for crazy, rich Asians. I was neither rich, nor Asian, but I could certainly qualify as crazy.

I was there to meet with two of the hotel's chefs about baking pies for the Fourth of July party. I found them on the far side of the lobby, at the Erawan Bakery. They were easy to spot, standing together in their bleached-white chef coats with their names embroidered above their breast pockets. Chef Ryan, a tall man with fair skin, clearly not Thai, was an executive assistant chef from Australia. And Jean-Marc, slender, graying at the temples, and looking like he would rather be riding a motorcycle than managing a kitchen, was the head pastry chef. He was from France.

"Would you like something? Pick whatever you want," Ryan said, pointing to the display of pastries. "It's all made here on site."

I perused the bakery display—ripe raspberry tarts, creamy and flaky mille-feuille, iced éclairs, macarons in a palette of pastel shades, and fluffy chocolate mousse. To look at the pastries, you could forget you were in Bangkok and think you're in Paris.

"I see you have pie," I teased. There were meat pies, small round ones filled with chicken and duck Thai curry. I half expected to see smiley faces on them, but there were none. There were also miniature lemon meringue pies, each the size of a hockey puck. Nestled in a shortbread crust, the lemon filling was as shiny as lip gloss and topped with three tiny dollops of meringue. It was pretty—too pretty. It almost looked fake in a shellacked, plastic surgery kind of way. So instead of pie, I ordered what looked most homemade—a trio of bite-size lemon bars dusted with powdered sugar, along with a latte.

"Saul sent us your list of pies," Ryan said.

I had told my embassy contact which pies I would make: apple, apple crumble, blueberry, strawberry rhubarb, Shaker lemon, s'more, and chess, which is a buttermilk custard. If I was truly recreating my Pitchfork Pie Stand, these are the pies I would need to make. "Were you able to get everything?"

"*Oui*," Jean-Marc said. "But it was not easy to get some of the ingredients. And we could only get graham crackers in a quantity of fifty pounds."

"Fifty pounds?" I needed less than five. I tried not to show my surprise—and my relief that I wasn't the one paying.

"When we finish our coffee, we'll give you a tour of the kitchen," Ryan said, "and then I need to get back to work. We're prepping for a banquet tonight."

The hotel's kitchen is located in what they call the back of the house. I had worked at a Hyatt resort once and was familiar with the maze of sterile concrete passageways that led to the offices and utility rooms hidden from the view of paying guests. The antithesis of the five-star façade that's curated for tranquility, the back of the house buzzes with hurried activity—a hive of worker bees serving the queen. Maintenance engineers carrying tools, maids rushing around with clipboards and key rings, laundry attendants pushing bins of sheets and towels, florists exchanging vases of old flowers for fresh ones, culinary staff wheeling loaded carts every which way to deliver their creations to the numerous restaurants, rooms, snack bars, and banquets.

The pastry kitchen, one of Erawan's many kitchens, was so far back in the reaches of a maze so complex, I didn't know how I would ever find it again without a guide. Cramped and crowded with limited counter space, the kitchen was tiny in contrast to its vast output of baked goods. I watched as a whole team of pastry chefs moved about the room, each one concentrating on his or her own creations. They were making breads, biscuits, dinner rolls, muffins, tarts, cookies, cakes, canapés, and the meat pies I had seen earlier in the hotel café. They were in a competition, but not like *The Great British Bake Off*. The thing they were competing for, as I would learn when it came time to bake my pies, was oven time.

Ryan bid his farewell and Jean-Marc took me into his coat closet of an office. There was barely room for one person, let alone three, but we squeezed in next to his assistant pastry chef who was sitting at the desk, typing something into the computer. "This is Samart. If you need anything, just ask him. I'm leaving for France, for my vacation," Jean-Marc said. He grabbed his leather jacket and motorcycle helmet from the hook on the door and, faster than you could say *au revoir*, he was gone.

"Nice to meet you," Samart said, as I stood there a little stunned after being abandoned by Jean-Marc. "I'm sorry my English isn't very good."

"I promise you, it's far better than my Thai," I replied.

Samart, a few inches higher than my five-foot-five frame, seemed tall for a Thai man. He was thin with a thick head of cropped black hair. His lips were full and his brown eyes were as warm as his smile. I liked him immediately.

"You're going to be here all week, starting tomorrow, right?" he asked.

"Yes," I said. "I'm going to make all the crusts first. Will you have enough refrigerator space for me to store them?"

He nodded. His eyes were so friendly, his manner so gentle, I immediately forgot about Jean-Marc.

"After that, I will have to prep all the fruit. And I plan to bake half the pies the day before the event and the rest that morning, if that's okay with you."

"I think so. We'll try to keep a little space for you to work. And I can get a couple of people to help you." Then, as if reading my mind, he said, "I'll walk you to the elevator, otherwise you might not find your way out."

Samart led me back to the lobby, and I retraced my steps through it to get outside into the sunlight. I was finally in the tropics and yet I would be spending the bulk of my time in a windowless kitchen in the artificially lit underbelly of the hotel. It was a classic case of "be careful what you wish for." I had been seeking cultural immersion and I was going to get it. And it would be worth far more than just enjoying the weather.

Before heading back to Julia's, I stopped to see what was drawing the crowd on the corner next to the hotel. Crammed together under a smoky cloud of incense, tourists and locals alike were lighting candles and praying—and talking on their cell phones. On either side of the corner, sidewalk vendors were making easy money selling incense and garlands of marigolds. Customers bought strands of the neon orange flowers to hang on the iron railing that protected the main attraction: a gold statue sitting on a throne beneath a bling-encrusted pavilion. This was the Erawan Shrine. More Medusa than deity, the statue's head had four faces, one for each of the four points on a compass, and eight arms, seven of them holding objects and one of them placed on its chest. Meet Brahma, the Hindu god of creation. This particular Brahma was known to Thais as Phra Phrom, one of the deities of the Hindu cosmology that was later absorbed into Buddhist belief. I had to do a little investigating to find out why a Hindu shrine was so popular in a country that is 95 percent Buddhist. I also wondered just how much the two beliefs merged. The history is so complex it would require a doctorate in religious studies to unravel it, but the universal belief—and the reason for the shrine's great appeal—is that regardless of your religion, by making an offering to Brahma, you will be rewarded with good fortune. I made a note to come back another day with enough *baht* to buy a few strands of marigolds.

The shrine was dwarfed by the surrounding behemoths built to worship that other god: capitalism. That the Grand Hyatt towered above the shrine was incongruous enough, but the billboard-size signs on the hotel windows for Rolex watches and an Alexander McQueen boutique were even more jarring as a backdrop. While the shrine appears to have been squeezed out by the hotel—and the Skytrain that whizzes by overhead on the elevated tracks—the hotel was there first. The original hotel, before it became a Hyatt, was called The Erawan, and during its construction in 1951, there were all kinds of delays and accidents. This scared off the workers, prompting the developer to consult an astrologist, who advised, "The karma needs balancing," so in 1956, they built the shrine to appease the spirits, and the project continued without further incident.

I was still getting over my cold, but I needed some exercise, so instead of taking the Skytrain—Bangkok's efficient and air-conditioned light rail system—I walked back to Julia's. I was destined to walk, it seemed, because just down the street from the hotel, marking the entrance to a church, was a Gothic archway. In front of the building next to it was a life-size portrait of Thailand's King and Queen in an *American Gothic* pose, minus the pitchfork. As if the message wasn't clear enough, a young woman in bib overalls walked past. I was starting to get used to the idea that my old house was going to haunt me all the way around the world. That and the fact that bib overalls were becoming a fashion trend. I would have to tell my mom. I took a few photos and kept walking.

Instead of getting tired from the walk, I was energized. The city was alive with traffic and commerce, noise and smells, that made my senses fire on all cylinders. Even the sweat running down my legs invigorated me. I meandered past the street-level storefronts of the high-rises, and sidestepped the stalls that lined the sidewalks, where vendors hawked everything from plastic washtubs to T-shirts to hair ties. I couldn't read the signs—the curlicue scroll of the written Thai language would take even longer to learn than comparative Eastern religions—but the lack of verbal information made me rely on my eyes, forcing me to look more closely at the visual details in order to decipher what was what. Some things, like the car wash, the drive-through pizza place, and Starbucks Coffee, were obvious. But other things, like the restaurant menus advertising fried duck's beak, red ant eggs, and tadpoles, I couldn't make out, even with their accompanying photos.

Street food was everywhere with setups ranging from shiny new food trucks to scuffed-up coolers secured to bicycles with bungee cords. In some cases, you could follow your nose to find the food. I sniffed out chicken sizzling on a grill—attached to a bike. The roasted meat gave off a scent so primal it made me salivate. Many of the food carts were makeshift restaurants. A few plastic chairs and tables set out on the sidewalk and, voilà, it was an instant café.

I stopped at a convenience store to buy a bottle of water, where a cat was sleeping inside in front of the refrigerator door. It didn't move, even when I pulled the door open. In the shop next to it, a dog was napping in the doorway. No one seemed to mind, or even notice, least of all the dog; everyone simply stepped over it as they came and went.

I liked that not every place in Bangkok was as polished or as glamorous as the Grand Hyatt or Julia's apartment complex. I liked how the streets were a little gritty, but still felt clean and safe. The organized chaos, colors, and smells of daily life made Sydney, which I loved, seem sterile, even dull, in comparison.

I wasn't expecting to walk past the American Embassy, but I recognized it when I saw the American flag flying out front and Marines guarding the walled compound. As I moved along the outer wall, an entire block long, I studied the mural that decorated the length of it. The art was a whimsical, almost childlike, montage depicting dual cultures: the American flag next to the Thai flag, the Statue of Liberty next to a Buddha statue, and the Marvel superhero Captain America next to a Thai girl riding an elephant. I was sure there would be pie somewhere in the mural, but I didn't find any. Repeated all along the wall were the phrases "Celebrating 180 Years of Thai-U.S. Friendship" and "Two Nations, One Friendship."

It turns out that Americans and Thais have been sharing goodwill since 1818, when the first American visitor, Captain Stephen Williams, sailed up the Chao Phraya River, seeking sugarcane. He left with a fully loaded ship and a letter from the Foreign Minister to President James Monroe proposing continued trade. We've been trading partners ever since. Fortunately, the nefarious sides of trading have lessened—sex tourism is on the decline and opium has been mostly eliminated—replaced by the crops of an even more addictive substance, one that I will never give up: coffee.

"Friendship of one government for another is an important thing," said King Bhumibol Adulyadej (Rama IX) in his 1960 address to the U.S. Congress, "but it is friendship of one people for another that assuredly guarantees peace and progress."

I didn't know it yet, but I was already contributing to that peace and progress in a certain Bangkok kitchen, building my own Thai-U.S. friendships.

Thailand, a constitutionalized monarchy since the absolute monarchy was dissolved in 1932, is a mostly peaceful country. It was never colonized by the French or British like its neighbors were, but its military has a habit of staging coups d'etat, including one in 2014, the year before my World Piece journey. These coups are usually bloodless, meant to force out a prime minister while relying on the king, in his elevated status, to serve as a stabilizing force while the quarreling sides work out their issues. But in the moment, from my superficial just-passing-through perspective, I felt only peace and love emanating from Thailand. I saw it in the little things, starting with the woman who swept the walkway every day at Julia's building. Whenever anyone passed by, she stopped what she was doing to bow in greeting. Needing one hand to hold the broom, she moved her free hand to her heart in a prayer position, fingers pointing up, and did a one-handed bow. This simple custom, such a gentle show of respect and humility, was one of my favorite things about the country, and I always, happily, returned the gesture with my own bow and hands in prayer. If using your turn signal promotes world peace, then bowing ensures it.

The staff in the Hyatt pastry kitchen was in full swing when I arrived for my first day of baking. A vision of white coats and white hats covering dark hair, hands moving in all directions, rolling pastry, kneading bread, and carrying trays to and from the ovens. Every inch of work space was in use. Where was I going to make my hundred some pie crusts? I looked for Samart to figure out how and where to start.

I found him in a corner bending over a row of petits fours, applying tiny roses to each with a tube of icing. "I'll need a large bowl," I told him.

"Is this big enough?" Samart asked, bringing me a stainless-steel bowl the size of a Volkswagen Beetle.

"That will work," I said. "I just need flour and butter. And some measuring cups."

"Measuring cups?"

"Yes, you know. Cups. For measuring."

"We don't have any," he said.

"None? How is that possible?"

"We weigh our ingredients."

In New Zealand, though they measure by weight, Mr. Z had a whole bin full of measuring cups. But here in this Francocentric commercial kitchen, there was not one cup to be found. Yes, I could estimate—I never measure precisely anyway—but these were pies for dignitaries. I couldn't take the risk of winging it.

Samart saw the look on my face and said, "Don't worry, we can use the computer and do the calculations."

I tried to stay out of everyone's way as I moved around the kitchen. The other chefs stayed focused on their own baked goods, but they were aware of my presence, stealing glances at this intruder, this foreigner, this blonde, encroaching on their limited space. I made ten batches of dough at once, making it the same way I make a single batch, blending the butter, flour, and salt, then adding ice water to hold it together, working lightly—all with my hands. No one said anything to me at the time, but word got back to me later that they had gone to their boss (not Samart, but Jean-Marc's boss) reporting the sacrilegious thing I had done. Aghast, they told him, "She makes the dough with her hands!" But to me, a food processor (or electric mixer of any kind) is the Antichrist of pie making, as you miss out on the most important parts: the tactile experience, the human touch, and—if you believe as I do—the ability to transfer energy, like love, into your pie.

I formed the dough into disks, making piles that grew into rows of piles, on my allotted twelve inches of tabletop. To make pies in bulk, it helps to complete one stage before moving on to the next, until you have everything organized and ready to put together. At my pie stand, I had the help of employees. Here, I was a one-person assembly line—so far.

On the second day, when I began rolling dough in earnest, the kitchen crew, growing used to my presence, became more curious. I had been crimping the edges for the single-crust pies when a young, bright girl approached. She was dressed like the others in the white uniform of jacket and shin-length apron wrapped around her tiny waist.

"We've never made American pie before," she said.

"Want to give it a try?" I asked.

She nodded shyly, smiling just enough to show her dimples. "My name is Lhin. I'm in training."

"I'm Beth."

After Lhin crimped a few crusts, which she accomplished with confidence and ease, another woman, a little older than Lhin and just as sweet, came over.

"I'm Nueng," she said. "I can help you, too."

From that moment on, we were a team. In between their duties of baking cheese sticks, shortbread crusts, and croissants, they helped me cut lemons into paper-thin slices for the Shaker lemon pies. Together, we peeled and sliced apples. We washed blueberries and hulled strawberries. We pressed graham cracker crumbs into pie plates for the s'more pies. Their crumbs, pressed so tightly and precisely, made mine look sloppy. I would never get hired here!

Each day in the kitchen, I watched a young man make the same cake, a fresh one every morning. He divided the batter into six cake pans, adding a different food color to each. After baking, he frosted the thin cakes as he stacked them—purple, blue, green, yellow, orange, red—adding a generous blend of mascarpone and whipped cream in between each. Using his industrial cake stand to spin it, he smeared more frosting on the top and sides until he had covered the whole thing in a cloud of white. From the outside, it looked like a tall vanilla cake, but to cut into it was to reveal the hidden treasure, a burst of all the colors, an edible rainbow.

I asked Samart about it later. "Are you making that to celebrate the same-sex marriage law that just passed?"

His blank look told me the answer before he spoke. "It's a regular item on our menu," he said. "We make this every day."

It was a good example of how narrow thinking works. In a lapse of consciousness, I was assuming that current events in America mattered here, as if life for Southeast Asians revolved around every bit of breaking news in the U.S.

The rainbow, chosen by the LGBTQ+ community in 1978 to represent equal rights, diversity, and acceptance, isn't just a symbol of gay pride; it's an internationally recognized symbol of peace, joining the ranks of many others—the dove, the olive branch, the "V" hand signal, and *the* peace sign (the ubiquitous circular line drawing), to name a few. It gained popularity with the 1960s peace movement, when American pacifists displayed banners in protest of the Vietnam War and Italians waved their *PACE* flags in their marches for nuclear disarmament. Throughout human history, the rainbow has been assigned positive meaning beyond peace and pride. Going all the way back to Biblical times, Greek mythology, the Inca Empire, and even earlier, it's been considered a connection between humans and spiritual worlds, a bridge between life and death, a sign of good luck, a promise of better times ahead, a signal of neutrality, or a blessing of marriage. The rainbow motif continues to express a desire for peace, inclusion, and social justice, but at its most basic level, a rainbow can simply be a bringer of happiness. Especially when discovered inside of a cake.

"Do you want to try a piece?" Samart asked.

"Yes, I would love to," I replied, aware that, judging by their lean bodies and their strong work ethic, the chefs didn't normally indulge in their own baked goods.

The young baker carved out a slice for me, watching as I dug a fork into it. The cake was light, creamy, not overly sweet, and went down way too fast. I ate without pausing in between bites and when my plate was empty, I looked up at the young baker and said, "That was the best cake I've ever had." He didn't speak English, but the clean plate and my smile communicated everything he had hoped to hear. He smiled back, dipping his head to conceal his pride.

I had been getting around Bangkok for over a week with this kind of non-verbal communication. Samart taught me how to count to ten. I wrote down the numbers phonetically: *neung, song, sam, see, ha, hok, jet, pat, gao, sip*. But apart from that and "thank you"—*kob khun kha*—I found myself in the rare territory of being at a loss for words. I had become a regular at an open-air café near Julia's apartment where I began to recognize the faces of the other regular customers. The women working behind the buffet line didn't speak English, and I had no idea what the dishes were so I couldn't even point to what I wanted, but we came to an unspoken understanding: they would dish up a plate of food and I would happily eat it, be it rice noodles, sticky rice, bean sprouts, chicken, fish, or pork. Whatever the mystery dishes were, they were always good, and always just a little too spicy.

In addition to my meals at the open-air café, my daily routine included a swim in the mile-long pool; a breakfast of yogurt and fresh papaya at home; a sweet, strong, slushy Thai iced coffee from a coffee cart; and, for four consecutive days, working in the hotel kitchen from late morning until late in the afternoon, sometimes into the evening.

To get to the Hyatt, some mornings I took a taxi, not the polluting three-wheeled tuk-tuk I remembered from thirty years ago, but a two-wheeled one. I didn't realize they had such a service until I was waiting for a cab one evening to meet Kate's brother Daniel, who had lived in Bangkok for ten years, for dinner. The doorman at Julia's indicated the traffic was bad—though traffic was always bad—and asked if I wanted to go by motorcycle. "Motorcycle?" I asked, noting I was wearing a skirt and sandals. "Sure!" The driver showed up instantly, handed me a helmet, and we were off, white lining between the long rows of stopped cars. Driving etiquette allows for all the motorcycles—and there are many—to cut to the front of the line at stoplights, all of them taking off at the same time, humming like a swarm of locusts when the light turns green. People warned me later, "There are a lot of knee injuries in Thailand because of that, so make sure to hold your legs in." I held onto the driver's waist, knees against the bike, and leaned into the curves with him the way I used to do on the back of Marcus's BMW. Feeling the wind in my face, I was blasted head on by molecules of air. If oxygen gives life, then all that air rushing past made feel fully, utterly, completely alive. No wonder Jack stuck his head out the window every chance he got. I was transported to a level of pure joy that I hadn't felt in decades. Thirty years earlier, I traveled around northern Thailand by motorcycle and here I was, once again, zipping around on the back of a bike. I was still that wild and brave girl after all!

Kate's brother was single and if he was as nice as his sister and parents I wondered if he might be someone I could fall in love with, though the fantasy vanished when he suggested meeting at an American-style sports bar. Daniel was indeed as nice as his sister and parents. He was tall and lean with that same big smile, shining eyes, and genuine Australian warmth, but the most memorable part of the evening with him was the motorcycle ride.

I didn't ride sidesaddle like many Thai women do. And I did not tell my mom about my risky mode of transportation, but I told Julia in an email. She wrote back, "I take a motorcycle taxi to work every day. Everyone thinks I'm crazy." And that is precisely why Julia and I are friends.

The motorcycle became part of my morning routine, but every evening after baking, I walked the hour-long route back to Julia's, always stopping at the Erawan Shrine before heading home. Inhaling the scent of sandalwood, I joined the other worshippers and said a daily prayer to ask for good fortune. I also expressed my gratitude to Brahma for my parents, for Jack, for Doug taking care of Jack, for Marcus, and for all the people who had been helping me on this trip: my hosts Charity, Kate, Foong, Julia in absentia, and adding a few more to my growing list, Samart, Lhin, Nueng, and the others at the Hyatt who were helping me make pie.

After all my prep was finished, it was time to start baking. I don't know who made the kitchen schedule—it wasn't Samart—but I was allotted the bare minimum of oven time. Worse, I got bumped from the second time slot I needed, which meant all seventy-five pies would have to be baked within three hours. "That's impossible!" I wanted to argue, but I would get use of all of the ovens at once, which made it doable. And as I started the baking process—filling the pie shells with fruit, putting on the top crusts, crimping the edges, and

brushing on the egg wash—Brahma rained down his blessings with
the best surprise: everyone in the kitchen pitched in to help! Samart
and the young man who made the rainbow cakes were assigned to
Shaker lemon, s'more, and apple crumble. Lhin and Nueng took
charge of strawberry-rhubarb, chess, and double-crust apple. And I
made blueberry.

They were all extremely competent, fast workers, and experts at
handling dough given they regularly made pies for the hotel. But
they weren't used to big, overstuffed pies like these. Theirs were bite-
size or mini pies, mostly filled with meat, though I did see a tray of
mini pecan pies come out of the oven one day. My pies were different
in that they weren't just big, they were the Beverly Hillbillies of the
pastry world—a little disheveled, never quite uniform in appearance,
but always earnest. Forced to ignore the precision that had been
drilled into them at culinary school, the staff graciously adhered
to my looser baking style, but when the blueberry pies came out of
the oven, oozing with dark berry stains all over the top, the young
French-trained chefs reached their breaking point, unable to hide
their dismay.

"You can't serve these," they said. "They are not perfect." Even
Samart disapproved.

I laughed. "Pie is not about perfection. This is exactly how a
homemade pie is supposed to look. Just wait until the event. I promise
you, these will be the first pies to get eaten."

Because the Fourth of July fell on a Saturday and the party was a
business affair, it was held on July 2, what would have been Marcus's
forty-ninth birthday. I could have spent the day dwelling on this
depressing fact, but I didn't have the time. An hour before the party
started, Samart, Lhin, Nueng, and I wheeled two plastic-encased
carts, ten-shelves high, fully loaded with pies, through the maze of
hallways getting wide-eyed stares from the other employees as we
went. We navigated the elevators and narrow doorways, until finally,
we entered the ballroom like a group of rock stars going on stage.

A table was already set up with an easel next to it propping up
a sign bearing my Pitchfork Pie Stand logo: a black and white line

drawing of the American Gothic couple with a slice of pie on the end of the pitchfork. We set out as many pies as we could, several of each flavor, until the table looked as if it might collapse under the weight of them.

One summer, I overheard one of my Iowa pie-stand customers telling another, "These pies are so heavy." "So heavy" may not be what some of us want to hear when it comes to bodyweight, but for pie it was a compliment. They were heavy, because when I worked in the Malibu café—the surfer version of culinary school—my pie mentor preached abundance and ever since, I fill the shells to their maximum capacity and a little beyond. Which explains why the bottom of my oven always looks like the aftermath of a volcanic eruption.

The pies for the embassy party may not have made the cut for the prestigious *Meilleur Ouvrier de France* pastry award, such were their homemade qualities, but they were so appealing, evoking such a Pavlovian response, they could have won any state fair ribbon—and were certainly worthy of my pie stand stamp of approval.

I had come into the ballroom earlier in the day to check out the table setup. A distinguished-looking man in a blue sport coat with a tiny American flag pinned to his lapel approached me. "You must be the pie lady," he said, extending his hand.

"Is it that obvious?" I asked, joking. I was wearing my bib overalls, like I had promised Saul, and to make sure I looked "Iowa enough," I wore my hair in braids.

"Glad you could come and make pies for us," he said. "I'm Patrick Murphy, the chargé d'affaires." Meaning he was an interim ambassador. "Saul told me about you."

"I haven't met Saul in person yet. Is he here?"

Saul had already spotted me and made his way over. "How did the baking go?"

"Great," I said. "You'll have to come by the pie stand tonight. I'll make sure to save you a slice."

"I have your security badge," Saul said, handing me a laminated card with a clip and an official seal that read "U.S. Department of

State, Diplomatic Security." It didn't have my name on it, only a number and my job title.

I laughed. "It says I'm with the band."

He laughed, too. "We didn't have a category for pie baker."

When I came back in the evening, the ballroom had been transformed into a fairground with stacks of hay bales, a ring toss game where you could win a stuffed animal, and several face-in-the-hole boards with various farm scenes, including one of a farmer dressed in bib overalls and a straw hat, holding a chicken. Samart and I posed with that one—Samart's face poking through the hole with the farmer's clothes, and me, already dressed in bibs, standing next to him in front of the board. Costumed characters milled about—a Holstein cow, a red delicious apple, and the California raisins, representing the dairy, apple, and grape industries, respectively. A spread of American snacks that I had watched my pastry friends make earlier in the day—corn on the cob, fried Snickers on a stick, and piles of donuts—was so bountiful you could get type 2 diabetes just looking at them. There was a lemonade stand in the middle of the room and Thai cocktail servers dressed as cowgirls carried trays of iced tea and beer through the crowd. A band played "The Star-Spangled Banner" before segueing into "Let's Groove" by Earth, Wind & Fire, while a state-fair-themed slideshow played above them on a giant screen. This parallel universe expanded further when pictures of John Deere tractors and the Sky Glider at the Des Moines fairgrounds, familiar scenes from my home state, appeared on the screen. Was I in a Bangkok ballroom or in Iowa—or both at once?

This crazy, cultural mashup, celebrating the 239th anniversary of America's independence, was attended by government leaders, business executives, trade representatives, and military officers of nationalities from Asia, the U.S., and beyond. Mingling, drinking, and eating pie, these were people in positions of power who could help make world peace a reality. Maybe in some micro way, pie would play a part in that. Maybe two adversaries would meet at the pie table and resolve their differences over a slice of something buttery and delicious. We often never know how the seemingly insignificant things we do can have a huge and lasting impact. I had already experienced that myself, forever influenced by the cleaning woman at Julia's apartment complex who bowed one-handed with her broom and would never know how much that meant to me.

Samart and I stood by the pie table, talking with guests, while Lhin and Nueng sliced and served the pie, remaining cool in demeanor but practically perspiring from trying to keep up with the demand. Two American gentlemen and two Thai women approached us. "We heard about the pie," one of them said. "We came all the way from the other side of the ballroom. They said you had blueberry."

"Yes, we still have some, but it's going fast," I said. I looked over at Samart with a playful told-you-so grin, causing him to laugh. "You better try a piece."

"I already did. We have to do quality control."

His laughter—along with all he had done to help accomplish this massive feat—catapulted me one giant leap closer to Nirvana. My path in life may be a mountainous one, the valleys so dark, the peaks so hard-earned, but at least I was in motion. And while there were days when the journey was a slog through a sea of moldy molasses, this particular evening was as joyful as a motorcycle ride.

On my last day in Thailand, I went back to the Grand Hyatt to say goodbye to everyone. This time, however, I was dressed like a hotel guest. I had ditched my overalls for a silk halter dress, cream with large black polka dots, so elegant no one would ever know I bought it for six dollars at Goodwill. I also blow-dried my hair straight and wore it down, my long locks covering my bare shoulders. When I walked into the kitchen, the baking team was busy, back to making the fancy hotel pastries and plating dishes of desserts, already moving on to the next big event. The disruption my pie baking had caused had been a mere pebble tossed in the river of their daily flow.

Samart was in the office at the computer and I startled him when I came in. "I didn't know it was you," he said, his eyes wide at my different look.

"I came to say goodbye, and to get everyone's contact info. Are you on Facebook?"

"Yes, I am," he said.

"Are you going to keep making pie after I leave?" I asked.

"I want to. I really liked it. We all did."

"Tell Jean-Marc if he puts it on the menu, his bakery sales will go way up," I teased.

"I have something for you," he said, handing me the page his printer had just spit out.

"The rainbow cake recipe!" I yelped. "I didn't think you were allowed to share your recipes."

He shrugged. "I know how much you liked it. And how happy you were about your new marriage law."

When I bid my final farewell to him, I did not do the customary Thai bow; I leaned in and gave him a big American-style hug. "Thank you for everything, Samart. I'm going to miss you guys." It was true, and I was sad about it. Sad in a good way, sad to leave the people who had accepted me, even liked me, for who I was, damaged soul and all.

I had started my stay in Bangkok with a cold—and with that epic episode of low self-esteem by the swimming pool. But after ten days—after the big success of the event; the relief that all the hard work was behind me; the friendships I made with Samart, Lhin, and Nueng; the nutritious diet, regular exercise, and restful sleep on Julia's crisp cotton sheets; and the exhilarating motorcycle taxi rides—I was feeling so buoyed, so healthy, so happy, that I moved with a new lightness in my step. And people noticed. As I was leaving the hotel, a gorgeous man—who had to be a decade younger than me—smiled at me as he was coming in. He stopped and said with an American accent, "I like the way you walk."

I smiled back and kept going, my dress swaying as I floated past so lightly I might as well have had wings.

CHAPTER 5

India: Part 1

> Yesterday I was clever, so I wanted to change the world. Today I am wise, so I am changing myself.
> —**RUMI**

I may have grown wings in Thailand but that airborne feeling was short lived, because upon arrival in India I crash-landed. My flight from Bangkok touched down in Mumbai after 10 p.m. and though I didn't like the idea of landing in an unfamiliar place at night, it was the only flight available.

I had wanted to go to India for years—curious about its traditions and mystical culture, attracted to all its bright colors, and charmed by its Bollywood films—but I used the same excuses I had made for putting off my round-the-world trip: I didn't have enough time or energy or money. The real reason was that I was afraid. I had heard about the poverty, the begging, the crowds, the smells, and, being an empath, I didn't think I had the fortitude to handle the sensory overload and the accompanying emotions. There were plenty of other, easier places to visit first. But when I finally committed to circling the globe, I also committed to making India one of my stops. It was time. No more excuses. I was going all in.

I wasn't even to baggage claim before I started sweating from nerves.

While waiting by the luggage carousel I made eye contact with a tall, olive-skinned man. His hair was just long enough to be pulled into a ponytail. He wore a dress shirt tucked into his jeans, and surfer-style loafers with no socks. Boho-chic meets businessman—

he was totally my type. After several stolen glances at each other we finally moved close enough to start a conversation. Within the first few seconds I found out he was a stockbroker who lived in New Orleans, he was half-Indian, he was in Mumbai for three weeks to visit his dad—and he had a girlfriend in Germany. *Damn.*

"Where are you staying?" he asked.

"The Four Seasons," I replied, sensing he was trustworthy enough to reveal such a detail.

"That's one of the best hotels in Mumbai."

"They're giving me a free room in exchange for teaching a few pie classes."

I wasn't intending to stay in such a luxurious place—again! My budget was too meager for even a few nights at a Motel 6, but Julia had worked there for a year and connected me with her old boss who was the general manager, an American who welcomed the idea of making pie with Indian food bloggers as a cultural exchange.

"My name is Johan," said the hot guy at baggage claim. "Here's my number. Call if you need anything."

We got our bags and when he saw that I was struggling to get a Wi-Fi connection to order an Uber, he said, "My Uber is already here. The Four Seasons is on the way to my dad's and we can drop you off."

Was I scared to hitch a ride with a stranger? *Au contraire.* I sat in the back of the taxi with him, in the cocoon of his protective (and alluring) presence, wishing I could spend my whole ten-day stay with him, wishing I had someone to help me navigate—and understand—this mysterious land. I was especially wishing he didn't have a girlfriend. I wished all this, because as we sped along the dark highway, catching ghostlike glimpses of the endless miles of slums, row after row of ragged shacks built right up to the edge of the road, I already knew I was in over my head.

My pie classes were scheduled for my second and third days in Mumbai, so I used the first day to sightsee. Having no clue where to start, I went to the hotel concierge desk, where a young and elegant woman—*Neetika*, her nametag read—offered to set up a four-hour tour. Dressed in a hotel uniform of a long, black silk skirt and a cabernet jacket, she wore her equally sleek long black hair in a ponytail. Power-red lipstick framed her perfect white teeth which gleamed as she greeted me with a smile.

"I'll call a driver," she said. "Just tell him where you want to go and he will take you there."

I want to go home, I wanted to say. I was tired. I was only halfway around the world, and I hadn't realized how much stamina this journey would require. I was an athlete, not a sprinter, but what I lacked in speed I made up for in endurance. At a slow and steady enough pace, I could go the distance and finish any race. But spending only ten days in each destination was the one-hundred-yard dash of world travel. How could I make any significant contribution toward peace at this breakneck speed? The muscles of both mind and body were cramping and I couldn't catch my breath, but I had faced greater challenges—like the grief of losing Marcus—and survived. That's what my dad called me, a survivor. I had made it this far and I wasn't going to give up. Or so I told myself. India would try to tell me differently.

"Can you recommend some places that I should see?" I asked her. "I didn't have time to read up on Mumbai before I got here."

"Of course, madam," she said.

She walked me out to a waiting taxi. An insect of a car, smaller than my Mini Cooper, its most prominent features were its scuffed-up bumpers and window decals proudly advertising "A/C cab." From the looks of the driver's light blue dress shirt, dark with sweat, along with my own skin instantly glistening from the heat as I stepped outside, I would be glad to have that air conditioning.

"Hello, madam. I am Maruthi." His face and belly were both pleasantly round, giving me the impression that he was capable of a good belly laugh when he wasn't in serious professional-taxi-driver mode. "It is a very nice day today. No rain. It is very lucky it is not raining. I will take you now."

"The weather seems very nice to me," I said, ignorant of why he made such a big deal about it not raining. "I'm Beth."

Neetika gave him instructions in one of the three languages spoken in Mumbai: Hindi, Marathi, and English. All I knew is that it wasn't English. There are 19,500 languages spoken on the Asian subcontinent, though the government officially recognizes only 22 of them. With almost 20,000 languages, it's a wonder anyone can communicate at all.

In addition to the places Neetika suggested, I told Maruthi I'd like to go to a boutique that sells India's popular tissue-thin-cotton tunics, and stop somewhere for lunch.

Maruthi smiled, wagged his head side to side, and said to me, "Yes, madam. Whatever you like, madam, we will do that." I understood this to mean yes, as in total confirmation. But in India, as I would learn, "yes" has a more ambiguous meaning, more of an acknowledgement that audible sounds came out of your mouth, not a literal comprehension of what you said.

Maruthi shifted into gear, entered into the pinball machine of traffic, and off we went, into the unknown.

Our first stop was Dhobi Ghat, an open-air laundry, where dhobis (washermen) scrub and flog sheets, jeans, shirts, saris—anything that needs to be washed—in large concrete tubs. It takes up a few square blocks and to peer down into it from the walkway above is to look into a coliseum of seven hundred workstations surrounded by mountain ranges of laundry, where upwards of eight thousand half-naked men slosh around in gray water. How they can keep so many items organized enough to be returned—with same-day service, no less—is as much a marvel as how anything can actually get clean, given everything is washed in this ramshackle arena and then either hung on miles of clotheslines in the city's smoggy air or laid out on sooty rooftops to dry.

Dhobi Ghat was started 140 years ago during British rule, which ended in 1947. But how and why this still exists in the twenty-first century, who can answer that, or *any* question, about India? Maybe because the system works and business continues to pour in from the likes of hospitals, hotels, and suburban housewives. In spite of the bleaching and ironing services available in the Dhobi Ghat, I assumed—and secretly hoped—my hotel had its own facilities for washing its sheets and towels. I snapped a few photos of the laundromat before Maruthi sped me off to the next site: the Banganga Tank.

Tucked into the quieter residential neighborhood of Malabar Hill, the Banganga Tank, built in 1127, was there long before any of the high-rises around it, and centuries before Mumbai became the busting-at-the-seams city it is today. To a first-time visitor like me, it looked like a rectangular swimming pool with stadium seating as it was surrounded by concrete steps on all sides. But the tank is no municipal swimming hole; it's a holy place based on the legend that a Hindu deity, Rama, was thirsty, and when he asked his brother for water, the brother shot an arrow into the ground and—*chamatkaar!*—a spring burst forth, his thirst thus quenched. Considered to be a tributary of the sacred Ganges River, even though the main waterway is over a thousand miles away, Indians bring the ashes of their loved ones and perform pujas (spiritual rituals) at the site. They also bathe in the water. And do laundry. But there was so much litter, both in the pool and all over the steps—bits of plastic, paper, clothing scraps, discarded food, not to mention a sour smell—that it prompted another of those perplexing questions encountered on my trip: If cleanliness is next to godliness, why wasn't this place of worship kept clean? And why couldn't I simply observe it with an open mind instead of being so judgmental? In spite of how it looked to me, there were plenty of people who saw it differently—like the handful of young men laughing and splashing around in their underwear, the group of women in saris immersed in conversation while eating lunch on the steps, and the mother in dirty clothes and no shoes who was busy picking the lice out of her young daughter's hair.

Holy fucking cow, I almost said aloud. Not even an emergency recitation of my *stay open, stay in the moment, don't judge* mantra could subdue my reaction to what I saw as a disturbing scene.

"Are you ready to go, madam?" Maruthi asked.

"Yes!" I replied, trying not to sound too eager—or too disrespectful. "Yes, I'm ready."

Next was the Chhatrapati Shivaji Terminus (a.k.a. CST). Formerly known as Victoria Terminus, the name was changed to reflect an Indian identity, which is also the reason the city's name was eventually changed from Bombay to Mumbai. A UNESCO World Heritage Site, the train station is an ornate monstrosity of brick and stone, the equivalent of ten Notre Dame Cathedrals combined (in my estimation), built in the Victorian Gothic architectural style with turrets, towers, arches, pointed windows, and topped off with a dome. It shouldn't have surprised me—*couldn't* surprise me given the way my travels had been going—that this building was known as the Bombay Gothic House. But any commonalities with my humble, rural-Iowa farmhouse ended with the name. The CST is so enormous and magnificent—so heavily embellished with gargoyles, bas-reliefs, and ax-wielding grotesques—that it's India's most photographed site after the Taj Mahal. Its tourism appeal got a boost after it was featured in the Oscar-winning film, *Slumdog Millionaire*, which ended with a Bollywood-style dance scene on the station platform as the credits rolled, back when Dev Patel was shy and scrawny and not the smoldering Adonis he is now. CST is also a hub of Mumbai activity—over three million commuters swarm in and out of the station each day. Conditioned by their quotidian usage, these commuters probably don't dwell on its historic symbolism. As for me, I could not appreciate its beauty when all I could see was a big fat remnant of oppression from a past era. Not just see it, but *feel* it.

The history is, of course, complicated and this is only my Wikipedia-deep understanding, but briefly, it's this: When the British Raj gave India its independence in 1947, it divided the country in two—India and Pakistan—with the intentionally malicious goal of fracturing the peaceful coexistence between Hindis and Muslims. This particular act of divide-and-rule even had a name: The Partition. The Brits *wanted* people to fight each other, and fight they did, causing seventeen million people to be displaced and one million killed. One million! To this day, seventy years on, the fighting hasn't stopped as Pakistan (Muslim) feels that the Kashmir region (also Muslim), which is located in the northernmost reaches of India (mostly Hindu), should belong to them.

It's this subsequent and lingering animosity that inspired a group of ten young men in 2008, to travel from Pakistan to Mumbai by sea, armed with AK-47s, grenades, and bombs, so they could express their feelings about the matter. The train station, where I now stood, was one of twelve locations on their hit list, where they opened fire on a crowd. Another target was the Taj Mahal Hotel, a historic luxury hotel filled with foreigners, where they took hostages for several days before setting the place on fire. In all, 174 people died, as well as all 10 terrorists—9 during the attacks and 1 by execution.

If there is any silver to be found in the tarnished lining of this colonial past, it's that the CST station, and the railway system that it serves, provided the infrastructure for India to rebuild its economy post-independence. And with the Brits corralling India's 20,000 different languages by declaring English as the official one, communications were greatly aided. Today, Mumbai is the financial center of the country and its largest port.

After the train station, we drove past the Taj Mahal Hotel, and though it had been fully restored and was once again thriving, I couldn't help think of its past horrors. We were on our way to another jewel in the crown of colonial conquest, the Gateway of India arch, on the Arabian Sea. The towering arch could be mistaken for a clone of Paris's Arc de Triomphe, but upon closer inspection one can see the Islamic influence in its design with keyhole archways and intricate stone latticework. Built to welcome British royalty, the arch had suffered its own tragic bombing in 2003, when a taxi filled with explosives killed 54 and injured 244. The attack was purportedly carried out by the same Pakistani terrorist group who orchestrated the one in 2008.

Maruthi parked and followed me toward the arch, speed-walking past me as we crossed the plaza, joining the hundreds of other vendors and tourists melting along with their ice cream bars in the oppressive heat. My light-blue blouse, dark with perspiration, now matched Maruthi's. Even more overwhelming than the heat was the chaos and noise—a Vitamix blender on high speed of honking horns, cars, taxis, horse-drawn carts, motorcycles, and people swerving around each other in every direction you looked.

I snapped a few photos with my phone, including a selfie with Maruthi, and we were off again. I sat in the back, sweating in spite of the "A/C cab." I watched Maruthi's crucifix swing wildly on the rearview mirror in rhythm with his Mumbai-style driving, impressed that his dashboard shrine of Buddhist figures and incense box held tight every time he swerved or slammed on the brakes.

Our last stop was on a sleepy, leafy street offering a respite from the crush of humanity and cars. No sooner had we parked than two young kids, a boy and a girl no more than eleven years old, rushed up to me. "Madam, madam! Would you like to buy something?" the young boy asked, holding up a small purse trimmed with embroidery and sequins.

"Don't buy anything from them," Maruthi cautioned. "They should be in school."

But they were persistent, and polite, and the purses were cute. "I'll take two," I said. "How much would that be in dollars?"

The girl, effortlessly converting the amount from rupees without a calculator, answered immediately. "Five dollars each. You should take more. They are good quality. I have more colors."

They may not have been in school, but their English and their math skills—and their salesmanship—were impressive.

I tucked my purchases in my bag and entered our destination: the Mani Bhavan Museum, a house where Gandhi often stayed between 1917 and 1934. Mahatma Gandhi—the lawyer, politician, social activist, writer, and patron saint of peace. It was fitting that Maruthi brought me here on the heels of visiting the colonial sites, because it was Gandhi who led the nationalist movement against the British Raj, a revolt he kicked off with his historic non-violent protest of the salt tax. Arrested by the Brits multiple times, he used hunger strikes while in prison to pressure them to listen to what he had to say—about treating people equally, about unifying the country, about peace—and his strategy worked. Even after India gained its independence, he used the tactic, going on another hunger strike to encourage peace between New Delhi's Hindus and Muslims. That was in January 1948. Two weeks later, he was dead—not from starvation, but from the bullet of a Hindu extremist.

The museum was part library, part bedroom, part photo gallery. Downstairs, wooden glass-front bookcases held volumes like *The Rise and Fall of the Roman Empire* displayed next to its Arab equivalent, *A Short History of the Saracens*. Farther down the shelf was H.G. Wells's futuristic dystopian novel, *The Shape of Things to Come*, several biographies about Leo Tolstoy; and many other illustrious works, underscoring how well-read Gandhi was. Upstairs, in an airy, white room filled with almost nothing but sunlight, was where Gandhi slept, wrote, meditated, and learned to spin cotton. A futon mattress sat on a star-patterned mosaic-tiled floor, and next to it, a stubby-legged desk so low to the ground that when he worked at it, he sat on the futon instead of a chair. Unlike the downstairs library crammed to the ceiling with books and old newspapers, the bedroom did not require Marie Kondo's services. It was sparse, as one might expect from a man who wore a loin cloth, yet elegant. A balcony as big as the bedroom overlooked a tree-filled courtyard, and a pleasant warm breeze drifted in through the open door. Gandhi's living quarters were much more to my taste than the hermitically sealed luxury hotel room where I was staying. Unfortunately, the museum was not a place where I could trade pie classes for lodging.

Maruthi waited while I climbed another flight of steps to the gallery, an entire floor filled with framed photos, dioramas, and plaques. I took my time, making my way around the entire room, stopping to read Gandhi's quotes, each one of them seeming to speak directly to me, to where I was in my life, and to my current challenges.

"True morality consists not in following the beaten track, but in finding out the true path for ourselves and in fearlessly following it."

I wrote it down in my notebook so I could read it every day for the rest of my trip.

"It is faith that steers us through stormy seas, faith that moves mountains, and faith that jumps across the ocean. That faith is nothing but a living, wide-awake consciousness of God within. He who has achieved that faith wants nothing."

In other words, money doesn't buy you happiness.

And there was one I especially liked, because it supported my insistence that pie should be made with hands and not food processors.

"What I object to, is the 'craze' for machinery . . . The machine should not tend to make atrophied the limbs of man."

I sent a picture of it to Samart in Bangkok with a winking face emoji.

What I didn't see on display was Gandhi's most popular, though paraphrased, maxim: "Be the change you want to see in the world." Words of wisdom that can be found throughout the known universe, on T-shirts, coffee cups, greeting cards, journal covers, graffitied on walls, tattooed on a friend's forearm, and, coincidentally, printed on a cotton dress I had brought with me (another hand-me-down from my sister).

For the record, what Gandhi really said was, "We but mirror the world. All the tendencies present in the outer world are to be found in the world of our body. If we could change ourselves, the tendencies in the world would also change. As a man changes his own nature, so does the attitude of the world change towards him. This is the divine mystery supreme. A wonderful thing it is and the source of our happiness. We need not wait to see what others do."

After reading all his quotes and missives, I had been instilled with hope, faith, and some much-needed optimism—until I came to the last display in the exhibit. It was a collage of photographs of Gandhi's death. Images of his blood-stained robe, the handgun used to kill him, a close-up of his hands in prayer *as he was dying*, and the headline of a newspaper that read, "Gandhi fell saluting his assassin."

He saluted his assassin? Fuck. I just stood there, frozen, my heart searing with pain. *Fuck. Fuck. Fuck. Fuck.*

"Madam, we will go back to the hotel now," Maruthi said, saving me from jumping out of the third-story window.

How about if you just take me straight to the airport? I wanted to say. Instead, I replied in a whisper, "Okay, that's fine."

I had paid for a four-hour tour which was to include a lunch stop at The Leopold Café—another site of the 2008 terrorist attacks—but Maruthi had me back at the Four Seasons in three. Which was just as well, because I didn't need to visit another murder scene. As it was, I was so close to breaking down in tears I couldn't have lasted another six minutes let alone sixty. Besides, it was starting to rain, a kind of rain, I would soon discover, that not only warranted Maruthi's earlier remark about the weather being nice, it would make his comment seem like a gross understatement.

Neetika spotted me as I walked into the hotel and asked, "How did you like it? Wasn't the Banganga Tank beautiful?"

Beautiful? Is that what you would call it? I couldn't stop seeing the images of the mother plucking her little girl's lice-infested hair, while young men purified themselves in the polluted water. Not to mention the buildings throughout the city, new and old alike, covered with mold, black and green layers growing as thick and unstoppably as vines on an Ivy League school. And the dogs lying on sidewalks, so skinny their ribs showed, so heavy with sleep they looked dead. How could any of this be considered beautiful?

"Well, um . . ." I began.

Don't cry, I commanded myself. My tears had been building over several hours. I needed to get to my room before I erupted in the lobby. *Just breathe.*

"Everything was so . . ." I chose my words carefully, "interesting." Which was an honest answer. "Thank you so much for setting up the tour, Neetika. I'm just going upstairs for a rest now."

"Enjoy, madam. Just let us know if you need anything."

A grief burst. That's what I would call what happened next. When I got back inside the padded cell of my room, it all came pouring out—the disturbance, the sadness, and the confusion over what I had seen of India so far. And to think it was only the first half of my first day, and what I had seen was only a few square miles of an entire subcontinent. The story of Gandhi's death had detonated a grief bomb inside me. It wasn't just *his* death I was grieving, but *all* deaths, the ones that came before and the ones yet to come—Marcus, Daisy, my parents, Jack, and so many more loved ones, past and present. This mushroom cloud of grief kept growing until it encompassed every single care or concern that had ever passed through my hyper-sensitive heart.

The Germans have a word for this kind of despair: *Weltschmerz*. Marcus had taught it to me, as he observed my tendency to grieve the injustices of life, all of them, not just the personal ones. "It means world pain," he said by way of consoling me. Hearing that the Germans had a word for it did help a little, as it meant I was not the only one who could feel this way. "It's the anguish you feel when the idealistic world you want doesn't live up to the way the world actually is." Weltschmerz is what dropped me further down into the abyss of unanswerable questions, the ones that are the ultimate source of all grief: *What is the point of all of this? How can we ever solve all these problems? Why are we even here on this earth? Why is world peace so elusive?*

My thoughts were interrupted by the rain. What had started as a few fat drops when Maruthi returned me to the hotel had developed into something I'd never before experienced. I heard it—and wanted to duck for cover—before I even knew what it was. What could have been mistaken for an Air Force squadron firing bullets at the windows was a solid sheet of water coming down with a force that could shatter glass. This was not rain—it was a biblical deluge! Had God just heard me questioning Creation and responded with damnation? No, this was simply normal weather for this time of year: monsoon season.

I had been warned. "You shouldn't go there in July," people said.

"I don't have a choice," I replied. "When you go around the world you can't time every stop around its ideal season." Case in point was going to New Zealand during its winter, a place I'm sure I would fall madly in love with in summer.

The rain, as thick and heavy as the room-darkening curtains, blocked my view. I could no longer see the city skyline or the ocean—sea and sky had merged into one gray blur—but I could still make out the blue tarps covering the makeshift village of shacks twenty-eight stories below. I stood at the window, wrapped in a fluffy white hotel bathrobe, insulated inside this water-tight, five-star sanctuary, looking down on one of the city's biggest slums where thousands of people, huddled beneath torn plastic, were getting pummeled by a rain more violent than I knew was possible; their homes flooding, their latrines overflowing, everything they owned, including their lives, about to be swept out to sea.

Everything about this was wrong. My heart sunk even further from the weight of this steaming pile of guilt placed on top of my grief.

I shouldn't be up here; I should be down there. Or maybe I shouldn't be here at all.

The extreme between luxury and poverty, right next door to each other, ripped my insides out. India has a population of 1.3 billion, and a caste system that keeps people in "their places." This segregation, endorsed by religion, is so extreme that the poorest are deemed sub-human and therefore "untouchable." For fuck's sake, how do you even begin to solve a problem this big?

You and your little pies are never going to make any difference. Give it up and go home, I heard myself saying. But then I thought of Gandhi. What would Mahatma "Be the Change You Want to See in the World" Gandhi do?

No. You are not a quitter. You're going to finish what you started. No matter how hard it is and how small your impact, you have something to contribute. You're still strong and healthy, and you're braver than you think. You can do this.

I jammed the complimentary earplugs that came with the room as deep into my ears as they would go to silence the rain, along with the honking horns and disco music that reached all the way up to the heights of my room, pulled a pillow over my head, and tried to sleep. I had a pie class to teach in the morning. And pie, as I had experienced

again and again, was an effective remedy for grief. No matter how
fucked up the world or how sad it made me, pie—making and
sharing it with others—always made me feel better.

When I baked pies at the Grand Hyatt Erawan in Bangkok, I
worked in the staff kitchen, where the only aesthetic part about it
was the baked goods, especially the rainbow cake. But at the Four
Seasons Mumbai, they put me in a front-of-the-house kitchen with
black marble countertops, sleek pendant lighting, and two wall ovens,
the kind you'd find in a suburban American home. This was where
chefs gave cooking demos to hotel guests—and where I would teach
my pie classes.

Niharika, the hotel's PR director, had invited six prominent food
writers and bloggers for an afternoon class, so I spent the morning
baking two cherry pies to be served to the participants—cherry, because
the fruit was in season. We would also be using peaches for the class,
which, like the cherries, were grown in the cooler climes of northern
India, not in the southern state of Maharashtra where Mumbai
is located. Niharika had arranged with the hotel chef to collect the
ingredients and have everything prepped, the cherries pitted, and the
peaches peeled and sliced. This was a necessary time saver as pitting
the cherries alone would have used up the entire four-hour class time.

As the bloggers started arriving, I stood behind the kitchen
island in my gingham blouse with my blond hair tied back and my
nerves still slightly jangled from the day before. Out of the six class
participants, two were men, Indians so handsome they could have
been mistaken for Bollywood stars. Saransh Goila, a boyish chef
with a smile as big as his social media following, had just published
a book called *India on My Platter*, about his backpacking travels
around the country to explore the various nuances of each region's
food. The other guy, Nikhil Merchant, a doppelgänger for a young
Burt Reynolds whose food writing could make the preparation of a

basic cheese sandwich sound like a sensual act, was in the process of opening a restaurant in Los Angeles.

Introductions were quickly made and the class got underway, creating a surge of positive energy in the room. Flour and butter merged to become dough. Cherries and peaches mixed with sugar to become filling. The sounds of animated chatter and laughter spread through the kitchen the way incense permeates a temple. This was my temple. Pie was my religion. And teaching situations, like this one, were my holy ground. I could be transported to a higher plane no matter what mood I was in before I started. Doug, who emailed me that morning to give me an update on Jack, had added a line acknowledging this. "Enjoy the pie classes," he wrote. "That's your private environment to relax, forget about the outside, and just do your thing." He was right. And that's exactly what I did. Like a prayer, the pie class reset my frame of mind and gave me a respite from my sadness. At least for the few hours I was in the kitchen.

When we finally got all the pies into the oven, we moved over to the dining area. I cut into the pies I'd made that morning while a waitress served tea: a warm, fragrant, milky chai whose combination of cinnamon, cardamom, and pepper complemented the sweetness of the cherry filling.

"I love chai," I told Nikhil, holding my teacup to my nose and inhaling its spicy perfume.

"When Americans order a chai tea latte at Starbucks, we laugh," Nikhil said. "Chai means tea, so it's redundant."

"I guess we think 'chai' refers to the flavor," I replied. "And Starbucks has so many flavor choices, you have to be specific."

He changed the subject back to pie, inspecting the cherry filling dripping from his fork. "I was quite surprised that pie making is so immersive and soul satisfying. I like how you talk about having imperfections. I always thought the crust had to be laser-cut sharp."

"Have you ever had American pie before?"

"Yes, in a classic American diner, at two in the morning after a night of drinking. Those were the days." We both laughed. Predicting my next question, he paused before putting another bite into his mouth and added, "Cherry is my favorite."

"What kind of pie does India have? I mean, if you consider pie to be anything with a crust that contains some kind of filling. Like, I would consider samosas are a kind of pie."

Samosas are a popular Indian staple of soft, flaky dough filled with a savory mixture of vegetables like potatoes, carrots, and onions, and fried in oil. They're listed as an appetizer on any given Indian restaurant menu in the U.S.

I waited for his answer as he swallowed.

"You're right. Samosas are Indian pies in the literal sense, but the samosa was not an original Indian creation. It originated following the invasion of Central Asian Turkic dynasties in the age of yore. It also has medieval affiliations with Persia and Iran."

Of all the people I could have asked, I had picked a samosa scholar.

"After making its way to India," he went on, "due to cultural appropriation and the transition through different states, it adapted itself to different forms and fillings depending on the produce from that state or part of the country."

"Wait. Samosas aren't Indian?" He shook his head. "Funny," I said, "that's like pie. In the U.S. pie is considered so all-American, when in fact it's an immigrant."

His culinary lesson continued. "There are many variations of samosas, so the East will have *shingharas*. In Hyderabad they have *lukhmi*—filled with mince and onion. The South is more Portuguese style, especially in Goa, where they're called *chamucas*, filled with meats. But there are many other fillings—jam, fish, chocolate, and *khoya*."

"Is khoya a fruit?"

"No, it's milk solids from boiled milk. Have you had a samosa yet?"

"Yes. I had one yesterday when I took a tour of Mumbai. The taxi driver stopped at a bakery. It was called something like Birj . . ."

"Brijwasi," he said. "I know the place."

"It was incredible, so flaky. They served it on a little metal tray with a dish of tangy dipping sauce. I also tried a little turnover kind of pie that was sweet, filled with ground nuts, and the outside had a little sugar glaze on it."

"That's gujiya," he said.

"Goo-jee-ya," I repeated. "That was especially good."

"My favorite Indian food is sev puri."

"I've never heard of it."

"It's a flat, flour disc layered with potatoes and onions and covered with chutney—any kind of chutney—herby green, garlicky red, sweet date, tamarind."

"Sounds a little like a mini pizza. That could qualify as pie," I said.

"It's finished off with crispy flour noodles on top called sev. It's crunchy and savory. It's so good. You find it on the streets of Mumbai. A plate is usually six pieces and I have a habit of eating two plates on my own—with no sharing."

"No sharing? Dude, did you not listen to my speech about how pie is meant to be shared?" This made him laugh, his black goatee parting like the sea to reveal the white pearls of his teeth. "If you don't mind me asking," I said, turning serious, "since my trip is about peace and cultural acceptance, do you see India as a peaceful country?"

I didn't mention that I had already looked up India's ranking on the Global Peace Index and that being 143 out of 162, it didn't rate as very peaceful.

"I do," he said. "It's a fairly tolerant country. The current conditions may not be entirely favorable, but the people are nice. As a race and culture, we are very calm, meek, and smart."

I agreed with him that the people were nice. I was struggling with everything in India so far except for one thing—that the people had been so kind.

"What about when you're in LA? Since you've been living there and opening a restaurant there, how do people act toward you?"

He nodded slowly, giving himself a moment to contemplate his answer. "LA is a culturally mixed place, so people are used to interacting with different races. When I'm there, I'm mostly surrounded by my family and friends, and my business associates. I see subtle incidents of racism, and sometimes I feel like an outsider when I'm in public, but as long as I don't give importance to it, it doesn't worry me." He grinned, raised a thick eyebrow, and said, "I'm known for food and spirits, basic human necessities." I laughed. "That makes it easy to connect with anyone," he continued. "Food is a universal language; I call it my first language."

"I totally get that," I said. "And I appreciate your honesty, Nikhil. When you get your restaurant open in LA, I will—." The alarm on my watch cut me off in mid-sentence. "That's my timer. I have to go check the ovens. I'll leave you alone now so you can finish your pie."

When the food bloggers' pies were done baking and set on the marble counter, they turned into a pack of paparazzi, whipping out their phones in a race to post images of their pies on Instagram. While they were busy with their phones, sharing their victory shots with the world, Niharika magically appeared with glossy Four Seasons shopping bags, just the right size for the pies, so the bakers could carry them home—a critical detail that had slipped my mind.

"Stay in touch," Nikhil said as he left with the others. "I hope to see you in LA."

"I'll be one of your first customers," I said.

As I was cleaning up, Neetika, the young concierge, came into the room. She always looked so polished, her eyebrows shaped into perfect crescent moons, not a hair out of place, her red lipstick never bleeding into the lines above her lips—because she had no lines. Her beauty was flawless. "How did it go?" she asked sweetly. "I saw people leaving with their pies. They smelled so good."

"Hi, Neetika. Your timing is perfect. I saved you a slice."

Her smile along with the smiles of the bloggers as they left, made me forget how troubled I was, and how uncharacteristically fearful I was feeling—but only temporarily. Because after everyone was gone and I was alone again, the fear came rushing back. I was afraid to leave the hotel? What was I afraid of? Was I being overly cautious or just wisely self-protective? The country doesn't have a great track record for treating women well and I had noticed how men far outnumbered women on the streets. Men were hanging out everywhere, and yet I never saw women walking alone. Even if Mumbai wasn't dangerous, it felt dangerous to me, or at least overwhelming. I kept wishing Johan didn't have a girlfriend, and that he would rescue me. I wished I could rescue myself.

I went back to my room and tried to call my parents. No answer. I tried reaching my best friend from childhood, Nan. No answer. I called my friend Dave in California, the artist who had designed my World Piece logo. After a few rings, he finally answered.

I described to him my confusion over India: the slum right next door to the luxury hotel; the anguish over seeing Gandhi's assassination photos; and how the sixty-dollar price for the plate of fish curry and glass of wine I ordered from room service, because I was too afraid to leave my room, was probably the annual salary for the nice man who delivered it to my door. I was a mess hotter than the ungodly spicy curry sauce on the fish.

As I sobbed into his ear, Dave just laughed. *Laughed.*

"You are on the Hero's journey," he said. "It's classic and you're hitting the low point right on schedule. Every journey has its struggle. Look it up. It's Greek mythology."

I knew about the Hero's Journey and Joseph Campbell's writings. But that wasn't it. This struggle felt different, unique to this particular place. Unsatisfied with his attempt at consolation, I sent up a signal flare of emails to friends and family, starting with Julia, who wrote right back.

> *Hi Beth,*
>
> *I loved India—every single minute—and would return in a second. I love how the people see beauty in everything and never seem to complain about their lives. I was never scared or had any problems at all. I think after a while you get used to it.*
>
> *Julia*

I also heard from my friend Janice in New Jersey, who had recently posted pictures on Facebook modeling her new sari and sharing her excitement about her upcoming trip to Tamil Nadu, gushing, "I'm counting the days until I go back to India. I feel so spiritually alive there."

To me, she wrote:

> *My visits revolve around my temple studies. When I'm there I let my guard down and I get a glimpse of the most human and divine parts of myself. Sometimes you have to be upturned in the wave to be able to turn inside. If you can, try to release into it.*

What was wrong with me? Why didn't I love India? Or was it that India didn't love me? Was there some other factor at play here? Was I picking up electromagnetic radio waves from some invisible energy field? Was I reincarnated from a past life here and this was some kind of karmic payback? Or was this just a place like no other I had ever experienced? I had no answers. But I still had my mantra, which I modified and expanded.

Stay open. Have courage. Send out good energy. Make pie. Get some rest.

The second pie class was double the size of the first. Niharika had told me she was expecting eight people, but the food bloggers' Instagram posts from the day before had created a buzz and we ended up with fifteen. They were all women this time, all of them beautiful with their smooth black hair and even smoother tawny skin, their clothes impeccable. Some wore tailored business clothes; others wore a traditional vibrant-colored cotton tunic over loose pants. Even their names—Sushmita, Arshie, Rohini, Poonam—were beautiful.

We stepped through the stages of the class: making and rolling the dough, laying it into the pie dishes, and piling in the cherries and peaches. When I went around the room to check the progress of each of the participants, Poonam and her friend asked about the filling. "Can we make it half-half?"

"Sure," I said, thinking they were going to mix the two fruits together. But when I came around a few minutes later, I burst into laughter. "I didn't know that's what you meant, but I love it." One half of the pie was bright orange—peach—and the other was vibrant red—cherry. "That's brilliant. Great job."

Their smiles were so wide, their faces radiating such warmth, I wanted to crawl into their purses and go home with them. Maybe they could show me their India, the true spirit of India, the India I hoped to find.

"We want to make a lattice top," Poonam said. "Can you show us how to do that?"

"Of course," I said, talking them through it. "First, roll out the dough like you would for a regular crust, then cut it into strips. Lay one strip across the middle of the pie and a second strip across in the opposite direction so it looks like a cross. As you add the next ones you have to pull every other strip back, lay down the new ones, then pull the first strips back into place. You'll see the over-under basket-weave pattern emerge after doing the first ones. Just work slowly and gently so you don't tear the dough. And if you do tear it, who cares? You can always cut out some hearts or other shapes and lay those over your problem areas."

I stayed with them until they got the hang of it and then wandered off to show a few others the same thing.

This pie class was like every other pie class I had taught in that no matter where I was in the world, no matter what nationality or language, everyone who participated was enthusiastic, focused, and creative—and they were always, without fail, elated by their finished pies at the end. This pie class, however, was not like every other in that we didn't have enough fruit. Perhaps the staff who prepped it determined that I must have overestimated the amount, that I couldn't possibly need so much. If I stopped to think about the poverty next door, it did seem greedy to make such big, fully-packed pies. But wasn't it for a good cause? Jesus. Every little thing in India, even if just a few extra pounds of cherries, could make you question your motives and morality.

Niharika sent a messenger down to the main kitchen asking for any ingredients they could spare. When they responded with half a box of Granny Smith apples, I got excited thinking they might have come from the Yummy Fruit Company in New Zealand, a connection to my first stop on the trip. But that notion was dampened when I saw that their little stickers read, "Grown in Chile." *Odd*, I thought, because New Zealand is a lot closer to India. But then I shouldn't have been that surprised given the Granny Smith apples I used in Bangkok came from the U.S. This prompted me to add "global trade logistics" to my list of life's perplexing questions.

No sooner did we get the fruit shortage resolved, smoke began billowing out of one of the ovens and the other oven quit working altogether. Niharika made a few urgent phone calls and said, "You can bake them in the main kitchen downstairs."

We loaded all the pies—some half-baked, some half-burned—onto a cart and I wheeled it through the windowless bowels of the hotel to the basement, where I was stopped at the kitchen door by one of the sous-chefs. "You cannot come in," he said. "You are not allowed."

"But we have to bake these pies. We were told we could use your ovens," I said, wondering how the message had gotten lost in translation between the time I left the demo kitchen and when I arrived downstairs. I suspected that what Niharika interpreted as a "yes" was one of those ambiguous head wags.

The young man left to consult his superiors. He returned, scowling. "Okay," he said, "but you must wear these," and handed me a hairnet, shoe coverings, and plastic gloves. If I had been shocked by the lack of cleanliness out on the streets, I was shocked, conversely, by the extreme attention paid to hygiene in the kitchen. The Four Seasons is one place in India where you would be safe eating.

I waited in the main kitchen for the pies to bake, while the class participants stayed upstairs eating the pies I had made that morning. I missed out on their conversations, but at least the pies were salvaged. They always are. I don't know how it happens, but they always turn out. A burnt edge can be sawed off with a serrated knife. A pie that didn't get enough sugar or got doused with too much salt could always be remedied by a scoop of ice cream. Pie is magical that way. It's forgiving. And it certainly does not need to be perfect. Each time I see an article about making the perfect pie—a headline I see all too often—I bristle at the notion of perfection. Fabric and rug weavers found in many cultures—Navajo, Pakistani, Indian, and others—deliberately weave mistakes into their work driven by the belief that only God or Allah is perfect. Baking mistakes don't need to be deliberate, they just happen sometimes; sometimes for reasons that have nothing to do with skill. But they never make the end result any less valuable or appreciated.

Again, after the victory shots and another frenzy of Instagram posts, all the participants filed out of the room, leaving a trail of fragrant and buttery fumes that drifted out from their Four Seasons shopping bags.

I wanted to go with them, spend time with them, these people who bubbled like hot pie filling with happiness, good health, and productive lives, people who were at home in this global powerhouse of a city, a city whose magic still eluded me. But I was alone again, left only with the lingering scent of their pies and the deafening silence of disappointment, resigned to spending the evening in my room, Rapunzel in my ivory tower. Maybe the pie-for-accommodation trade wasn't such a favorable bargain in the end. I was grateful—of course, I was grateful—but I was too insulated and isolated from the culture. How could I, like Julia suggested in her email, "get used to it" if I wasn't immersed in it?

With my two pie classes behind me and my next scheduled events not on the calendar until the following week, I had four days to fill in between. I called Johan, the hot guy from the airport, to get some ideas for where to go and what to see—hoping he was free to hang out.

"My girlfriend is arriving tomorrow. But you should get out of the city and see a little more of India," he suggested. "You should go to Goa."

I emailed Nikhil, the food blogger. "You should go to Goa," he replied.

Finally, I asked Niharika, the hotel's PR director, who said, "You should go to Goa."

So I went to Goa.

Goa is a state on India's west coast, a popular beach destination, and only a short (and cheap) flight north from Mumbai. The flight was around fifty bucks; my overweight baggage fee was twice that. Upon landing at the Goa airport, I took a taxi to my hotel, rolling down the windows to feel the warm, moist wind in my face. The landscape was so green—vibrant tropical hues of ferns, flowers, palm trees, and rice paddies with a pair of long-horned oxen pulling carts through them.

Oh, so this *is the India I've been missing.*

I exhaled all that city stress; I even broke into a grin. But in an instant—which is the amount of time it took my taxi to cross the yellow stripe on the road—my smile vanished as I watched a car coming straight toward us, my enchantment with the pastoral scenery replaced with the certainty that I was going to be killed in a head-on collision. A well-timed swerve saved us. But my driver continued to pass everyone he could, remaining in the wrong lane and refusing to budge even when there was oncoming traffic. Besides the horror of his advanced game of chicken, his driving was erratic, jerky, and downright maniacal, as he played a bonus round of Scare the Tourist—at which he was excelling. He must have been immensely pleased with himself.

I was totally carsick by the time he dropped me at my hotel. Except that it wasn't my hotel. When I found the manager of the place, waking her from a nap, not only did she have no record of my reservation, she said, "We're closed. It's monsoon season."

"Yes, I know it's monsoon season." Just as the words left my mouth, the fire hydrant in the sky opened its valve and the rain pummeled the palm leaves, the hibiscus, the grass, nothing was spared. We barely stayed dry ourselves under the metal roof of the old Goan-style bungalow, getting splashed from the buckets strategically placed to catch the drips. "But I booked a room here through Expedia. I already paid for it."

She paused, considering what could be done, and finally said, "Our sister property, Casa Vagator, is open. It's about five miles up the beach from here. Come. I can drive you there."

Yin and fucking yang. For every difficulty, there was kindness. Maddening confusion? Kindness. Frustration? Kindness. Closed for the season? Kindness. This place was giving me emotional whiplash.

She took me to the edge of civilization, to a hotel surrounded by jungle and perched on a small cliff above the beach. They had a room available—almost all the rooms were available. Because who in their right mind would come to the beach during monsoon season?

The rain forced me to stay inside, so I stretched out on my bed to read *Shantaram*, by Gregory David Roberts, a novel based on the author's real-life experiences as an escaped convict from Australia who lived in Mumbai's slums. (The story is better than it sounds.) The book had been a parting gift from Neetika, the concierge. I wanted to see India in real life, not just read about it, but at least the pages—all eight hundred of them—were keeping me occupied. Even so, it was hard to read with all the noise outside. There was a construction crew on the roof, a jackhammer gone wild. Or was it a freight train? Were there trains here? No. The deafening sound that made me fear the roof would cave in was, once again, the monsoon. No wonder I had seen so many cabins and kiosks, discotheques and cafés, juice bars and dress shops, covered with tarps. Some were shrink-wrapped like mummies in cellophane, preserved for the duration of the season. Even more worrisome, if the roof did collapse and I got buried in the rubble, no one would know where I was since I wasn't at the hotel where I was supposed to be. I hadn't been able to tell anyone, because with each passing downpour, the power went out, taking the internet down with it, which was only available in the lobby anyway. I needed to get in touch with my parents, especially because my dad's melanoma surgery was taking place the next day.

In between rainstorms, I went out to the pool for a swim, but a family of hotel guests had taken over the area, their laundry laid out to dry on the pool's concrete deck like it was the Dhobi Ghat, taking advantage of the precious few minutes of sun. So instead of swimming, I walked over to an elevated wooden platform overlooking the ocean. The deck served as the hotel's cocktail lounge during the high season, but the wind was blowing so hard no wine glass, table, or chair, would stand a chance of staying in place.

I pointed my face into the gale and began contorting myself into twisting triangles and warrior yoga poses.

India is the birthplace of yoga and meditation—Westerners flock to India's ashrams for spiritual cleansing—but why would I need to go to yoga boot camp when I could have my own private yoga studio overlooking the Arabian Sea, where the wind was so strong it could blast any toxins right out of my pores? I didn't have the attention span for an ashram anyway. I've always found my own best form of meditation and way to quiet my mind comes from riding my bike or rolling pie dough, lulled into a calmer state by repetitive motion— not by sitting still with my eyes closed. Which, as I had experienced when sitting by the pool in Bangkok, can have the unsettling effect of a séance. Nor did I believe in following gurus. Gurus are people, too, and I'd seen too many of them collecting their followers' tithes only to buy a fleet of Rolls Royces. (To be fair, even Gandhi wasn't a saint. He went through a phase when Italian leather shoes were his material vice.)

Even if ashrams were my thing, I wouldn't have needed to come all the way to India, as the American Gothic House is only twenty-five minutes away from the world headquarters of Transcendental Meditation (a.k.a. TM), a meditation technique started sixty years ago by Maharishi Mahesh Yogi, who had been a spiritual guide to The Beatles. He bought a college campus in Fairfield, Iowa, and created the Maharishi International University, where people can get paid to meditate for five or six hours a day—not for inner peace, but for *world* peace. My butt goes numb just thinking about it. Called "The Maharishi Effect," practitioners of TM, believe that peace can be achieved if the square root of 1 percent of a population simultaneously practices advanced meditation techniques. The *TMhome.com* website states that in 2007, in an attempt to prove it, 1,725 participants (the square root of 1 percent of the U.S. population at the time) gathered in one place. Incredibly, this collective consciousness approach may actually work, as homicide and violent crime numbers decreased from 2007 to 2010. For that four-year period, the homicide rate dropped 21.2 percent and violent crime was down 18.5 percent. (Though those double digits are a bit of a public relations spin as *per year* the rates dropped 5.3 percent and 4.6 percent, respectively.) It may seem far-fetched, but meditating for peace could possibly be successful as there is still so much we don't understand about what we cannot see, about physics, energy fields, and life beyond our planet. Whether through group meditation or mindfulness in general, the one consistent thing that shows up in my research is this: *World peace starts within yourself.*

India was showing me that I had a lot of work to do on that front.

Taking in a deep breath of salty air, I stretched out my arms in opposite directions, and turned to gaze out over my front arm, past the tips of my fingers, directing all my pent-up energy out through my middle finger—in a positive way. This was my superpower pose, Warrior Two, or in India's ancient language of Sanskrit, Virabhadrasana II (pronounced: veer-ah-bah-DRAHS-anna). *Vira* means courageous hero; *bhadra*, friendly; and *asana*, posture.

While I was stretching and bending—and posturing like a courageous, friendly warrior—a skinny mongrel of a dog walked onto the platform. She watched me for a while and I called her over, which had the opposite effect. She ran away as if I were about to swing a cricket bat at her.

After a few more standing poses, I settled into a seated position in an attempt to meditate—I could at least try for five minutes—and just before I closed my eyes, I saw the dog again. She was below the platform, where a puppy emerged from underneath, then another, and another, and another. There were four puppies total, maybe a month or two old: brown, black, white, tan, each one a different color. It was impossible to look inward with these cute little things within reach. I figured snuggling with a puppy would calm my nervous system faster than those slow Ujjayi breaths, so I climbed down off the platform to go pet them. They saw me coming and scurried back into hiding, but curiosity prevailed. Eventually, one at a time, they poked their heads out, took a few steps toward me like it was a dare, then ran back under. They never let me touch them, but at least I got my dog fix—along with so many fleabites it looked like I was wearing pink polka-dot knee socks. My legs would itch for an entire week.

I took pictures of the puppies to send to Doug. I also sent him pictures of the cows I had seen wandering freely down the dirt roads earlier, their bony ribs showing, their backs humped, their bicycle-handlebar horns with tips so sharp and pointy they could spear a fly—and people walking past them as if the cows were just everyday pedestrians. Any time I saw anything farm-related, be it a tractor (like the ones I had seen in Australia and New Zealand) or corn (like the ears roasting on a grill outside Goa's Basilica of Bom Jesus church), I snapped a photo for Doug. I liked having a reason to stay in touch besides just checking on Jack. He seemed to like it, too, though his replies were often about his own adventures, decidedly more sensible ones, like kayaking on the knee-deep waters of the local river, riding his bike down the gravel road at sunset, or filling his silos with chopped oats. Mostly, he kept me updated on Jack and how much he loved swimming in the muddy pond, how he and Doug's dog Mali teamed up to hunt frogs, how they looked forward to their treats of fresh liver after their walks. I cringed to think of the slimy, bloody organ meat that the dogs slurped down like ice cream. He always added that everyone at "Camp Doug" was cheering me on. His emails, always so brief, were like Tic Tacs: tiny refreshing mints that didn't last long enough and left me wanting more, always waiting for him to dole out another.

During a brief cloudless patch, I decided to take a tour of the area by motorcycle taxi, remembering how much that had lifted my spirits in Bangkok. The man at the front desk called one for me and I waited at the hotel entrance for it. After half an hour, I went back to the front desk. "He's coming," he told me. I went back outside. Fifteen minutes later, when the driver still hadn't shown up, I went back to the front desk. "He's here," the man said. Maybe "here" meant "somewhere in Goa." I waited for ten more minutes before I lost my resolve.

As I walked back to my room, brimming with frustration and tears, large drops of rain began splattering the walkway. I thought of my friend Kathy Eldon's favorite adages from her Iowa Lutheran upbringing. "What's for you won't go by you," she would tell me. "Rejection is God's protection," she would say. In other words, it was a blessing the motorcycle taxi didn't come, because if I had been out on that bike in the rain—not just rain, *monsoon*—I would have been So. Very. Fucked.

No matter how much I resisted, India wanted to be my spiritual teacher—though it had a warped way of instilling its lessons.

After the downpour, when the electricity came back on, I ran up to the open-air lobby, hoping to get an internet connection so I could reach my parents. The signal was sporadic and too weak to use video, and after several aborted calls, I was finally able to piece together news about my dad's melanoma surgery.

"He's home from the hospital, but he's been sleeping a lot," my mom said. "He's napping now . . . Oh, I hear him getting up. Let me put him on the phone."

"I'm doing fine, Boo," he said. He didn't sound fine. He sounded tired and his speech was slurred. "The surgeon said . . ."

The line went dead. I called back. "What were you saying?"

"The surgeon wasn't happy with the margins, so I have to go back for another surgery in a few weeks."

"Oh . . ." I didn't know what to say. That didn't sound good, but I wasn't there to know exactly what the doctor had said and what that might imply. I should have been there.

"Don't you worry about me, Boo Bear," he said. "I'm in good order. What about you? How are things going? Where are you?"

"I'm still in India. Everything's going great here. A little rainy, but otherwise fine." I would save the truth for the pages of my journal.

But my mom knew. "You take care of yourself," she said sternly. She had a mother's instinct for picking up on every syllable in my voice, able to discern exactly how I was doing.

"I better go before we get cut off again," I said, before my mom could analyze my well-being, or lack thereof. "Let me know as soon as you get your next surgery scheduled. I love you guys."

"We love you, too, honey," they said.

I sat staring at my blank computer screen long after they hung up, replaying the conversation in my mind. *Don't worry about me, Boo*, he had said, but from this flooded beach town nine thousand miles away, I was more worried than ever.

The taxi driver for the return trip to the Goa airport drove safely. He stayed in his lane, passing no one, and, even more importantly, given the wet weather, he kept his speed down. And his windshield wipers worked. He stopped at a roadside kiosk where, behind the window of a glass cabinet, I spotted a pile of samosas, crispy fried triangles filled with the promise of a hearty snack. I bought four—two for myself and two for the driver. They were wrapped in printed newspaper, the way New Zealanders used to wrap their fish and chips before they switched to clean white paper. (It made me wonder how Charity was doing. I had emailed her a few times but she didn't—or wouldn't—reply.) The newspaper pages were covered in the swirly script of one of Goa's seven languages, but all I could decipher were the pictures of politicians, cricket players, and Bollywood stars. I don't know if it was the novelty of the newspaper or the roadside appeal, but this samosa—loaded with soft veggies and spiced with cumin—tasted even better than the one from the Mumbai bakery.

After haggling over the taxi price—he had promised one rate, then doubled it—I dragged my luggage inside to the ticket counter, ironically looking forward to my return to Mumbai.

Oh, but not so fast, Grasshopper. Swami India isn't done dishing out its lessons.

"I'm on the five o'clock flight," I told the ticket agent, handing him my passport.

"There is no flight at that time, madam," he replied.

"What? That can't be right."

"Let me see your itinerary." He looked at my printout, pointed at the number, and said, "It says right here. Your flight left at five a.m."

What? Noooo!

I couldn't believe it. I had made the rookie mistake of misreading the flight time. I don't know how it could have happened given that for the past ten years I had kept my watch set to military time—the twenty-four-hour clock—which almost every other country in the world uses except for the U.S. I could glance at my watch and always know without having to calculate that 17:00 is five o'clock in the evening—and that 05:00 is five in the morning.

"Well, can't you just put me on the next flight to Mumbai?"

"No, madam. You have to buy a new ticket."

"That's ridiculous," I snapped. "Surely you can just change my ticket." Then I tried pleading. "Come on. It was an honest mistake."

"I'm sorry, madam."

"Give me a break," I grumbled.

I was relentless. The poor guy was just doing his job, loyal to his company's rules, and I—a guest in his country—was being a total jerk, argumentative to the point where all he could do was direct me to the ticket office. There, a woman in uniform informed me, "That's our policy, madam. You have to buy a new ticket."

With these words, every previous frustration I had tried to ignore or stuff down came rushing to the surface. I wailed, unable to stop the monsoon-strength tears from pouring down my face. My chest heaved up and down and my fists clenched as I threw a tantrum as uncontrollable as a two-year-old's.

"Sit down," the woman said. "Please. Sit down."

I stayed standing.

"SIT DOWN!" she demanded. I slumped into the chair. "Please," she said gently, handing me a bottle, "drink some water."

I took the bottle from her and blubbered through my tears. "Every . . . single . . . day . . ." I could barely speak. ". . . something goes wrong here."

"There must be a reason," she said.

Really? What would that be? What reason could there be for getting *this* upset at every turn? Was I jinxed? Had someone put a curse on me? Were my expectations so unrealistic? But my friend Nan had emailed me a few days earlier, saying almost the same thing. "If you can't adapt to India there's a reason why," she wrote. "You're too good a traveler."

Well, I wasn't *that* good of a traveler showing up twelve hours late for my flight.

In the film *The Best Exotic Marigold Hotel*, I always saw myself as the Judi Dench character who eagerly and easily adapted to life in India; she got a job, learned some Hindi, and moved about with confidence. In reality, I was the Penelope Wilton character, the rude, judgmental, anxiety-ridden wife who couldn't cope, became hysterical, and left India in a huff. I didn't want to be her.

One thing was obvious: I had lost my *Jai ho*. And I was determined to get it back.

CHAPTER 6

India: Part 2

Deepa Krishnan is an energetic woman with a streak of gray running through her short black hair who, after eighteen years of working in corporate finance, started Mumbai Magic Tours. According to her company website, she trains and employs college students from slums to lead food, craft, and textile tours so they can earn income while they're in school. Her other tours are led mostly by women, making her network of female guides the largest in India. She is involved in many humanitarian-aid efforts, initiating rainwater-harvesting projects in rural villages, and heading a non-profit that provides education to low-income students. Also a talented Indian cook, she appears on local television food programs. I learned of her through an Indian journalist who suggested that, because of the food connection, I reach out to Deepa. When I emailed her about my mission, once again, pie opened the door to a new opportunity as well as a community.

"You can stay with us," Deepa insisted. "My daughter is away at school. You can have her room. And we'll have a family dinner. We will cook the food together and you can teach us how to make pie."

And so, after the cloistered five-star hotel and the semi-disastrous side trip to Goa, I would finally, for my last few days in the country, get the true Indian immersion I had been seeking.

Deepa lives in a quiet part of the city in a high-rise apartment building. Her place looks mostly Western in style with its couch, dining room table, chairs, and lamps—though her galley kitchen was miniature by America's supersize standards. And there was no oven—well, there was, but it was a toaster oven. Another difference was the absence of closet space; Deepa had only a cupboard, smaller than an armoire, yet it held a designer-boutique's worth of saris made of cottons and silks, ironed, folded, and grouped according to color and pattern. She pulled out a few saris from the stack to show me, her hands reflexively stroking the kitten-soft fabrics. A purple and white gingham pattern caught my eye—I could spot gingham a mile away. "I love this one," I said.

"I like that one, too. But I like all of them." She smiled, then picked out an elegant burgundy and orange one with gold trim to wear for the day's festivities.

I went to my bedroom to shower and change into clean clothes—my sister's hand-me-down dress with the Gandhi quote seemed the most fitting for the occasion—but when I dug through my suitcase to get it, I discovered everything was covered in a reddish-brown powder. Every single thing—my jeans, my underwear, my toothbrush. Somewhere between Goa and Mumbai my Costco jar of cinnamon had spilled inside my bag. Had it occurred to me that I'd be in the country where cinnamon comes from—harvested from the dried bark of the bushy trees that grow in southern India and Sri Lanka just off India's southern coast—I wouldn't have brought it along.

Oh, India. Why do you continue to challenge me so?

"We're going to start," Deepa called from the kitchen.

When I joined her, she had already pulled out a dozen spice jars and bowls of batter and had heated up a skillet on her stove. "We're going to make some Indian dishes," she said as she pulled containers of chopped herbs and grated carrots out of the small refrigerator.

Standing at the sink was another woman, barefoot—per the protocol in Indian homes—wearing a cotton smock, her gold hoop earrings reflecting the sun. She was washing dishes. "This is my maid, Shamla," Deepa said.

Is a maid just a maid, or was this a close-up look at India's caste system, the hierarchical designation of humans—a glaring and long-standing obstacle to equal rights?

Shamla smiled at me so warmly, even giggling a little, that her apparent contentedness settled my porcupine quills and I packed the question away for later.

Deepa explained the steps of what she was making, pie-like things—stuffed breads, pancakes, chapatis, and noodles. She started with khandvi, a paste of chickpea flour and yogurt that she smeared directly on the counter and cut into strips that she then rolled into pinwheels. I stood next to her, watching and trying to take notes, but I couldn't keep up, partly because I couldn't spell anything and partly because each dish she made had a complex combination of spices from her collection of red chili powder, dried green mango powder, pomegranate powder, tamarind, mustard seed, onion, turmeric, ginger, and something called asafoetida (stinking gum spice).

"Coriander and cumin are the two basic spices in Indian cooking," she said. "But all these spices are not native to India; they came with the Portuguese."

There were the blurred lines of origin again, the cross-cultural blend of foods, like when Nikhil disclosed that the Indian samosa is not Indian. In America, there's been a trend of attacking others for cultural appropriation. Don't even think about opening a Mexican restaurant if you're not Mexican, and don't bother to write that young adult novel you worked so hard to research about the Gullah community when you're not of the West African-American Carolina heritage yourself—unless you want to be a bullseye for vitriol and have your book contract canceled. The accusations aren't always fair because our human species is like garam masala: an inseparable blend of many flavors and colors that's better and more balanced when all mixed together. How are we supposed to learn about each other, understand each other, and come to respect, and even love each other if not for sharing these recipes and stories, even if they didn't originate with us? If we had always been guarding our cultural identities so tightly, we would never have known the joys of eating a juicy "American" hamburger (whose origins lie in Germany) served with a side of French fries (from Belgium) dipped in ketchup (invented in China as a fermented fish sauce before evolving into the tomato sauce we know today).

Deepa had to work fast as some of her family had already arrived, including her mother and three aunts. The women all wore short-sleeved saris draped diagonally over one shoulder, leaving a bit of bare midriff showing. The long skirts wrapped around their legs, and gold bangle bracelets jingled on their wrists. Each one's hair was a little grayer than the next, and each wore it in a long braid down their back. On their foreheads, just above the center of their eyebrows, was a red dot—a bindi—made from the scarlet powder of plants. A bindi signifies that a woman is of the Hindu faith and married, but it can also be a symbol to bring one's attention to the third eye, which sees the things the physical eye cannot, like one's inner life. I was already examining my inner life so closely I didn't need a bindi—I needed blinders. A bindi isn't all about labels or X-ray vision, however; some wear it simply as a fashion statement.

As more family members filled up the living room—uncles, aunties, husbands, cousins, young mothers, a toddler, a teenager, and a newborn—the apartment grew as noisy as the traffic outside. Shamla shuttled the platters of food out to the dining room table to make room in the kitchen for Deepa, who was emptying her shopping bags loaded with flour, sugar, and apples.

"Now, let's make some pie," Deepa said.

Because the kitchen was small and counter space limited, there was only room enough to teach two people at a time. Deepa and Shiv, a young man from downstairs, were the first to volunteer. Shamla, wedged in a corner of the kitchen, offered to peel the apples. Shiv rolled up his sleeves to make dough while his wife nursed their seven-week-old baby in the living room. And Deepa, draped in her elegant sari, pushed her silk wrap back to keep it out of the butter and flour. As the two worked together on the same pie, the four aunties poked their heads in occasionally to watch and inquire about the work, commenting on the smooth surface of the dough and the evenly crimped edge. From the looks of their first effort, one would assume that Deepa and Shiv had been making pie forever.

Once the pie was in the oven—make that toaster oven—Deepa's sister Roona and Roona's daughter Ramya wanted to give it a try. "We don't have any more apples," Deepa said, "but I do have some mangoes."

"I've never made a mango pie," I confessed, "but you can put virtually anything in a pie shell, so let's try it."

Roona, like Deepa, was a businesswoman. She was the COO of a big bank, but it was eighteen-year-old Ramya who was calling the shots, declaring, "We're doing a lattice top." They worked in tandem, four hands moving deftly to peel the slippery orange mangoes, slicing them into a bowl and stirring in a bit of sugar—just a little though, because the fruit was already sweet. I had them add flour to thicken the filling. I would have preferred cornstarch or tapioca, but like the American pioneers had done, we used whatever was available. Roona's manicured silver nails and Ramya's tattooed hand weaving strips of dough across the top, and crimping the crust on opposite sides of the dish, reminded me of Kate making a pie with her mom in Australia. It wasn't world peace, exactly, but I liked to think the experience would create a loving memory, one that, in Ali's case, even dementia could not erase.

I asked Ramya about the tattoo that covered the back of her hand. "It's a mandala," she said. The configuration of geometric symbols and circles looked like something I might have drawn with my Spirograph in childhood, only this design was more intricate, more artistic, and way more permanent. "It represents the infinity of the universe," she explained. "It's a spiritual compass to remind us of truth and compassion." This was a young woman who believed so wholeheartedly in peace, harmony, and love, she engraved a symbol of it on her skin.

There was something about the mandala, and about being around Ramya and her strong, self-assured female relatives that put me at ease. Men prevail over women outside on the streets, but in this apartment, the women ruled—smart, highly educated, powerful women. Among them was Lavanya, Deepa's niece, a PhD candidate, who was there with her four-year-old son.

"I hear you're a feminist scholar. What does that entail?" I asked Lavanya, who was leaning against the kitchen doorway watching Roona and Ramya construct their mango pie.

"I study feminism in the Indian context," she said. "There's a huge class divide and other dimensions that separate Indian women from each other. The problems Indian women face are diverse, and feminist responses are diverse, too."

"But is there anything being done about it?" I asked.

"Yes, efforts are being made to make public spaces safer for women, and we're trying to change mindsets about dowries, arranged marriages, and divisions of labor, as well as dismantle the caste system."

"Sounds . . . I don't know . . . like why are women still so oppressed?" I asked. "And I'm not talking just India. I thought we'd have gender equality by now. And don't even get me started on social justice. Do you think there's any hope that anything will really change?"

Lavanya nodded. "I'm trying to raise my son to be sensitive, and teach him how to treat others with kindness and respect. I talk to him all the time about gender equality. I taught him about consent and he now says I need his consent to put broccoli on his plate!"

We all laughed.

"At least we're talking about these things," Lavanya continued, "and that gives me solace."

"*You* give me solace, Lavanya."

"The pie looks like it might be done," Ramya said, turning the subject back to a more tenable one.

I took a look and saw the mango juice bubbling up through the lattice work. "I think you're right."

The pies baked quickly and evenly in Deepa's little countertop appliance. I would never underestimate a toaster oven again! We sat them, apple and mango side by side, on the windowsill to cool. This was no farmhouse scene from a *Saturday Evening Post* magazine cover; this was a fourteenth-floor window, barricaded by security bars, that opened wide to Mumbai's city lights and honking horns, with the sari-clad aunties looking on. The juxtaposition of the scene made me feel like I was finally back on track with my mission. This was exactly what I had set forth to do: initiate a cultural exchange on a deeply personal level. To be in this home, embraced by this extended family—and to feel safe—made me glad I didn't follow my friend Nan's advice before I went to Goa. "Cut your losses and leave," she had said. If I had left, I would have missed out on this evening, which I considered the whole point of the trip.

It was finally dinnertime and the family settled in—on couches, chairs, around the table, anywhere one could squeeze in—to indulge in the assortment of Indian dishes Deepa and Shamla had made. There was no silverware; everyone ate with their hands or used chapatis, an Indian tortilla, to scoop up their food. I had just shoved a handful of rice into my mouth when Ramya laughed, pointing to the rice grains stuck to my cheek. "You don't need to put *all* your fingers in your mouth," she said. "Let me show you. Just hold your fingertips to your lips and push the rice off with your thumb." She also demonstrated with expert dexterity how to one-handedly tear a chapati, still warm, fresh off Deepa's stove.

When the pie was served, every member of the family's four generations readily lined up for a slice. Deepa handed out plates and, because it was Western food, forks. I watched as Ramya took a bite of apple pie, holding a silver fork in her mandala-tattooed hand.

"Wait," I told her. "I have to take a picture." This meeting of symbols was to capture world peace in a single snapshot. "If I ever write a book about my trip, this is going to be my cover." Ramya just smiled, making a little moaning noise as the apples and cinnamon hit her tongue.

At the end of the meal, Deepa poured everyone a glass of buttermilk. I took a sip and wrinkled my nose at the sour taste. "It's a daily ritual, the secret to Indian digestion," Deepa said. "It keeps us in good working order, otherwise with all these spices we would have ulcers."

Everyone around the table laughed—the old men in their trousers, the grandmothers in their saris, Deepa's husband Pramod, Ramya, Lavanya, all of them—collectively nodding and murmuring, "Yes, yes, that's true."

Upon my arrival in India, I had driven past a slum at night. When I stayed at the Four Seasons, I looked down onto one. And at the end of my stay, as if by some act of providence, I visited one. Not the one next door to the hotel, but the Dharavi slum—the one of *Slumdog Millionaire* fame and third largest slum in the world—of which Deepa offered tours through her company.

Of Mumbai Magic's many bright, young guides, mine was Razak, a tall, lanky college student, still growing into his manhood from the looks of the downy black fuzz on his upper lip and chin. Clean cut in his plaid shirt and jeans, he was a fourth-generation resident of the slum, though the first thing he told me was, "It's not a slum, it's a neighborhood."

We began the tour by walking across an elevated sidewalk that traversed six lines of railroad tracks, lined on all sides with litter and laundry laid out to dry on the monsoon-free day. Once we reached the other side of the tracks, we entered into a city within a city. I wasn't scared, nor did it feel even remotely dangerous. It was daylight and I was with Razak, a gentle soul with whom I instantly bonded as if he were my little brother.

Out of the twelve million people living in Mumbai, it's estimated that as many as one million of them live packed into this area of five hundred acres, often with as many as fifteen people living in one room. From an aerial view, it may appear as if the dwellings are all shanties made from scrap material, but seeing them up close, I was struck by how many structures were solid, made of concrete, some two stories, some with glass windows. Yes, there were many shacks cobbled together from corrugated metal and plastic tarps, but even the less sturdy-looking ones had satellite dishes on their roofs. The main walkways winding through Dharavi were paved, bustling with delivery trucks, motorcycles, and bicycles, but many were narrow dirt alleys, so narrow that the sun couldn't reach through. There were open troughs of waste water—a blend of toxic sludge and raw sewage—running alongside the paths and tangled root wads of wires dangling precariously overhead. They had electricity. And Wi-Fi. And goats. Handsome, long-eared white goats with leather collars and bells around their necks, lazing around in the doorway of a shop like the dogs did in Bangkok.

As we walked along, my eyes were wide with overwhelm—an amalgam of wonder, revulsion, heartache, and admiration. What I did not expect to see was so much industry and so many industrious, enterprising people working in thriving small businesses, like plastic and aluminum recycling, leatherworks, fabric dyeing, clothing manufacturing, pottery, glassmaking, tool and die machinery-making, and more.

In a one-room workshop, a group of men sat cross-legged on the floor, taking apart cassettes—some were mini-cassettes, those long obsolete tapes used for dictation—separating the hard plastic from the metallic tape. They sorted the tiny bits into designated buckets, a tedious task, but for them every scrap had value—including the garbage that was everywhere, which people picked through looking for more material to recycle.

"One industry's waste is another industry's new material," Razak said. "Have you heard of American Tourister? They make suitcases here." From the recycled plastic, I presumed.

"Really? That's very cool. When I need a new suitcase, that's what I'll get."

In another room, a row of men sat behind sewing machines stitching garments out of magenta-colored cotton. The cloth must have come from a workshop I had seen earlier, where two men with long wooden poles leaned over vats of hot-pink dye, swirling swaths of fabric around in the liquid, occasionally lifting it like noodles to check for doneness.

It was all so mind-blowingly impressive, especially in such crude working conditions. Anyone who thinks that poverty is synonymous with laziness needs to visit Dharavi. And the people, not just the workers but all around, did not look destitute. They looked busy and purposeful, living normal days filled with work, school, family, housekeeping, shopping, and cooking. They looked healthy. And clean, mostly. Many of them seemed to be wearing freshly laundered clothes. There was a man with an ironing board, set up outdoors under a staircase, where crispy shirts hung from hooks. Trousers were pressed, folded, and stacked with military precision. And people were lined up waiting for his services.

Razak pointed out an open-air temple that was packed with idols representing a variety of religions, including Islam, Hinduism, Buddhism, Judaism, and Christianity. "This is the Eighth Wonder of the World," he said. "There were riots in 1992, people fighting in the name of religion, so the temple was created as a reaction to that, to show that God is one, just called by a different name."

The riots he was referring to were known as the Bombay Riots, incited by a group of right-wing Hindu extremists after they illegally tore down the Babri Masjid mosque, a tactic straight out of the British "Divide and Rule" playbook. The slum itself, however, has a history of being inclusive given its residents have migrated from other parts of India. They all work and live shoulder to shoulder in this small space regardless of religion or caste. Away from their rural villages, it's easier to break free from the hierarchy and unjust traditions. And with the slum's 69 percent literacy rate, young people are getting educated enough to speak out and say, "The caste system is not right and we don't have to accept it."

Razak and I kept walking. "We have our own fire station, hospital, schools, restaurants, bakeries, and cinemas," he said. I wasn't surprised these establishments existed here after having already seen produce markets, spice markets, playgrounds, and banks with ATMs. "We also have a police station, but the crime rate is low. Because of all the labor, there's no time to commit crimes."

I wanted to laugh, but the truth behind his statement was too biting. I could still picture the men picking apart those mini-cassettes. And that was probably one of the cushier jobs, especially compared to the women's daily chores of cleaning and hauling water, a necessity given the slum's absence of plumbing.

We continued, peering inside the various micro-industry workshops—one guy tanning leather, another guy welding machine parts, another one sharpening blades. The paths were wet or gunky in places, with what I didn't want to know, especially as I was wearing flat sandals.

"You want to drink something?" Razak asked.

It was so hot, and though the sweat wasn't visible, my shirt was soaked with it. "Oh, yes, please," I said, without stopping to think I could get sick. I had not adhered to the tourist maxim to avoid India's street food at all costs and so far I had been fine, but this wasn't just the street, it was the slum.

"Do you like sugarcane?"

"Sure," I said. I was so thirsty I didn't care what I drank or where it came from.

We walked over to a juice stand where a man fed woody stalks of sugar cane into a metal press. A contraption of two metal cylinders attached to a rubber belt, it was likely manufactured in the neighborhood. With the belt spinning, it crushed the plant between the rollers until every last bit of liquid had been drained out. The man served it to us in coconut shells, their outsides brown and rough with hairy fibers. Of our natural drinking cups, I could hear Razak's words from earlier: "One industry's waste is another industry's new material."

"This is good!" I told Razak, tipping back my coconut shell. It was as refreshing and quenching as lemonade, and not as sweet as I expected. But did it make me sick? Oh, I would get sick soon enough— terribly, horribly, utterly sick—but it would have nothing to do with the cane juice, or with India.

The tour was supposed to last an hour and a half, but it was so fascinating, I was so comfortable there, and I liked being with Razak so much that we spent twice that much time. I finally understood why the author of *Shantaram*, Gregory David Roberts, would want to live in a slum, and it wasn't because it made a good hiding place from the thugs who wanted to kill him.

I understood, because it was in the slum where I found India. The real India. The magic of India I had been missing. Dharavi isn't a slum, and it's even more than a neighborhood—it's a community. And community is what unites us, what helps us feel secure, what encourages us to work together and support one another, what makes us feel like we belong. Isn't that what we all long for as humans? To feel like we have an integral place that anchors us when the rest of life is so hard and confusing? Even I, as an outsider, felt a sense of belonging in the slum, such was the palpable strength and surprising solidity of its ecosystem.

For nine days, I had thought I was the Penelope Wilton character from *The Best Exotic Marigold Hotel*, but finally, on day ten, down on the ground, under the cover of the blue tarps, I discovered that I could be the more accepting Judi Dench character after all, the one whose guiding principle applies to life regardless of where you live: "We get up in the morning. We do our best. Nothing else matters."

CHAPTER 7

Egypt: Layover in Cairo

> From the equality of rights springs identity of our highest interests; you cannot subvert your neighbor's rights without striking a dangerous blow at your own.
> —CARL SCHURZ

A
s my flight from Mumbai approached Cairo, I scanned the horizon, desperate to get an aerial view of the pyramids and the Sphinx, but all I saw was haze—a thick and blurry tan-colored fog saturating the sky. Was it smog? Or was it sand? If there was a city down there, I couldn't tell. I couldn't see a thing except for an atmosphere choking on its own particulate matter. As we neared the ground, I imagined our landing—and how it would feel to be buried alive in a sandstorm. *Death by suffocation.* Another one for the ever-expanding list of Things I Didn't Think of That Might Kill Me.

I was reminded of flying into LA on a particularly brown, smoggy day and how from the air I dreaded my return to the air pollution, but once I landed and was immersed in it, I didn't notice it as much. Cairo, I assumed, was like that, and surely a mesmerizing place once you're down in it, even if you couldn't breathe because of the dust. But as anyone who loves the desert knows, a life lived in shifting sands has its own kind of magic.

I was impatient to get off the plane. I had a five-and-a-half-hour layover and hoped it would be enough time to take a quick tour of Cairo by taxi. Once inside the airport, I went straight to the immigration desk in the transit area and asked the two men in olive-green uniforms for a day-visa to go into the city. The supervisor looked at his watch, wrinkled his face, and looked at the other man who shrugged his shoulders. I waited expectantly, silently willing him to say yes, until, finally, he said, "No. There's not enough time."

I am standing here in the birthplace of pie and I can't leave the airport?

According to the *What's Cooking America* website, "Pie can loosely be traced back to the ancient Egyptians during the Neolithic Period or New Stone Age beginning around 6000 BC. The Neolithic Period is characterized by the use of stone tools shaped by polishing or grinding, the domestication of plants or animals, the establishment of permanent villages, and the practice of such crafts as pottery and weaving."

The earliest pies used inedible crusts to preserve and transport meat, but evolved into free-form galettes made with oat, wheat, rye, and barley, filled with honey, and baked over hot coals.

The kind of pie you find in modern-day Egypt is called *feteer meshaltet*, which translates as "cushioned pie." It's made with multiple layers of dough using ghee, essentially concentrated butter, that makes a melt-in-your-mouth pastry so flaky it requires a wet washcloth to wipe off the crumbs. It's served flat and round, or rolled up like a crepe. It can be plain, with the dough soaked in honey, or filled with anything from meat and cheese to chocolate. I had seen it in photos, but never tasted it. *If only I could leave the airport!* I should have thought to bribe the immigration officers with the promise of bringing them baked goods. But it was too late.

Alas, I would see no pyramids, no Sphinx, nor would I get to sample feteer meshaltet or any pie in the country of its origin. Then again, if a Cairo taxi ride was anything like the one in Goa, it was probably just as well that I stayed put in the airport bubble. More impenetrable than a bubble, the airport windows were so thick and so heavily tinted in an otherworldly shade of green, I couldn't tell if I was in Egypt or if I had landed on Mars. Between the opaque windows and the haze outside, I couldn't even see planes landing.

I couldn't get on Wi-Fi, so I spent the time writing in my journal, trying to make sense of my time in India. But after filling a record-breaking twenty pages and getting a cramp in my hand, it was to no avail. (Seven years later I am still trying to make sense of it!) But it would be Lebanon, my next stop, that exacerbated my questions about the human condition, what we are capable of, and why we are the way we are.

The café where I sat was like an island in the middle of the concourse. As I sat at my table writing, and taking tiny sips of my eight-dollar cappuccino to make it last as long as possible, a little Egyptian girl kept skipping by. Dressed in pink running shoes and carrying a Little Mermaid purse over her shoulder, her long dark ponytail bounced in time with her steps. For at least an hour, she never stopped skipping—or smiling.

A few years earlier, I went grocery shopping with a guy I was dating. I was in a melancholy mood and to shake me out of it he made me skip with him across the parking lot into the store. "It's impossible to be sad when you're skipping," he said. He was right. By the time I reached the door I was laughing.

I wasn't skipping or laughing now. I was watching this young girl with a lump growing in my throat. She was so unselfconscious now, so full of innocence, but as she grew up, what would her life be like? Would she have equal rights as a woman, or would she be oppressed by a male-dominated culture? Would she have the independence and freedom to form her own beliefs? Or would she be conditioned to adhere to mandated familial, cultural, or religious doctrines?

I was raised Catholic, but born a feminist, and by age thirteen knew I could not subscribe to any religion that prevented women from becoming priests. My parents honored my views, for which I was grateful, as many of my friends' parents weren't so flexible. I was always aware of my freedom and my privilege—my skin color, nationality, and socioeconomic status—that came only by the luck of where my ball landed on life's roulette wheel. But I was also a woman. And I felt the disadvantages—and dangers—of that.

The list of abuses toward women is long: rape, sexual harassment, genital mutilation, child and forced marriage, physical abuse, human trafficking, domestic servitude, forced labor. And let's not forget about physically damaging fashion trends like foot binding and corsets.

In some countries and cultures, mainly Middle Eastern and Asian ones, women are sometimes killed by their own family members for the perceived dishonor upon their relatives. They call them "honor killings"—and the murderers face no repercussions! Some of the reasons, Human Rights Watch explains, might be that the victim refused to enter an arranged marriage, was the victim of sexual assault or rape, or had an affair—even if only allegedly. The reasons could be more trivial, like dressing in a way deemed inappropriate or displaying behavior seen as disobedient, which could be simply talking to someone on the street. What if that someone had initiated the conversation, merely asking her for directions? She might never be allowed to explain herself before being shot, beaten, or stoned to death. Some women are prevented from being born in the first place—feticide, it's called, the killing of a female infant. This still happens all over the world, though mostly in India and China. And to think we are living in the twenty-first century!

I can't even. And yet . . .

And yet, "The secret to world peace is women," declares an article from *GlobalCitizen.org* titled "Five Activists Tell Us Why Women Must Lead the Fight for World Peace." "If you Google 'the secret to world peace,' you get a raw deal: Four out of the first five articles offered up to you by the internet gods were written by men," writes the author, James Hitchings-Hales—who is male. "It's been right before our eyes all along. But it's merely a whisper in the halls of power, hardly applied in any practical or political sense, and often systematically discouraged."

Lavanya told me only 14 percent of India's parliament is women. In her studies, she's learned that "it will take the gender gap one hundred and eight years to close—if it doesn't keep widening. Religion and politics are all run by men," she said. "It's all masculinity." Simply put, to quote a female politician in Iowa who spoke to me off the record, "The problem is testosterone."

By no means is this meant to disparage men, but according to a UN Women study, "The evidence is inarguable: When women are involved in negotiations, the probability of a peace deal being sustained over two years increases by 20 percent. It's 35 percent more likely that the deal will last over fifteen years when women are represented at the negotiating table." We have a long way to go though, because between 1992 and 2018, of those involved in major peace processes only 13 percent of peace negotiators, 3 percent of mediators, and 4 percent of signatories were women.

Laurel Stone, a researcher on conflict management, genocide prevention, and women's security, writes that because women address societal needs rather than caving in to what warring parties want, their impact on peace is more significant, more positive. She also notes that the likelihood of peace enduring increases not just when women participate in the process, but when gender electoral quotas are established.

By quotas, that should not mean just a few token females, but complete gender equality, which is just common sense considering that the world's population is made up of equal parts men and women.

Stone says, "Long-term policies empowering women to move past victimization and into leadership positions are key to establishing a more peaceful society over time." The world needs more female CEOs, more women in politics, more women making decisions about the well-being of our people and our planet.

As I watched the little Egyptian girl skipping across the terminal in her pink running shoes, I liked to think that she will become the president of her country one day. One can only hope.

My flight to Beirut was announced, so I tucked my journal back into my carry-on, the words on its pages so noisy you could almost hear the book shouting, its remaining blank pages lying in wait for my deluge of ink as I continued my way around the globe. I took one last glance at the little girl, said a silent prayer for her, and made my way to my gate.

CHAPTER 8

Lebanon

> Peace does not mean an absence of conflicts;
> differences will always be there. Peace
> means solving these differences through
> peaceful means; through dialogue, education,
> knowledge; and through humane ways."
> —**DALAI LAMA XIV**

In Seattle, Washington, during the summer of 2012, Barbara Abdeni Massaad, a Lebanese cookbook author, photographer, and humanitarian, took a lunch break from the restaurant-consulting gig that had brought her to the U.S. for a month. She was browsing the shelves at the Elliott Bay Book Company, where a book with a heart-shaped pie against a gingham background caught her attention. She began reading the story about a woman who used pie making as a way to cope with her grief over the sudden loss of her young husband. There was only one copy left, and Barbara wanted to buy it, but she hesitated as it had a coffee cup stain on the cover, compliments of a previous customer who took it into the bookstore's café, ignoring the signs politely asking people not to. Barbara bought the book anyway and upon finishing it, she contacted the author—me—to offer her praise, and an invitation.

"If you ever want to come to Lebanon," she wrote in her email, "I would be happy to host you."

So when coming up with the list of countries I would visit, before announcing my trip to anyone, before the first offers from others (like Charity in New Zealand) came pouring in, Barbara's home in Beirut already held an unassailable place on my itinerary. That's because Barbara's work embodied my mission; but instead of pie, her vehicle for kindness was soup.

Two years earlier, on a cold January day, Barbara was watching a TV news program from the comfort of her heated apartment in Beirut. The newscast was airing footage of the largest Syrian refugee camp in Lebanon, located in the Beqaa Valley, a mountainous region on the Lebanese-Syrian border. A hot, dusty, and fertile place in the summer, winter had descended upon the camp, covering the makeshift village of tents with snow and ice. The refugees were dressed in clothes far too light for the weather, and you could see their breath as they huddled around tiny stoves trying to warm their hands. If not for the news caption stating otherwise, you would have thought they were in Siberia. Upon seeing these images, Barbara felt a stirring in her heart, a mix of outrage and compassion. "I HAVE TO DO SOMETHING!" she shouted.

She jumped into action, loading up her Land Rover with blankets, warm clothes, and all the vegetables, broth, and spices needed to make hot and nourishing soup. The refugees were grateful, so she kept returning, making the two-hour drive into the mountains every week, gradually winning the trust of the camp's inhabitants. In between cooking for them, she employed her professional photography skills and made portraits of the Syrians, capturing every generation, from infants to the elderly. These portraits became part of her internationally award-winning cookbook, *Soup for Syria: Recipes to Celebrate Our Shared Humanity*. Her goal for the book, featuring soup recipes from celebrity chefs like Yotam Ottolenghi, Alice Waters, and Paula Wolfert, wasn't to make money for herself. Instead, the profits—100 percent of them—are donated directly to the refugees.

Who wouldn't want to spend ten days with someone like her!

Barbara offered to take me up to the refugee camp so that I could bring them pies. I had done something similar in Newtown, Connecticut, in 2012, after the Sandy Hook Elementary School shooting, that horrific massacre of 20 first-graders and 6 adult staff. I had been so moved to do something, *anything*, to help ease the pain of their grief, that I enlisted my friend Janice Molinari (the same Janice who loves India so much). I drove from Iowa to New Jersey, where Janice opened up her home to strangers, secured use of neighbors' ovens up and down the block, and over the course of several days, with the help of over 60 volunteers, we made 250 apple pies. We packed the pies into my twenty-four-foot RV and handed them out by the slice to the residents of the town. The gesture of compassion was so warmly received and appreciated, I thought I could replicate the concept, albeit on a micro scale, by bringing pie to the Syrians.

After booking all my stops and applying for the necessary visas, I signed up with the U.S. Department of State for its Smart Traveler Enrollment Program (STEP) to receive travel notifications for each country. Before leaving India, I got a STEP advisory warning Americans to avoid travel to Lebanon. It was deemed too high-risk, a level four out of four. Of course, it was a risk; it was the Middle East. The unrest had been hanging around there since . . . let me calculate . . . since the dawn of humanity. Several decades earlier, Lebanon had endured a brutal civil war from 1975 to 1990, at the cost of 120,000 lives. That war, like most wars, was incited by religion, tribalism, and artificially drawn geo-political borders. Things were, for the moment, relatively quiet in the small country, if only on the surface. The warning likely had more to do with its neighbor; not Israel this time, but the other one, Syria, where a war was—and, after a decade, still is—raging.

At the time of my visit, Lebanon ranked at 145 on the Global Peace Index, two spots closer to the bottom than India, with Syria coming in dead last. I promised myself I wasn't going to put myself in harm's way—that was my policy whether at home or away—but I figured that, because I would be with Barbara, I would be safe. Safe, however, is a relative term.

My flight landed at dusk. Gliding across the Mediterranean Sea, the sun's last light glazed the water like icing on a cake. The sky rotated in a color wheel of pastels from peach to pink to lavender. Looming ahead was the land, a gold-spun quilt of sand and cedar that had once served as a launchpad for explorers like Lawrence of Arabia and Freya Stark, the pioneering female travel writer, when the main mode of transportation had been camel. Dangerous or not, I, too, wanted to be an explorer of the Levant, as these ancient Holy Lands are referred to in the Old Testament. Something about the colors and light already felt familiar, like I was coming home, like some part of me already knew this unknown place. I didn't believe in reincarnation, but could Lebanon have been my ancestral home with memories embedded deep in my mitochondria? Time, diaspora, and the mingling of tribes had turned me into a DNA mutt, but maybe I held some trace of Lebanon in my cells. More likely, the instant familiarity had more to do with how Beirut's backdrop of coastal mountains looked a lot like Los Angeles, and how skimming the Mediterranean before touchdown was similar to LAX's overwater approach.

Inside the airport, I immediately spotted a woman with long, curly hair so red it radiated a halo of flames. With big brown eyes magnified by round spectacles, she was dressed like a Phoenician goddess in a flowing flowered sundress, paired with rope sandals, the footwear of Jesus. And she was drinking an espresso from a paper cup. Her energy was so electric, she practically levitated above the waiting crowd.

"Habibti!" she squealed, wrapping me in her embrace. "You're here!"

I knew that habibti meant darling, and just the sound of the word made me forget about the STEP warning.

"Did you get my email about catering the Indian dinner? We're going to be busy. I thought you could help me."

"Yes," I said. "And I'm happy to help with whatever you need."

"I know you had a hard time in India, habibti. And of all things, we have this Indian event, but maybe this is meant to be."

India wasn't going to let me go. It had to be karma. There was no other explanation.

Stay open. Just stay open. You've got this.

It was dark by the time we reached Barbara's apartment. She lived on the outskirts of Beirut, on a mountainside, where high-rises grew thicker and higher than the pine forest above them. Below, a blanket of city lights shimmered in every direction far into the distance, until reaching the edge of the sea where the yellow glow abruptly ended. What lay beyond was as black as outer space. A stray cat appeared out of nowhere, greeting us as we approached the building's entrance.

"That's Tchu Tchu," Barbara said. As the orange cat continued on its way into the night, she added, "He's my cat."

Yeah, sure he is, I thought, hoping that beneath her beatific persona she wasn't a crazy cat woman—or just plain crazy.

It was late, but her family had waited up, and as we walked in the door of her apartment I was introduced to her husband, Serge, her two teenage daughters, Mia and Sarah, and her eighteen-year-old son, Albert. Smiling politely, they all welcomed me, including the dogs. "That's Belle," she said of the black cocker spaniel licking my legs, while a Mexican jumping bean of a Chihuahua bounced around my ankles. "And that's Pepito," she said, trying to make herself heard above its bark.

And there it was, another of life's perplexing questions: How can a dog so small make such loud noise?

"Sarah and Mia are leaving tomorrow for—"

Just as Barbara started her sentence the room went pitch black—not just the room but the whole city. Without a word, Albert turned on a flashlight and Serge casually lit candles.

"Sarah and Mia are leaving tomorrow for Girl Scout Camp," Barbara continued. Even in the dim light, I could see she was unfazed by the sudden lack of power. Likewise, she could see my confusion. "It's just a power cut, habibti. We have them regularly."

"Regularly? Why?"

"The power plants can't keep up with the demand. It will come back on in a few minutes," she reassured me. "Or maybe a few hours. Definitely by tomorrow."

The lack of electricity and the persistence of this critical issue would be only one of Lebanon's crises I would learn about first-hand in my short stay.

The next morning, lured out of bed by the heavenly scent of coffee brewing—the power having returned—I heard something scratching on the apartment door. Barbara opened the door and in walked the cat from the parking lot. "Good morning, Tchu Tchu," she said as he sauntered past her.

"That's amazing! How do you have an outdoor cat when you live on the fifth floor?" I asked.

"He climbs through the gated door downstairs and usually takes the stairs. Sometimes he rides the elevator if anyone is going up."

He rides the elevator, as if he's just another tenant in the building. I shook my head and laughed, but Barbara brushed it off like it was just, well, normal.

A good way to gauge people's capacity for empathy and desire for peace is by the way they treat animals. I already knew it and the cat merely confirmed it: Barbara was not crazy—no crazier than I was anyway. She was one of the most empathetic and peace-loving people I would meet on my journey.

We ate a breakfast of thick, plain yogurt called labneh (pronounced "leb-nay"), drizzled with olive oil and sprinkled with za'atar, a Lebanese spice mix of sesame seeds, thyme, and dried sumac. Bright-blue ceramic dishes blazed with fresh tomatoes, mint leaves, honey, homemade pita bread, sliced cucumbers, and black olives. Sitting among them was a basket of homegrown apricots, orange with ripeness. The Mediterranean diet is not only one of the healthiest, it's one of the most colorful. Every morsel, so fresh and clean, rendered the table setting a tableau of vitality, the vibrant hues more stimulating than the coffee.

"The apricots are from our home up on the mountain," Barbara said. "We need to use them before they go bad, so I was thinking you could make a pie."

"I'd love to. And if you need any other help, I can pitch in," I offered.

"Do you mind walking the dogs while I get the girls ready for camp?" she asked.

"Yes! Absolutely. I need my dog fix."

So off I went, down the five flights of marble stairs, Belle and Pepito on leashes with Tchu Tchu, the cat, following behind, while

Barbara's other cat, Chicamoo, stayed home, hiding in the linen closet. As I made the loop around the neighborhood, giving the dogs time to sniff the base of every pine tree, I held my face to the sun and wondered how Jack was doing. I longed to be walking him, my *own* dog. The place that Jack held in my heart ached constantly, a dull throb that I wasn't always conscious of, even though it accompanied me every mile of my trip. But staying in the moment, walking Barbara's dogs—their tails wagging so hard they might lift off like helicopters, their curiosity as elevated as the mountain range behind us, their poop secured in plastic bags—I found myself appreciating something I had not yet experienced in the seven weeks I'd been traveling: normalcy.

Normalcy is the breakfast dishes being washed and put away, Barbara sitting at her desk checking her email, and Mia yelling at Sarah that she can't find her shoes. Normalcy is the two sisters posing for a photo in their *Guides du Liban* (Girl Scout) uniforms—navy blue skirts, white blouses, and blue striped kerchiefs around their necks—and dropping them off at their school, where a crowd of kids waited to board the fleet of yellow school buses that would shuttle them into the countryside for a week of summer camp.

What was not normal, not for me, was the way people talked. French and Arabic are the national languages of Lebanon, and English is widely spoken, but people regularly speak all three languages at the same time. A typical sentence could contain words or phrases from each, all mixed together. I had just taught Barbara how to use the dictation function on her phone and teased, "You're going to confuse the hell out of your phone if you dictate like that."

"Okay, habibti," Barbara announced after the girls boarded their bus, "now we're going to buy supplies for the Indian dinner, and then I'm taking you to lunch at one of the best places in Beirut."

We made our way down into the city and with Barbara driving I could stare out at the passing scenery, taking in as much as I could see of Beirut out of the window of a moving car. What appeared to be the centerpiece of the city was Lebanon's largest mosque, Mohammad Al-Amin Mosque, its shiny blue dome nestled in between four minarets standing sentry, their pointy tips pricking the sky. Right next to it was Saint George Cathedral, a newly constructed Catholic church, its bell tower, topped with a skyscraper of a cross, built to compete with the minarets in height, as if religion were a contest you could win. Given the number of wars waged in the name of one's definition of god being superior to another's, one could argue that organized religion is an obstacle to world peace.

We passed by the old souk, rebuilt as a Rodeo Drive shopping mall, any hint of its traditional wares that I had imagined, like spices, baskets, and rugs, were obliterated by Gucci and Rolex boutiques and a cineplex movie theater. Most notable was the absence of people; the souk was empty, as if there'd been a bomb threat. Farther on, we crawled through the city center, clogged with traffic, past commercial office buildings, some of which looked like they'd been built in a hurry and not built to last, as if they knew they'd have to rebuild again anyway. Beirut showed signs of neglect and fatigue, a Sisyphean weariness after its civil war, evidence of its toll visible everywhere.

Road blocks and military checkpoints dotted the city, manned by armed soldiers in green fatigues and berets—a fashion holdout from Lebanon's days as a former French colony. With automatic rifles strapped around their chests, the men, young and serious, stood behind concrete barricades and rolls of barbed wire. Fortresses of sandbags surrounded long-abandoned buildings. I couldn't help but see a glass-half-empty view of Beirut given the many obvious remnants of bombings: the black scars of fire, pockmarks left by bullets, broken windows, gaping holes in walls, piles of rubble on the ground. This was not the glamorous "Paris of the Middle East" it was reputed to be. That jet-setting, martini-sipping era, half a century earlier—back when I was in grade school and before the war—had passed.

Still, I felt no sense of danger—except for the driving. There were almost no stoplights, but the few in operation served merely as a suggestion, as if stopping on red was considered optional. Every intersection and on-ramp was a free-for-all, a battle of wills to see who could go first—and everyone wanted to go first. It was the chaos of India's traffic without the noise. In Lebanon, no one honks their horns. Instead, they just accelerate and—*inshallah*—trust God's will that they make it to their destination alive.

The restaurant Barbara was taking me to for lunch, Onno, had been a favorite of Anthony Bourdain; he had made a point to dine there whenever he was in Beirut. It's in the Armenian Quarter—Bourj Hammoud—an industrious neighborhood of narrow streets with a cat's cradle of electrical wires crisscrossing overhead. Laundry hung from balconies and faded awnings shielded busy shop fronts from the relentless sun. But what I noticed most, as we circled around the block several times in search of a parking place, was the signage. Banners stretched across the roads, as well as graffiti painted on the buildings, with the words, "Fuck Turkey." I had arrived on the one hundredth anniversary of the Armenian genocide, a travesty for which Turkey has never apologized, let alone acknowledged, continuing to this day denial of its role in the mass murder. While I regularly pepper my speech with the F-word, in this case, using the term "forgiveness" in place of "fuck" may be the only way to heal these century-old scars. Like many in America, a country so young and geographically far removed from world history, I hadn't learned about things like the Ottoman Empire or the Three Pashas. The Pashas were three military rulers who, after staging a coup in 1913, took over the Ottoman Empire. Determined to ensure a pure Turkish ethnic identity, they initiated what was, essentially, the Holocaust of World War I.

How is it that people can't grasp that the goal of a pure ethnicity is pure folly? In 1999, Joseph Chang, a statistician at Yale University, published a paper on how he had used mathematical analysis to conclude that we all share a common ancestor. In 2013, University of Southern California researcher Peter Ralph, along with geneticist Graham Coop, provided DNA-based evidence to confirm it—that, indeed, everyone on Earth is related.

If the DNA research had been done a hundred years earlier, would it have mattered? And why is it so hard to convince ourselves that as humans, we are *one* species sharing *one* planet? We share

99.9 percent identical genetic makeup with a mere 0.1 percent sliver that allows for variation, which means we are all slices of the same pie. Even when it's a divided one, like Poonam and Rohini's half cherry, half peach in Mumbai, a pairing of very different but equally appealing colors and flavors can coexist side by side. To reduce our species to one single race—even if it were possible, which thankfully it's not—would be like eating rhubarb pie every day; you'd get sick of it. Variety is the spice of life—of *all* life in all forms. It's called ecology, the interrelationship of all organisms and their environments, a symbiosis that's essential to—and should guarantee—world peace.

While the lunch at Onno was worthy of Anthony Bourdain's praise—*mezze* (small plates meant to be shared) made with combinations of chickpeas, lentils, eggs, dried meat, slivered almonds, tangy sauces, and fragrant spices—I could barely eat. My appetite was lost to the world outside, the one where peace was elusive, achingly just out of reach.

But a morsel of peace was closer than I knew. Because right after lunch, Barbara and I went next door to an art gallery called The Vintage Shop, where industrial art pieces hung on the walls. Signs with metal letters illuminated by a backdrop of lights, each of them bearing only one word: PEACE. No sooner did we step outside of the gallery, a young man walked toward us wearing a T-shirt that made me stop him and ask for a picture. He smiled as I snapped a photo of his shirt. The word "WAR," in all caps, was crossed out with a red slash; beneath it was the word "PEACE" in equally bold letters.

There was that yin and yang thing again. For every push, a pull. For every aggression, an act of kindness. For every grievance, a plea for forgiveness. For every act of violence, a prayer for peace.

We shopped at a grocery store for the Indian dinner ingredients— beans, lentils, rice, chicken, and spices—and unloaded them at Makan: Art Space, the restaurant where Barbara was serving the Indian dinner. Three dinners, actually, as what I had thought was a one-time catering gig was actually a multiple-night pop-up. I helped Barbara prep, working alongside her son Albert, who inherited his mother's passion for food. Barbara wasn't just a cookbook author, she was president of the Beirut chapter of Slow Food, a movement that promotes local food traditions and access to good, clean, and fair food in over 160 countries. Barbara was friends with its founder, Carlo Petrini.

Albert was heading to culinary school in France the following week, but he was already a pro and taught me how to curl my fingers back when chopping, so as to slice the carrots and onions and not my skin. I may have been confident in my pie skills—apart from the occasional oven burn, I could make a pie without ending up in the ER—but I was not professionally trained as a chef, pastry or otherwise. Which is why I protested when Barbara assigned me the job of making the dessert—rice pudding for fifty people. "Just stir constantly," Barbara instructed me. But when the rice burned on the bottom of the pan, requiring the massive stock pot of milk, rice, and sugar to be thrown out, I was relieved of my duties.

Rice pudding disaster aside, the cooking experience underscored how each new country on my trip was connected to the last. In New Zealand, Charity had given me Sam Cawthorn's contact info in Australia. In Australia, Kate had introduced me to her brother in Thailand. From Thailand, Julia hooked me up with the hotel in India. And India had tied itself to Lebanon by way of Barbara's catering gig. I didn't know what would connect me to the next countries— and to whom—but there would be more surprises, coincidences, and connections ahead. If I was learning nothing else on my journey it was the affirmation that humanity is one big spider web of silky threads, almost eight billion of us constantly spinning new patterns, building upon the old ones, all caught in a collective net.

While Barbara continued to log twelve-hour days in the restaurant kitchen, simmering chicken thighs, skewering kebabs, and rolling out chapatis, I took over the kitchen in her apartment. Except for the company of Barbara's dogs and cats, I was alone in an uncharacteristically quiet home, allowing me to get into my zone, peeling, rolling, crimping—the kind of rhythm that always calms me, no matter where in the world I'm baking, even when it's in a Beirut kitchen with no air conditioning making a dozen apple pies on a ninety-nine-degree day. Even when I have to lie on the cool kitchen-floor tiles several times to keep from passing out.

Before putting the pies in the oven, I decorated their tops using the angel cookie cutter I was given as a gift when baking in Newtown, Connecticut. The cutter had become a sacred token as it represented the victims who were killed by the gunman. We adorned nearly all of the 250 pies we made with an angel, sometimes adding the initials of the Sandy Hook victims. In Lebanon, although the pies were to acknowledge living people, I treated each angel cut-out with reverence, gently pressing the dough in place as a prayer for the people who would be receiving them.

Early on a Sunday morning, Barbara and I packed my twelve pies into the Land Rover. I had made fourteen, but Belle pulled one off the kitchen table and it landed upside down on the floor—much to Pepito's pleasure. And the cat, not Tchu Tchu but Chicamoo, the shy one, used one of the pies as a bed, leaving her paw prints as evidence. We also loaded several bags of donated toys and clothes into the car. Leaving the bright-blue Mediterranean Sea behind us, we set off for the Beqaa Valley refugee camp, climbing higher and higher into the mountains, passing through military checkpoints and winding through land so dry, brown, and barren that the only thing growing there, besides the scraggly patches of shrubs and grasses, was my apprehension.

As we passed through the town of Bhamdoun, a summer resort town (one of many mountain escapes where Lebanese go to flee the coastal heat), I noticed the familiar green and white Siren of the Starbucks logo. "Drive-thru," the sign read in English.

Starbucks? Where am I?

"That's sad," I commented to Barbara, pointing out the coffeehouse. "Globalization undermines local businesses and turns unique places into generic ones."

"I understand what you're saying, habibti. I'm not in favor of it either. Part of our Slow Food mission is to stop it from happening, but to Lebanese, having Starbucks build stores here feels like an acknowledgment of Lebanon's existence."

A quarter mile on, the ubiquitous golden arches rose into the sky. It wasn't only Starbucks that had found its way to the Lebanese outback; McDonald's was there, too, instantly recognizable even when its name was written in Arabic. I had yet to visit a country that didn't have a Starbucks and McDonald's, not to mention KFC, Subway, Domino's, and the like. It made me bristle at first, but I understood what Barbara was saying about inclusion.

Climbing higher still on the Beirut-Damascus Highway, we passed under an overhead road sign that read *"Frontière Syrienne."* Marcus had traveled in Syria before we got married—before the war—and loved it. He visited the Krak des Chevaliers, an eleventh-century castle from the Crusader era only one hundred miles away from where Barbara and I were now. In a photo he took there, he captured a ray of sun boring through an arched passageway, the stone walls glowing orange-red, unchanged since the days of knights riding through it on horseback. Blown up to poster size and framed, the photo hung in our Stuttgart apartment. The romance of that image made me want to visit Syria, but now the words "Syrian Border" sounded forbidden and foreboding, swimming in my belly with the same sensation I had when skydiving for the first (and only) time. I was back in that moment, standing at the open door looking down at the ground ten-thousand feet below, alarm bells going off in my brain screaming, *Are you crazy? You could die!* We were an easy air-strike distance from the front lines. I had never been this close to an active war zone. I hadn't told anyone I was coming here—more to the point, I hadn't told my mother. I would wait until we were safely back in Beirut, which in itself was a relative concept given I had already ignored the U.S. State Department's warning advising Americans not to travel to Lebanon at all. Barbara had been to the camp at least fifty times. It had to be fine. Perfectly safe. Nothing at all to worry about.

Lebanon's Beqaa Valley is home to vineyards, manicured green rows of grapes, and upscale wineries designed like French châteaus that attract tourists—but it's no Bordeaux. It's home to Lebanon's largest refugee camp, inhabited by over 300,000 out of the 1.5 million Syrians fleeing from the war in their country next door. These were the ones desperate enough, determined enough, lucky enough, to have escaped with their lives given almost half a million of their fellow citizens have perished—so far.

On one side of the valley, a cluster of tall apartment buildings sits on a mountain slope, while on the other side, the refugee camp sprouts out of the parched soil. Power lines run through the center like lines on a map, dividing the two vastly different worlds. A dragon's breath of wind blew a cloud of dust across a field where women worked, some hunched over, some sitting on the ground, digging in the dirt.

"Potatoes," Barbara said as the women dropped their unearthed treasures into burlap sacks. "Some of the refugees find work as field hands for the local farmers," she explained.

Around the perimeter of the field, an old man in a windbreaker and fisherman's cap tended to his goats. Their long hair and shaggy coats looked too hot for the scorching heat, but they didn't seem bothered as they browsed for what snippets of vegetation they could find. In the distance, much larger herds of goats grazed alongside flocks of sheep, dutifully attended by a handful of other shepherds. I wondered what the animals were providing—yogurt, labneh, milk, or meat—and if it would be shared with the refugees.

Barbara turned onto a dirt lane that took us between rows of tents, temporary housing constructed of two-by-four wood frames that held up walls—if you could call discarded billboards "walls." Advertisements were still partially visible, scraps of what the ads promised—cruise vacations to the tropics, luxury cars, the latest smart phones—as the vinyl fabric flapped in the wind. Many of the tents were covered in plain blue tarps, some were white, and some had UNHCR logos—the acronym for the United Nations High Commissioner for Refugees. Every roof was weighted with spare tires to keep the shelters from sailing away.

We stopped to visit a young couple whose baby boy had been sick. Barbara had been paying for his hospital bills, and for the special formula he needed once he finally got the diagnosis that he was lactose intolerant. We went inside their tent, bringing an apple pie with us, and sat on the straw mats and floor pillows that covered the ground. There were no chairs, no refrigerator, no bathroom, only a thin bedroll for sleeping, but everything was clean, and the bed was neatly made, the blankets pulled taut. My own house was never this tidy. Lavender-and-white-checked fabric lined the interior like wallpaper, a decorative touch that made it feel homey. In lieu of a closet, the wife's dresses—a collection of long and glittery prom gowns—hung on nails pounded into the wooden frame. While Barbara held the baby in her lap and chatted in Arabic with the couple, I was focused on the pleasant warm breeze that drifted through the tent, invited in through an open flap. Besides being clean, the tent was comfortable, the weather perfect for sleeping. But it was summer, not winter. Not the frozen hell it would become when temperatures plummeted and snow and ice added further punishment to already tenuous circumstances. It would take a lot more than soup to stay alive in these conditions.

Barbara pointed to me and the apple pie, explaining how it was a gift for them. That was my cue. I handed it to them and smiled. They smiled back as they accepted the gift. "*Shukran. Shukran*," they said. I didn't need translation to know this meant thank you. The way their eyes shone told me everything.

We moved on, driving down the dirt road until we came to a cluster of women all wearing headscarves with patterns of paisley and flower prints in rich colors, leaving only their weathered faces exposed. Babies in slings were strapped to their bodies, with their toddlers in diapers clinging to their legs. One of the women was pregnant, her belly so big her baby was likely due within weeks. We stopped to greet to them, they gathered around us, focusing on me. They looked closely, inspecting me with a friendly gaze. Finally, one of them asked a question that made Barbara burst into laughter.

"She wants to know if you're Angelina Jolie," Barbara translated for me.

The women knew of the actress not from her films, but from her visits to their camp. But me confused with Angelina Jolie? I laughed, too, because as a five-foot-five blonde I looked nothing like her. The only thing I had in common with Angelina Jolie was that I was standing on the same soil she had, at this same temporary tent city that was not temporary enough as the Syrian conflict raged on. Months had become years, refugees kept arriving, and the camp continued to grow, spreading across the valley like the mountain's shadow at sunset.

"Beth is a pie baker," Barbara explained to them while I stood silent, relying on my smile as a means to communicate. "She is traveling around the world promoting peace. She made apple pie for you. In her country, pie is a symbol of comfort and generosity. Would you like to take a pie?"

At least I'm pretty sure that's what she said. The only word I understood in the midst of her Arabic was the French word, *gâteau*, which translates as cake, but there was no need to argue semantics.

I handed out pies in plastic grocery bags to several women in the group. When they peered into the bags, their expressions changed from excited to quizzical as they studied the strange food: the golden-brown crust, the globs of thickened apple filling that had oozed out, the angel decorations on top. Barbara assured them the pie was good, wholesome, made with high-quality ingredients, and made with love. She promised them they would like it.

Trust. It was not something to take for granted here.

Their bodies convulsed with nervous laughter under their long dresses as the women, and their children, continued looking at both me and the pies with wonder. *Who the hell is this woman who is not Angelia Jolie? And why is she giving us pie?* they must have been thinking. But what had I expected? They had never even seen a pie, and had no idea what this American pie was or what it represented. This wasn't turning out to be the experience I had had in Newtown, Connecticut, the one I had hoped to duplicate. *Duplicate?* What was I thinking? A Syrian refugee camp was not the same as a wealthy New England hamlet, even if they were linked by different types of suffering. But the women did seem touched by the culinary gifts.

We climbed back into the Land Rover and hadn't driven more than ten feet when a crowd of men ran toward us, an angry mob wielding clubs and sticks. Some were waving machetes as if they were swords, stabbing at the air as they converged and surrounded our vehicle. I held my breath as they approached, bracing myself for impact, for torture, for certain death. But our car was simply a rock in a river to them; they weaved around us and kept on running. One man, his face dark with rage, his eyes narrowed, his brow furrowed tight, pounded on my window, his punch so hard I reeled back to avoid his hand coming through the glass. The glass held, but he shook his fist at us, yelling something I couldn't understand. The way his lips curled back in a snarl was translation enough. He ran off as more men, brandishing their rudimentary weapons, raced past. An old, leather-skinned man rapped loudly with his gnarled fingers on Barbara's window. She rolled it down only just enough for him to shout inside, "GET OUT OF HERE! IT'S NOT SAFE!"

Impossible to make a quick U-turn on the single-track road, Barbara had to inch her big SUV around, shifting into forward, then reverse, forward, reverse, forward, reverse, until we were at last pointed in the opposite direction. She pressed the gas pedal to the floor, her wheels shooting out a cloud of dust as she whisked us away from the erupting violence.

"Where they are going is exactly where I was going to take you," she said calmly. *How could she be so calm?* "I know the families down at that end of the camp. I think it might be some family feud." She paused and added, "I've never seen that happen here before."

My pies were supposed to bring peace, I wanted to say, but I said nothing. I just sat there, eyes wide, pulse racing, mind processing, heart breaking, hope crumbling, asking myself the question I ask far too often: *Why can't we all just get along?*

"We'll figure out another place to give away the rest of the pies," Barbara continued.

About a half mile down the track, we came to the edge of the camp where a bored-looking vendor stood next to a pile of watermelons in the blazing midday sun. I wondered how many customers he expected to get on this lonely stretch of road. Just beyond the watermelon stand, we spotted two boys, no more than nine years old, walking alone. Barbara pulled over to talk to them. Black-haired with deeply tanned skin, they were dressed in clean T-shirts, jeans, and sandals. At first glance they were handsome and healthy boys, but a closer look revealed their eyes, black and burning with anger—younger versions of the man who had just pounded on my window. They, too, were carrying weapons, toy guns so authentic looking I thought they were real.

We got out of the car. Barbara, her red hair blowing like one of those inflatable tube men at a car dealership, greeted the boys, disarming them with her exuberance.

"We are giving away pies. Do you want to take one home with you?" she asked. A short discussion in Arabic followed. The boys eyed us with suspicion, then looked down at their feet, kicking the dirt, stalling as they tried to decide. Would their answer be *na'am* or *la*? Yes or no? Finally, deciding that although we may be a pair of strange women, we were probably not out to kidnap them—or kill them—they nodded slowly and mumbled something to Barbara, still uncertain about the acceptance.

Barbara turned to me and said, "They're going home in opposite directions, so let's give them each one."

"It's pretty disturbing to see them running around with toy guns," I said to Barbara as we drove off with half a dozen pies left to distribute. "At what point will they be carrying real guns?"

She didn't answer my question, which was fair, given I'd meant it as a rhetorical one.

A few blocks outside the camp, we encountered two women and their brood of children walking along the road, so we stopped to ask if they would like some pies. The women, like the others we'd met, wore long kaftans in especially bright colors. These were magenta and cobalt blue and bejeweled with rhinestones and sequins that sparkled like mini disco balls against the monotone background of the desert. Islamic fashion was a growing industry; Muslim women, determining that if they were going to follow the Quran-dictated dress code to cover themselves from head to toe, they were at least going to do it with style. Their scarves were wrapped so tightly around their heads and necks that only a small oval of their faces showed, faces that were as embellished as their dresses. Thick smudges of black kohl lined their eyes, dark pencil exaggerated their eyebrows; they wore bright lipstick, too. By comparison, Barbara and I, in our short sleeves, khaki pants, and lug-soled hiking shoes, with only sunscreen to enhance our faces, must have looked downright uncivilized to them.

Once again, Barbara did the talking. When she motioned to me, I held open a bag to show them the pie. They leaned in to look and nodded. Yes, they'd love some, they indicated with their big smiles and soft eyes, readily willing to trust in us. We gave them four pies, enough so that everyone in their big family would get some, and then, using the single most powerful and lasting form of communication— touch—we hugged each other to say goodbye. I didn't realize it then, but it would be one of the most memorable exchanges on my journey.

"We'll go deliver the toys and clothes to my friend's place now," Barbara said. "He works with the refugees and he'll distribute the donations."

We drove across the valley to one of the many high-rise apartment buildings that overlooked the camp. Barbara's friends, a family of eleven, were Syrian refugees as well, but because the father, Turkey, worked for a humanitarian organization, they were provided the luxury of real housing. The apartment, spacious but barely big enough for such a large family, was new, nicely furnished, and most essentially, it had heat and plumbing.

"Barbara!" they all shouted, rushing to welcome her, while I stood to the side, holding the pies we brought them.

She put her arms around the kids and, after the initial excitement passed, told them, "I have some things in the car for you."

Turkey sent the younger boys scrambling down the stairs to unload the bags she brought, while their sisters, taking the pies, hurried to the kitchen to prepare coffee for us. We settled onto the couches in the living room, where the oldest of the kids, Wissam, joined us. Wissam had been in his third year of university studying engineering when he fled Syria with his family. His changed circumstances sent him in a new career direction, a creative one. Since arriving in Lebanon three years earlier, he had started a theater and musical group for kids in the refugee camp, both to entertain and to educate them. He had also been making short films, documenting the kids and their situation, and posting them on the YouTube channel, Salam Ya Sham, the name for his cultural arts foundation.

"Let me show you my latest video," he offered.

I didn't know what to expect, but it certainly wasn't *this*. I stared into his laptop for the two-and-a-half-minute duration, trying to hold back my tears, as Syrian kids spoke to the camera.

"*Salam*," they implored.

Wissam translated for me. "*Salam* means peace," he said. "They're saying 'We miss peace. We need peace. We all have a right to peace.'"

Salam is also the word for hello, making every Arabic greeting a solicitation for a more amicable world.

"Habibti!" Barbara pulled away from the private conversation she was having with Turkey. "I just realized the reason you are here. You can help Turkey and his family get to the United States."

I almost choked on my Turkish coffee. I set the tiny china cup down on the coffee table and looked up at her helplessly. "I . . . I don't know how that works, but I can try to find out." My first thought, however, was of Wissam, of his film, and the important work he was doing with the kids in the camp. *These kids needed him!* My next thought was that in spite of knowing that the family was looking for—and deserved—a better life, what did the U.S. actually offer? America has its own demons and divisions, and its Global Peace Index ranking drops lower every year. Granted, the U.S. isn't ruled by a ruthless dictator (so far) and doesn't have a war raging on its soil, not a physical one anyway. With lax gun control and its skyrocketing number of mass shootings, Americans need only dodge bullets, not bombs. And immigrants in America aren't always given a warm welcome. We are guilty of our own acts of cruelty toward outsiders, and as far as I knew, refugees were not offered apartments as big and as nice as the one Turkey and his family were living in. And yet in Lebanon, Wissam told me, they never felt safe, they couldn't have bank accounts, the country could never be "home."

The enormity of resolving this family's situation flattened me like the man'oushé we had stopped to eat on the way up the mountain. Man'oushé is unleavened bread named for the indentations of the baker's fingertips left in the dough, their prints made invisible under the layers of dried herbs of za'atar, fresh vegetables, tomatoes, mint, and olive oil. That had been only a few hours earlier, before my view of the world was blown open.

If Angelina Jolie hadn't managed to make a dent in the situation, how could I?

"Salam." The kids' voices from the film kept replaying in my head. "Salam," they repeated over and over. "Salam."

After we left, Barbara, being the bold and courageous Lebanese that she is, decided to take us on another lap around the refugee camp. The camp was like a second home to her, which is why, on this summer day, she wasn't going to let a few measly sticks, knives, and clubs stop her from moving around the place and visiting the people she cared so much about.

I have never encountered trouble during my travels, which I attribute to avoiding it in the first place. If I so much as get a whiff of danger, I run the opposite direction. But here on the Syrian border, I was so fixated on turning my pie giveaway into something meaningful, I didn't protest when she announced we were going back into the troubled area. Besides, I was with Barbara, a warrior, Wonder Woman climbing out of the trench to face the battle with nothing but her bravery and her bracelets for protection.

Just as we turned the corner back into the camp, a flash of movement caught my eye. We came upon it right as it was happening, bearing witness to something I had never seen before. At the exact moment we turned, one of the boys with the toy guns was throwing his apple pie into the ditch—*my* apple pie, a pie I had made with such tenderness and care. I had invested myself in those pies, filling them with my wishes to provide happiness and nourishment to those in need. I had made those pies to promote peace. But there it was, one of my homemade pies, airborne, in flight—and heading straight for the ditch! To watch it sailing through the air in an upward arc before plummeting down, felt like being in a car wreck when objects spin unnaturally out of place, when time takes on a different dimension, when everything moves in slow motion yet in reality moving so fast the brain can't compute what is happening. My pie was about to be totaled!

"Barbara! Look!" I shouted, pointing toward the wreckage.

She slammed on the brakes and came to a stop next to the boy. "What are you doing?" she demanded.

Her words shrunk him to half his size, his armor crushed as quickly as the pie, the youthful innocence he had worked so hard to conceal on full display. "My mom told me to get rid of it," he stammered.

Barbara continued the interrogation, and the reprimand, while all I could do was watch as his mouth turned down in confusion, sadness, and remorse; his dark eyes dripped with tears that streaked his young cheeks. As if we had melded into one being, my own eyes filled with tears, and I sat frozen in the passenger seat, as voiceless and confused as the boy. He was troubled, unsure who he was supposed to answer to—Barbara, this force of nature with the wild red hair and freckly white skin, or his own mother?

Unrelenting, Barbara kept scolding him. "She came all the way from America and she worked hard to make these pies for you. She wanted to do something nice for you. We are going to go back to your tent and I'm going to talk to your mother."

Fortunately, Barbara translated this last part for me, and it compelled me to butt in. "We are *not* going to talk to his mother! Just let him be. We've done enough. Let's just go."

And so we drove away, the boy still crying, me still crying, the Land Rover emptied of its twelve pies—eleven of them given to refugees and one lying in a ditch, another casualty of Syria's bloody, senseless, heart-wrenching war.

The next day I got an email from Doug.

> *Beth, I am so humbled by what you have done. Taking pie to a refugee camp is incredible! And to think I complain about the weather. Jack is doing good, but he misses you. I do what I can. I take him for rides in the truck and give*

him back massages. That usually settles him. Please stay as safe as possible on your amazing, compassionate, humane endeavors. Everyone at Camp Doug looks forward to your safe return on September 1.

A heartfelt XO,
Doug

It was more emotion than he had ever expressed, and he had never written "XO" before. I wrote him back right away.

Thanks, Doug, but I don't feel I've done anything. I'm just a traveler passing through. What difference can I make by handing out a few pies? I feel almost silly for doing it. I'm still so troubled and trying to process what happened at the camp. It was basically, "Here have some pie" and then we were speeding off in our air-conditioned Land Rover. Even more troubling was that we stopped at one of the wineries afterward. I admit it was relaxing to be in the air-conditioned restaurant surrounded by the lush green of the vineyards and it gave Barbara and me a chance to talk. We chatted nonstop about the world, life, love, marriage, grief. But drinking a bottle of rosé in the elegant setting while all those displaced people were only half a mile away living on dirt in tents? It was like staying at the Four Seasons in Mumbai and looking down on the slum. You can't help but feel a terrible guilt. Seriously, I'm still confused by the whole thing.

His reply was a quick comeback to my lament, and a surprisingly insightful one coming from this stoic farmer.

Beth,
You are TRYING to share!!! Remember the saying about one butterfly wing beat halfway around the world . . . You may be that butterfly! ;-)
XO, Doug

Back in Beirut, I continued the morning routine at Barbara's, walking Belle, Pepito, and Tchu Tchu around the neighborhood. Outside the building, I had noticed a little beach cabana with garbage cans parked in the shade of its striped awning. "That's a cute way to store the cans," I thought. Each morning, however, I observed the trash pile growing, spilling out of the cans and onto the ground, spreading beyond the confines of the cabana. "They need a bigger cabana," I mused. But what I was witnessing was something more serious. Beirut was facing a new war: a battle over where to put the garbage. The city's old landfill had reached capacity and was closed before designating a new one. This neighborhood cabana was only a microcosm of what was happening all over Beirut.

The next time we drove to the city center, mountains of garbage bags, reaching the height of second-story windows, lined the streets for blocks on end. On the sidewalks, in the medians, on the corners, everywhere you looked there were heaps of steaming, rotting garbage. It began affecting Beirut's nightlife as people liked to dine al fresco in the many outdoor cafés. But no one wanted to eat outside with the stench of garbage spoiling their meal. The country had been without a president for over a year and the parliament members couldn't—or wouldn't—make a decision to stem the public health crisis. It would take several months and citizens protesting in the streets to come up with a solution, which was, simply, to reopen the old overflowing landfill.

No amount of garbage could deter Barbara from going to her Italian friend's birthday party. I tagged along, joining her group of friends at a cozy corner bar, in a quiet neighborhood with minimal trash. Inside the bar, we squeezed around a small table, where we were promptly served glasses of prosecco. When Barbara was summoned by another friend across the room, I turned to talk to the guy on my left. I could tell by his accent—and his blond beard—that he was from another part of the world, so I asked him where he was from.

"I'm from Switzerland," he said. "From Bern."

"Oh? I'll be in Bern next week."

"Where are you staying in Bern?"

"I'm staying with my friend, Uschi. She lives near the Paul Klee museum."

"Uschi?" he asked, rummaging through the filing cabinet in his brain. "Uschi Kamer?"

"WHAT? Yes! Oh my god, you know her?!" My sorority-girl squeal made the bar go silent; every head turned in my direction.

"Is everything all right, habibti?" Barbara asked, having rushed over.

"He knows my friend in Bern! How crazy is that?"

"My wife, Heba, works with Uschi," he continued. "She's on an assignment here."

"Heba is my good friend," Barbara said.

Heba, a tall, dark, beautiful Lebanese radiating the same kind of female strength as Barbara, came over and joined us. "We're going back to Bern next week," she said. "Maybe we'll see you there."

"I still can't believe it!" I said, shaking my head. "What a small world!"

The tiny bar was too small to contain my excitement. I wanted to run to the top of Mt. Lebanon and shout, *YOU SEE?! WE ARE ALL CONNECTED!* as if I had discovered the answer to the meaning of life, or found the solution to world peace. At the very least, I interpreted it not as mere coincidence, but as personal confirmation that I was not the lost soul I often felt myself to be, forever tumbling downstream in the white water, bouncing off the boulders, occasionally finding an eddy, but never finding my place. This convergence of people, of common friends, signaled that even if I was merely a speck of dust in the cosmos, I belonged here, exactly here, at exactly this time, in a bar in Beirut, halfway around the world from the place I called home.

This encounter in the bar, fleeting as the excitement was, gave me the fuel I needed to keep going, because Lebanon had challenged me as much as India, maybe even more. The power cuts, the garbage fiasco, the aggressive driving, the aftermath of civil war, the heavily armed military presence, the lack of government, the ongoing secular tensions, the refugee crisis, the anniversary of the Armenian genocide, and, of course, the fight in the camp and the pie in the ditch, all conspired to undermine any hope I held out for world peace. It would take me a long time to focus on its many positive parts, though as I flew off to the next country, I took with me a small but consoling conclusion: life goes on—*no matter what*. Even in an unstable place where danger lurks uncomfortably close, you still go to work, you walk the dogs, you shop for groceries, you go to Girl Scout camp, you attend birthday parties, you make pies, and you exchange hugs with strangers in a refugee camp. That's all any of us can do, no matter what life throws at us. We keep going. We just keep going.

We get up in the morning. We do our best. Nothing else matters.

CHAPTER 9

Greece

> What you leave behind is not what is engraved in stone
> monuments, but what is woven into the lives of others.
> —PERICLES

reece is the birthplace of many things: Western civilization, the Olympic Games, modern medicine, myths, classical literature, philosophy, and luminaries like Plato, Socrates, and Aristotle. Even democracy itself was born here, though Americans often get the credit like they do with pie. Greece was not the birthplace of pie—that was Egypt in 6000 BC—but historians believe that Greeks were the first to make an edible crust. They added butter, butter, and more butter, until, eventually, it evolved into the flaky, croissant-like phyllo dough that Greek pastries are known for today. Somewhere in my research, I had read that the first recorded pie recipe could be found in Greece, its ingredients of honey and sheep's cheese etched onto a stone tablet, and I was going in search of it. That was the plan.

Plan. The word alone portends the possibility of failure.

When I was organizing my trip, my friend Kee Kee put me in touch with a high school friend of hers from Madison, Wisconsin, Christopher Bakken. Christopher is a professor of English, the author of several books of poetry, and an expert on Greece, both the country and its food. He said I should meet his friend in Athens, Christina Panteleimonitis, who restored a three-hundred-year-old mill for her handmade pasta business. Pasta, even by my loosest definition, didn't qualify as pie, but Christina also had a mission to search for old Greek recipes and I thought she might be helpful in my quest. I also liked that her company supports women. Christina replied to my email saying she would be happy to give me a mill tour, and that she would take me to the pastry shop next door as the owner's mother makes pie. "Pie is *pita* in Greek and she makes every kind, the traditional way from phyllo," she wrote. She added that I should reach out to her friend Georgia Kofinas, a Greek-American cookbook author. I wrote to Georgia who, in turn, invited me for a Greek meal at her Athens home on the night of my arrival.

I asked each new contact if they knew where I could find the mythical stone tablet with the pie recipe. "No idea," they all answered, making me wonder if I had imagined it. I wasn't deterred though. Greece would be the shortest leg of my trip (my Egypt layover doesn't count). I had only five days instead of ten, but with its main archaeological museums clustered in Athens, I figured I'd be able to hunt it down.

Before leaving Lebanon, my email inbox filled up with more STEP alerts, this time for Greece. The country was in the midst of a financial crisis and the media had been reporting that Greeks were so desperate for money they were mugging tourists for their cash. I was well aware of the media's fear-mongering tendencies, sensationalizing, even exaggerating news to hook viewers. In 1994, I was in Paris when the Northridge earthquake shook Los Angeles and to see the footage of the collapsed buildings on CNN, replayed over and over, you'd have thought the entire city had fallen into the ocean and that everyone was dead. I eventually got wise to the fact they were showing the wreckage of just one or two apartment buildings. It was bad, yes, but it wasn't *that* bad. It's almost never that bad. I also factored in that Greece is ranked thirty-three positions higher than the U.S. on the Global Peace Index. (In a few years, Greece would outrank the U.S. by one hundred!) I wasn't going to take the clickbait. And while a crisis—like Greece's temporarily crippling circumstances—would normally prompt me to hand out free pie to provide comfort and kindness, I was still discouraged, even chastened, by what happened in the refugee camp in Lebanon. I wasn't ready to try again.

I requested a window seat on every flight I took, but I wasn't able to get one for my inbound flight to Greece. I had never been there, but I had dreamed of its beauty— over two thousand islands surrounded by a marine blue sea, whitewashed stucco houses, blue doors, dome roofs, secluded beaches tucked in rocky coves, and the cast of *Mamma Mia* singing and dancing its way down stone paths that led to boat docks. A window wouldn't have mattered since we took off from Beirut at 4:30 a.m. and I was asleep until we landed in Athens just before sunrise.

I had used the remainder of Marcus's frequent flyer miles to book a hotel near the National Archeological Museum, a strategic decision for finding the pie recipe, or whatever crumbling relic was left of it. The night before leaving Beirut, I went online to confirm the hotel and discovered I had missed a critical detail. The area, while a museum zone by day, was a red-light district by night, and therefore "unadvisable for solo female travelers." At least the STEP advisory meant the more cautious tourists had canceled their trips and I could get a last-minute Airbnb during the high season.

I found a place on Drakou Street in a central but quiet neighborhood of solid, well-preserved homes, all with terracotta rooftops, window shutters, and designs carved into heavy wooden doors outfitted with brass knockers. The first thing I did was ditch my luggage at the Airbnb, ridding myself of the beast of burden, so I could explore the city a little.

I walked a few blocks and sensed no danger. I didn't see any criminals, street beggars, or anyone asking for, or stealing, cash. The streets were quiet as I made my way over to the Acropolis, one the most famous archaeological sites in the world. Rooted high on a rocky hill that overlooked the city, the Acropolis is a village in the sky safeguarded by a stone fortress where revolving populations of kings and gods and religious leaders had lived. Inhabited since prehistoric times, the citadel has survived wars, earthquakes, and vandalism— the financial crisis would mean nothing to this tenacious stronghold.

Rows of cypress trees pointed upward like rockets ready for blastoff, the silvery leaves of olive trees fluttered in the hot wind, the scent of pine hung in the air. I breathed it all in as I did a lap around the perimeter of the hill, hugging the iron fence, where on the other side an old woman in a straw hat swept the sidewalk. I almost expected her to stop and bow like the woman in Thailand did, with her broom in one hand and the other in prayer, but she didn't notice me, didn't even look up. A handful of tourists promenaded around the cobblestone walkway, and I could see more people dotting the skyline of the craggy outcrop, their cameras pointed at the Parthenon's rows of marble columns. Built in the fifth century (construction started in 447 BC) to honor the goddess Athena, it's a miracle that the Parthenon is still standing. It wouldn't be if not for the cranes and scaffolding that surround the temple, employed in a continuous effort to keep what remains of the structure from collapsing.

The Acropolis Museum at the base of the hill was easier to access, but I didn't go inside as it was interesting enough, and free, to walk on its thick glass floors that covered the archaeological dig below. Standing on the horizontal window, I peered down past my Chuck Taylors to scan the partially buried treasures—hoping to see a stone tablet with a pie recipe. I don't know why I was so obsessed with it when I don't even like recipes, let alone follow them. I saw no tablets or any remnants of that kind down in the dirt. The site had been cleaned up, the soil brushed off any findings, the debris removed, leaving only the foundations of homes, bathtubs, sidewalks, and staircases, all used by people thousands of years earlier. Who were these people? What kind of lives did they live? Were they happy? What did they eat? What did they do for healthcare? All I knew about them was that they had turned to dust—as we all will one day. Wrapping my head around history this ancient could make me tired on a good day, and after the red-eye from Lebanon, I was spent. Too tired to take in anything more, I walked back to the Airbnb, promising myself I would return to the museum, and to the Acropolis, another day. I would pay the admission fee, climb up the steep hill to the ruins, and explore it later.

If only I had known there would be no later. If only I had added "Never put it off until later" to my list of travel rules. The mantra could have been—should have been—*Seize the day*. Because after my dinner with Georgia Kofinas later that evening, the only thing in Athens I would see was my ceiling fan.

In a quiet, modest neighborhood, just outside the city center, an attractive, trim, gray-haired woman in black slacks and sensible shoes waited outside the Neos Kosmos metro station watching for any passengers coming out of the exit. It was dusk on a Friday night in summer, but between the layoffs from the financial crisis and being peak vacation time, the usual Friday night faucet of rush-hour commuters had been reduced to a trickle. I was the only passenger to get off at the stop.

"Beth?" the woman asked. My face lit up with the relief that I had arrived at the right place. "I'm Georgia. I'm parked just over here," she said in an accent that was still distinctly American, even after living in Greece for forty years.

In her tiny car, we zig-zagged our way through the maze of narrow but tidy streets. Unlike the historic district of my Airbnb, the apartment houses here were built in the seventies and eighties. There was no sign of danger in this area either, no muggers lurking by the ATMs, but in this residential suburb, there were no ATMs or tourists in sight. And any businesses—bakeries, boutiques, and butcher shops—had already closed for the evening, their doors and shutters pulled tight and locked.

Georgia's apartment was modern, with everything new and up-to-date, but the man who met us at the door was from another era altogether. Dressed in black, his face narrow and long, appearing even more elongated by a white beard and long bushy side burns, he looked like an illuminated figure from a gold leaf painting—a Greek Orthodox icon who had stepped off the canvas and come to life. The only thing missing was the halo. He held his reading material in his hands—a Bible, perhaps, but I don't remember. It could have been *The New York Times*. Because even though he looked Old World Greece, he, like Georgia, was American.

"This is my husband, Papastavros," Georgia said, introducing us.

"Nice to meet you," I said, nodding my head in a small bow.

"He's a Greek Orthodox priest," Georgia added.

"Oh? My brother's father-in-law is a Greek Orthodox priest," I said. "He lives in California."

"We lived in California," Papastavros said. "Where is he?"

"In Petaluma. But his church is in Novato."

"Father Constantine? At Nativity of Christ?"

"YES!" I screeched louder than I meant to.

"He is a friend of mine. We were at theology school together years ago."

"No way! I can't believe it! I have to text my brother and tell him." Patrick, who lives in Seattle, replied immediately when I told him where I was and whom I was with. "That's crazy! We're in Petaluma with him right now."

I almost dropped my phone. How was it possible, just a few days after meeting friends of Uschi's in Beirut, that it was happening again? What kind of planetary alignment was taking place? How fast was the world shrinking? What message was I supposed to take from *this*?

In his article "Coincidences: What Are the Chances of Them Happening?" British statistician David Spiegelhalter concludes, ". . . think of all the people you have ever known. Then think of all the people that you have had some connection with, such as attending the same school, being friends of friends and so on. It will be tens of thousands. If you are the sort of person who talks to strangers, you will keep on finding connections. If you are not, then think: you might have sat on a train next to a long-lost family member, and never realized it."

My trip around the world was all about talking to strangers. My connection to the Kofinases wasn't a sign from God; there was no hidden meaning. It happened because I had had the courage to fling myself out of the familiar and into the unknown, to choose courage over fear. In my quest to immerse myself in each place, to be part of the local culture, to get to know the people there, I was, indeed, finding connections. According to Spiegelhalter, it could happen to anyone. The question now was not *will* it happen again, but *when?* And at what point would I stop being surprised by it?

Georgia would write to me later, describing numerous other connections she and Papastavros had with my brother's in-laws, her description of them as impossible to untangle as a switchboard of telephone cables. She was best friends with Father Constantine's first cousin, and his brother-in-law was her husband's professor at the seminary in Boston. "So, my dear," she concluded, "it's not just coincidence that we met."

I was in the kitchen with Georgia a little later, watching her cook, when Patrick texted me a photo of his mother-in-law, Kay— or Presvytera as a Greek priest's wife is called. She was holding Georgia's cookbook, *The Festive Fast: A Guide to Olive Oil and Vegetarian Cuisine.*

"Look at this, Georgia!" I held the picture in front of her as she stirred fresh calamari bubbling in garlic broth.

Peering over her glasses, she said, "Everything I'm making tonight is from that book. We're fasting now."

"Is it a holiday?"

"No, it's a Friday."

It may not be the practice by Greeks in other parts of the world, but in Greece, every Wednesday and Friday are fast days. Greek Orthodox fasting, however, is not a cleansing diet; there's no starving, no liquids-only, no counting the minutes and hours until you can eat again. There's little deprivation, only the abstinence from meat, dairy, and fish (though shellfish is allowed). And the "strict fasting" on certain days of the year still isn't all that strict; only oil is added to the list of foods to avoid.

This was not one of the strict days, as every dish on Georgia's fasting menu was drowning in olive oil: a school of silvery sardines, a tomato and cucumber salad, eggplant with stewed tomatoes and capers, they were all swimming in it. So was the squid, marinated and sautéed with the splash of Ouzo that Georgia added to the pan, because fasting did not mean abstaining from alcohol either.

For dinner, we moved out to the balcony covered by a large white awning, its shade no longer required since the sun had gone down. The table sat in the middle, surrounded by a botanical garden of potted plants, including an olive tree whose slender leaves fluttered in the breeze. The table, set with a white cloth, blue glassware, and blue napkins, all but disappeared under the dishes of food that filled every last inch of space.

Papastavros gave a blessing, but once we settled into the meal, the formalities fell away, exposing his Californian side. He poured us each another glass of white wine and said, "It's too bad we're leaving on our vacation tomorrow. We would have loved to show you around."

"You really should get out of Athens and go see some of the islands," Georgia chimed in. "There are so many beautiful ones." She started naming a few, but I couldn't keep up with the names. Lesbos, Patmos, Kythnos, Andros, Poros, Naxos, Mykonos—it was all Greek to me.

"I'd love to see more of the country, but I only have five days— four as of tomorrow—and I want to find that pie recipe on the stone tablet."

"That's tricky," Georgia said. "We do have ancient sources about pita, which travels into the etymology of the word pie. Its development is quite interesting which involves phyllo pastry and flatbread."

I didn't know where she was going with this.

"I've got plenty of information and experience on making Greek pitas," she continued. "I can't really bring myself to call them 'pies,' unless we go into a philological discussion about the root of the word."

Philological? Her vocabulary was lost on me, as difficult to understand as the Greek island names. But I should have anticipated her scholarly interest in literature and linguistics after receiving her first email when she used the word gastrosophy, which is the science or art of good eating, as I learned after consulting a dictionary. The art of good eating—that was an easy one, and I was presently practicing it like a religion as I continued sampling Georgia's many dishes.

For dessert, she brought out a plate of fresh fruit piled high with slices of peaches, apricots, and cherries, and baklava, a mixture of ground nuts and cinnamon wrapped in flaky phyllo dough, saturated with honey. The baklava would be the closest thing to pie I would eat during my stay. And it would be the last thing I would eat for the next five days.

What happened next is the stuff of a classic Greek tragedy. In my case, it was that my bowels failed me again. Before arriving in Greece, my intestines had been moving like LA's start-and-stop traffic: mostly stop. But that was merely a prelude to the real drama. My stomach was revving up for a Formula One race.

I woke up the next morning feeling sick, so ill that I emailed Christina to postpone my tour of the mill. I told her I was sure I'd be better by the next day, but I was still sick the next day, and the day after that.

I lay in bed, hour after hour, beneath my ceiling fan. I watched its blades slice through the late July air, spinning around at a dizzying speed, yet barely producing a breeze. As the days passed, I drifted in and out of sleep, mired in fever and sweat, and hallucinating from whatever travel bug I had picked up. Or was it food poisoning that was responsible for hollowing out my insides? I spoke to Georgia and she and her husband hadn't gotten sick. Calamari—if it was from the calamari—would make an effective weapon in warfare: one tainted bite could incapacitate an entire army. Even if it wasn't the seafood that was trying to kill me, I would never eat squid again. And I would never mention it to Georgia.

During a brief window of lucidity, I checked in with my parents over Skype.

"Hi, Dad. How's your recovery from the second surgery? You feeling okay?"

"I'm good, Boo. The plastic surgeon did a fantastic job with the skin graft on my head. You can't see it under the bandage, but it looks like a daisy."

I tried to smile, to act like I wasn't concerned about him dying, to act like I wasn't about to die myself.

"We are just heading out to the doctor for Mom to get her eye—" He stopped talking abruptly.

My mom wasn't on camera, but I could hear her off to the side shushing him, as if him telling me about a basal cell on her temple or a sarcoma on her forehead would somehow be harmful to me.

Heeding my mom's warning—he knows how to keep the peace in their marriage—my dad changed the subject and continued, "How are you doing, Boo? You don't look so hot."

"Yeah, I'm sick. I've been knocked out for the past few days. Remember when I left and couldn't poop for two weeks? Now I have the opposite problem. It's coming out like water and I'm going so often I can't leave the house. I can barely make it to the bathroom across the hall. And what's really embarrassing is my hosts use that bathroom to shower. I feel bad for them. I'm their worst guest ever."

He laughed his deep belly laugh that worked like instant medicine, giving me some temporary relief. "That's no fun," he said.

"I'm so tired, I can't even make it to the kitchen to get a cup of tea. I'm tempted to change my ticket and just fly home from here. Plus, I'm worried about you and Mom."

"You just keep resting, Boo. You've been pushing hard. I'll make a martini tonight and toast to you and your health." I could hear my mom moving around the room, probably putting together a matching outfit for whatever appointment she was having that she didn't want me to know about. I would have to email my sister to find out.

"You don't look well," my mom said as she appeared on the screen, her peach T-shirt accessorized with a peach-and-red print scarf, and a rhinestone-encrusted red cap, her exercise in matching fully executed. "You're so pale. I'm worried about you. Can you get to a doctor? Make sure you get enough fluids." She turned to my dad and said, "Tom, we have to go." Looking back to the screen, she added, "You keep in touch and let us know how you're doing." And then she disappeared from view.

"It was good to see your face, Dad. Thanks for being there for me. I look forward to seeing you in . . . gosh, it's still a month and a half from now."

"We love you, honey. Call again soon."

When the video screen went black, I closed the lid to my laptop, rolled onto my stomach, and buried my face in the pillow so my Airbnb hosts wouldn't hear me crying.

Worst. Guest. Ever.

After another two-hour nap, I got dressed so I could walk down the block to buy Gatorade at the corner market. But the effort of sliding a sundress over my head exhausted me so much that I made it as far as the door of my room, four steps away, before turning around and going back to bed.

After another two hours of sleep, I was rested just enough to shuffle down the hall to the kitchen, using the wall to support myself. The well-worn floor planks creaked beneath my feet, announcing my arrival to Kostas, my Airbnb host, who was sitting at the table eating olives and reading the newspaper. Tufts of gray hair in disarray, his belly pushing against his white T-shirt, his khakis wrinkled, he looked like he, too, had just woken up from a nap, but this was the first time I had seen him—maybe he always looked like this. I envied him for his good health, and for the luxury of being in his own home, a beautiful one at that.

"Oh, you're up," he said. He set down his paper and stared at me, assessing my condition before speaking. "We were worried about you, but we didn't want to bother you. Have you eaten anything? Can I make you some toast? And what about some tea?"

The kindness in his eyes almost leveled me, but instead of collapsing onto the floor, I managed to settle onto a chair.

One of the biggest fears I had for my round-the-world trip wasn't getting mugged, it was getting sick—so sick I might die. I was convinced India would be the place my body rebelled against foreign bacteria, but I came away from Mumbai with my intestines unscathed. Moreover, I was afraid of getting sick in a place where I was on my own. I was alone in Athens, and sicker than the time I got acute amoebic dysentery in Kenya thirty years earlier. But this is the thing that you learn when traveling: You are never alone. You can lose your faith in humanity, but there will always be someone with empathy to remind you that our species is not a complete lost cause. You can even be in a country that Americans are warned is too dangerous to visit and find a sympathetic being quick to perform an act of mercy—like make you a piece of toast.

"And let's get you to a doctor," he said as he watched me nibble on the toast like a mouse, taking tiny bites for fear of what might happen once any food hit my stomach. The bathroom, I was well aware, was at the opposite end of a very long hallway.

When my body was emptied to the point I could safely leave the house without a diaper, I went to the doctor. An eccentric man older than Hippocrates, he had me lie down on his table, where the sound of the tissue paper covering it crunched in my ears as he poked my belly. "Does it hurt?" he asked each time his fingers walked to a new place on my abdomen.

"It's tender," I replied.

"It's just something travelers get. It's nothing serious," he announced in his thick accent.

Nothing serious? I clenched my teeth with what little strength I had left. I had hoped for a more conclusive diagnosis, not a dismissive wave of his craggy hand that was already scribbling a prescription for an antibiotic. He handed me the paper and instructed, "Do not eat anything but white rice and Coca-Cola for the next week."

On my way back to the Airbnb, I passed a grocery store, where I bought rice and Coke. In the cookware section I found a pie dish— an American-style one, shallow with a tapered edge—and bought it as a thank-you gift—and apology—for my Airbnb hosts. In my depleted state, the three pounds of groceries I carried back to Drakou Street felt as heavy as my seventy pounds of luggage.

With only a few more blocks to go, wobbling like I'd spent all day in a bar and not a doctor's office, I passed a gift shop that sold items carved from Greek olive wood. Desperate to get back to my room and sleep, I wouldn't have stopped, but a basket in the window beckoned me inside. In the basket, and in several others like it, rolling pins stood on end like flowers in a vase. The wood, in earthy, rich hues, was sanded into a smooth texture, and the natural artistic swirls of grain meant each rolling pin had its own unique pattern. I picked one up and rubbed my hands along the surface. It felt warm and alive, like oily skin, and pulsated like it was still breathing. A tree had sacrificed its life to become this beautiful pie-maker's tool. I wanted one. But I was too weak to carry even one more pound and my luggage was already at the maximum weight allowance. Reluctantly, I put the rolling pin back in the basket. On a shelf higher up were baskets of small spoons, also carved from olive wood. Some had long handles and perforations for draining liquid, like for fishing olives out of a jar, perfect for my dad's signature three-olive martinis. A teaspoon, I could carry. For my dad, I would carry the whole world home on my back.

I called my artist friend Dave when I got back to my room—the same Dave who laughed at me when I called him from India in tears. "I'm going to try to change my flight and stay longer," I told him. "To make up for the days I lost."

"You didn't lose any days," he corrected me. "You spent the energy elsewhere, so you haven't lost anything. Do you remember those 1970s game shows where the contestant would go into a booth with cash blowing all around, and they had to grab as much as they could? The ones who realized they weren't going to get it all relaxed a little more. And they ended up getting the most. Just relax," he said, laughing at me again.

I got his point. But if it was supposed to make me feel better, it didn't.

Even more insulting, the airline ticket agent burst into maniacal laughter when I called. "You must be joking. It's the high season. There are no seats available for two, even three weeks out." Seems that I wasn't the only one to ignore the travel advisory. Good. Because tourists would provide some first-aid to the country's financial crisis. Though with my meager purchases of rice, Coke, a pie dish, an olive spoon, and a metro ticket totaling less than twenty-five dollars, I hadn't done much to contribute to the struggling economy. I would just have to come back. But for now, I had to stick with my schedule and fly onward for what would be the seventh and last flight of my round-the-world ticket before the final one back to the U.S.

Before packing up, I called Doug to check on Jack.

"He's doing good. We've been to the pond every day this week."

I pictured my little terrier swimming in that green water with a big stick in his mouth, more like a tree limb heavy enough to sink him. I wished I could teleport myself to Iowa and to the quiet and restfulness of the farm, to float in the stillness of the pond, and recover there instead of pushing on to yet another country. And then another. It was my last flight, yes, but I still had four stops in Europe to go.

"Do they celebrate Pi Day there?" Doug asked. He was always surprising me with his knowledge. He had never lived anywhere other than his farm tucked away in a remote pocket of rural Iowa, and yet he spouted facts and recounted history as if he were a Rhodes scholar.

"I hadn't even thought about that!"

I felt so ignorant. How had I missed that connection? It was so obvious. Pi—or π—is the sixteenth letter of the Greek alphabet, and because it is the first letter of the Greek word for periphery, it was chosen to symbolize the mathematical number that measures the ratio of the circumference of a circle to its diameter. The reference to pi, an irrational number that can't be rounded to less than eight decimals, has been simplified to 3.14. Leave it to American math geeks to figure out that 3.14 is also March 14, thereby declaring the day as National Pi Day—celebrated, of course, with pie. But not in Greece. They write the day before the month, so 3.14 would be 14.3. Instead, they celebrate Pi Approximation Day on July 22, as 22/7 depicts the fraction of pi. I had arrived on the 24th and missed it by two days.

"The earth is round and you're traveling its circumference," Doug replied with a quickness that impressed me. "So that counts."

Ten pounds lighter after my intestinal distress—wishing the airline would let me apply my weight loss to increase my baggage allowance, as I still wanted one of those olive-wood rolling pins—I dragged my bag and my body the three blocks from my Airbnb to the metro station. The uneven paver stones and the sidewalk that buckled over tree roots, made the three blocks harder than the last three miles of a marathon. Ah, the marathon, another Greek invention. By the time I reached the station entrance, I needed another nap.

I stood in the midday sun working up the energy to descend the station's Mt. Olympus-size staircase, oblivious to the people weaving around me as they came and went. I'm normally careful when I travel, staying vigilant, holding my purse close, and avoiding eye contact or moving away when sensing unwanted attention. But I was sick and vulnerable, an easy target if someone wanted to take advantage of me—or rob me. I was wondering how I would summon enough strength to make it all the way to the airport, let alone to the train, when a woman grabbed my large suitcase. She pulled the handle right out of my hand. I was too weak to hold onto it, and too exhausted to chase after her as she started down the stairs—with my bag. Dressed in plain clothes—a skirt and blouse in drab shades of brown and mauve with a neckerchief tied around her neck—she didn't look like a mugger; she looked like a peasant. A peasant with the strength of Hercules and the speed of Hermes.

She stopped and looked back at me, motioning with her head for me to follow her.

"No," I protested. "I can manage by myself." Even a stranger could tell this was a lie.

She shook her head, said something in Greek, and continued down the long cavernous stairwell that took us deeper and deeper underground, wheeling my heavy bag behind her as if it were filled with helium, while I struggled to stay upright holding just my carry-on. When we got to the bottom of the stairs, she motioned to me again to keep following her—as if I had a choice at this point. I kept my eyes focused on my bag, watching her feet plowing through the crowd in her low-heeled black shoes, her brown polyester skirt brushing the back of her calf muscles.

If the Greek goddess of kindness, Charis, were of flesh and bone, this was her, swooping down from the heavens and coming to my aid. She led me all the way to my platform and pointed at the overhead sign to show that I was getting on the right train, heading in the right direction, bound for the right destination: the airport.

"I . . . uh, I . . .," I stuttered as I looked into her face, plain and make-up free, a face that radiated beauty, the real kind that comes from within. There was so much I wanted to say, and to ask. What was her story? But all I had time for was a quick "Thank you," and as I said it, I regretted that I hadn't learned how to say it in Greek. She replied with something akin to, "You're welcome," and then she vanished into the crowd.

I knew right then that whenever I would get discouraged about the world and frustrated by its imperfections, I would think of this humble woman and her random act of kindness. And I would remember this: Do not despair. You are never alone. There are good people walking among us. And they will appear when you need them most.

CHAPTER 10

Switzerland

> Climb the mountains and get their good
> tidings. Nature's peace will flow into
> you as sunshine flows into trees.
> —JOHN MUIR

For the European leg of my journey, I didn't need to spread out a map of the continent, close my eyes, and see where my finger landed, the way I did thirty years earlier. I knew where I needed to go. Even though I wanted to go home—more than at any other time on my trip—I couldn't get back to my own family for recovery. Luckily, my surrogate family, the Kamers in Bern, Switzerland, were just a short flight, train, and taxi ride away. Eve and Uschi Kamer are the sisters I lived with in Bern, and had traveled with to Thailand decades earlier. Uschi is the one whom the couple in Beirut knew in that small-world coincidence. Visiting them would be a welcome respite. And after defying the State Department's travel warnings for the last three countries, landing in one of the most peaceful countries in the world—also ranked as one of the happiest—was sure to help.

I flew from Athens to Frankfurt, Germany, and with the train station right inside the airport it was easy to get to Bern. As I waited for my train, I noticed that the one on the next track was headed to Stuttgart, the same train I had taken so many times to be with Marcus during our courtship and marriage. I was planning on taking it again after I recovered, to visit Marcus's grave, in spite of Barbara's scolding. "Why would you want to go there?" she asked. "You'll just open up that wound."

"Because I want to thank him for making this trip possible," I told her. "And say a final goodbye to him. I see it as closure." But the sign above the platform—the word "Stuttgart" lit up in LED lights as bright as the glare of Barbara's disapproving look—knocked the wind out of me. It wasn't until I was on board and pulling out of the station, in a different direction, toward the Swiss Alps instead of Southern Germany, that I could breathe again.

As the train gained speed, I relaxed into its smooth, gentle motion, lulled by its quiet hum, transfixed by the vineyards and green fields streaming by my window screen. Who needs sedatives when you can just ride a Swiss train? I appreciated this kind of reliable public transportation—regularly inspected for safety—all the more after the suicidal taxi rides in India and the no-rules driving in Lebanon. I appreciated feeling safe in general. It made me think about how we take safety for granted when we live in places with minimal corruption and maximum OSHA laws. And how we don't realize, until we venture out from our neighborhoods and step into unfamiliar or less fortunate worlds, how much we have to be grateful for. When we take the time to acknowledge that gratitude, it leads to compassion, and compassion leads to world peace. It's no accident that World Gratitude Day falls on September 21, the same day as the International Day of Peace.

I arrived at Uschi's after dark, and she greeted me at the door of her apartment building. "Dahhhling! You're here!"

We had called each other darling, always drawing it out with a dramatic affectation, ever since that first summer I spent in Bern. Uschi had helped me enroll in an intensive, month-long French course, after which I went to the South of France to put my new language skills to use. I found a job in Cannes as a deckhand on a small yacht, and the British actress Joan Collins came on board for lunch one afternoon. Normally I was cleaning toilets, babysitting the owner's kids, and, on occasion, having sex with the French chauffeur, but this day I was assigned the job of keeping the guests' champagne glasses filled. Hidden behind her huge sunglasses and wide-brimmed hat, it was impossible to tell who she was, but the way she spoke gave away her identity. She was all "dahhhling" this and "dahhhling" that. I had relayed the story to Uschi and the word stuck. And like Barbara greeting me with "habibti"—also meaning darling—it was a most comforting word.

"You smell like cinnamon," she said as she hugged me.

"Yeah, I know," I replied flatly without bothering to explain.

"You don't look well. Let's get you to the doctor. And you can spend as much time here as you need. It will be like a *Kur*."

A *Kur*, I knew from Marcus, is a month-long medical leave, generously covered by European health insurance. *Kurs*, he liked to tell me, were responsible for many marriages breaking up, because spending a month alone at a *Kurhaus* (a medical spa) made for an ideal hookup place.

"It will be Kurhaus Kamer," she said, laughing. It was safe to say there would be no hookup during my *Kur*. I had more important desires than getting laid, like being able to keep food in my body— and having a fully formed poop.

Uschi is two years younger than me, a half foot taller, and carries herself with poise. I was a hyena next to this elegant giraffe. She was single, probably because she had been traveling most of her life— earlier as a flight attendant for Swiss Air (we often saw each other on her New York and Chicago layovers) and for the past ten years as a finance administrator with the Swiss Agency for Development and Cooperation (SDC) in its Humanitarian Aid department, with projects taking her to Lebanon, Egypt, Jordan, Sri Lanka, and beyond. The Swiss constitution states the country should help alleviate hardship and poverty in the world, contribute to the respect for human rights, and promote the peaceful coexistence of nations and democracy, and the SDC is charged with implementing this mission. In other words, Uschi is doing her part to promote world peace.

No matter what she was doing for work, Uschi put the five languages she spoke fluently to good use. In Switzerland, she could use at least four of them on any given day since there are four national languages: Swiss German, French, Italian, and Romansh. She doesn't speak Romansh—almost no one speaks this ancient language from the deep mountain valleys—but she uses her English, as it is widely used in cities like Bern that attract international workers and visitors.

Uschi is a born nurturer, and the way she liked to take care of me—even from the time I first met her—made her seem like a big sister. Upon seeing my pale face and my clothes hanging off my body, she put those caretaking skills into overdrive.

For the first few days, while Uschi was at work, I slept—sleeping the long, rehabilitative sleep of someone who just bequeathed half her insides to the Athens sewer system. When I wasn't sleeping, I was soaking in Uschi's extra-long bathtub, helping myself to the assortment of Weleda and Dr. Hauschka German botanical bath products that filled her cupboard. It took a week, but I weaned myself off my restricted diet of boiled white rice and Gatorade (I switched from Coke), gradually adding Swiss staples of Gruyère cheese, crusty baguettes smeared with salty butter, and the greatest health elixir of all: vitamin C—C as in chocolate. Every good Swiss has a supply of chocolate on hand—the average Swiss consumes twenty pounds of it per year (Americans eat half that)—and I knew where Uschi kept hers. I broke off pieces from her assortment, starting off with plain milk chocolate and working my way into the darker, more exotic ones infused with hazelnut, almond, orange, and honeycomb. I savored each square, melting them on my tongue and not swallowing until I'd turned them into liquid. I was sneaking bites like an addict, hoping she didn't notice how quickly her stock was dwindling before I had a chance to replenish it.

Uschi's apartment was halfway up a mountain at the edge of the city, bordered by pastures and public gardens. I stayed in her guest room, leaving the window open for the summer breeze to enter—and for my toxins to exit. I fell asleep to the soft jingle of the sheep bells worn by the whole flock grazing right outside, and woke to church bells chiming all over the city.

Once I felt a little stronger—boosting my immune system not just with chocolate but with iron supplements after a follow-up blood test at a Swiss clinic showed I was anemic—I started exercising. You don't need to join a gym in Switzerland; the mountainous country is like one big StairMaster and there were steps right behind Uschi's apartment leading to the top of the local mountain, the Gurten. In my first foray out of the house, I climbed the steps slowly, pausing every four or five steps to catch my breath, moving uphill past the clusters of houses and flower gardens built into the hillside. I followed the perimeters of picket fences, opening and closing their gates to pass through. I only meant to take an easy half-hour walk, but something—the sun, the blue sky, the fresh air, the scent of the flowers, the storybook charm, maybe all of it combined—lured me upward. When the houses ended and the staircases gave way to dirt trails carved into switchbacks, I kept going.

I came to an open meadow where a herd of cows grazed, feeding on the grass and wildflowers that would nourish their milk—the milk that would be made into chocolate and that other Swiss icon, cheese—that would, in turn, nourish the people who ate it.

I stopped to take photos for Doug. Cows had become "our thing," our way of connecting without words. Doug sent me photos and videos of Jack trying to herd his cows, my fierce little terrier running up and down the fence line barking at them, the dog as oblivious to his size as the cows were indifferent to him. Seeing images of Jack always split my heart into two halves—one half was a helium balloon knowing that he was so happy, the other was a cinder block as I remained uncertain about the future, about what would happen when I came back for him, about where we would go after "Camp Doug." Still, whenever I encountered cows—in the pastures of New Zealand, on Lynne and Edgar's dairy farm in Australia, in the middle of a Mumbai city street, and here on this Swiss mountainside—I took photos for Doug.

Doug's pictures weren't always of Jack and his cows. Sometimes he would send me pictures from his tractor while mowing alfalfa, cutting stripes into a green field that stretched all the way to the horizon. He sent photos from the top of his grain silo with a panoramic view that could have been Switzerland, if you squinted and imagined that the towering cumulous clouds were The Alps. Other times he would send me videos of hay bales being shuttled on a conveyor up to the barn mow. Doug made me more aware of farming and all the hard work it entails, which opened my eyes a little wider as I moved through each country. I paid more attention to details, like how the topsoils of the world come in all different shades, though none are as black as Iowa's.

I may have been focused on pie, set on proving how its global history connects us as humans, but agriculture, in all its forms, is the world's foremost universal thread. Every country on the planet needs to feed its people. Humanity and civilization developed because of farming and our continued survival depends on it. And, of course, without farming to provide flour, butter, sugar, fruit, and eggs, there would be no pie.

On the opposite side of the cow fence, a herd of tourists waited at the base station of a funicular for a ride to the summit. I watched them file into the train, and though I was tempted to climb aboard, my determination to improve my health and build up my strength prevailed. I kept walking—climbing, stopping, panting, and climbing more—until I reached the top of Gurten Mountain, where a signpost declared, "Elevation 2,835 feet." From the way I felt on the climb I had thought it was double that, but it was high enough to get a view so surprisingly spectacular, I reflexively jerked back and gasped. Across the valley—beyond miles of emerald green fields, ribbons of glacial-blue rivers, silver mirrors of lakes, and grazing cows—were the Alps. Towering above everything else were the Eiger, Jungfrau, and Mönch peaks, three of the Alps' biggest rockstars, covered in snow that reflected the sun.

I staked out a quiet spot on the grass, away from the picnicking families, away from the palace-like restaurant where the cog train deposited its passengers, and sat down to take in the alpine panorama. I put my face into the wind like Jack would do and lifted my chin toward the sun. I didn't care if I burned my corneas; I did not want to stop looking at this scenery, this real-life Shangri-La, for even a minute. Damn, it was good to be alive—*still* alive—still healthy enough to make it to this elevated spot. Because after India, where nothing seemed to go right, and Lebanon, where my faith in humanity took a nosedive, and Greece, where I depleted any remaining reserves, I would not have thought it possible to feel this good about life again, this calm. But up on the mountain, insulated from man-made distractions, feeling closer to whatever spiritual power exists, there it was—as rare as a snow leopard, as fleeting as a zephyr—the elusive goal: inner peace. I wanted more of this.

Every morning I hiked to the top of the Gurten, though I was never able to capture that level of serenity again, but at least I was building back my physical strength.

I spent my afternoons in town exploring the city. Uschi's neighbor loaned me a bicycle for the duration of my stay, which I rode into the city center, an easy coast downhill, but a strenuous climb coming home. One day, while pedaling uphill, I got passed by an octogenarian. She cruised right by me on the steepest section, not a drop of sweat on her brow. *How could this be? Am I still sick or am I that badly out of shape?* Watching her leave me in the dust, I looked more closely and saw, hidden in the frame of her bike, a small electric motor. I refused to ride the funicular up the Gurten, but I would have said "hell yes" to a power-assisted bike.

Bern is the capitol of Switzerland. It's a medieval city, with buildings still intact from the twelfth century—an age that's unfathomable in America. With its Gothic church spires, rows of attached houses with red roofs and wooden window shutters, cobblestone streets, arched passageways, and gilded clock towers, Bern is the poster child of UNESCO World Heritage sites. Built on a horseshoe bend of the Aare River, the old part of the city is surrounded on three sides by the glacial-blue waters gushing down from The Alps, accessed by steep stone staircases, grooved from hundreds of years of foot traffic, that lead down to the water. Fountains topped with stone-carved Renaissance figures bubble at street intersections and large pedestrian-only plazas are utilized for farmers' markets and outdoor seating for the many restaurants. Everything is so well preserved you feel like Claire in *Outlander*— like you've passed through the rock and landed in the past, in a time where you'd see men dressed in tights and tunics, and women in kirtles and cloaks, instead of sweatpants, sneakers, and mini-skirts.

Based on the hundreds, maybe thousands, of bicycles crammed into the public bike racks around the city, I wasn't the only one getting around on two wheels. The overflowing bike racks underscore why Switzerland ranks as one of the top-three most eco-friendly countries in the world. For one thing, in Europe it's less common for people to own cars—an unthinkable concept to Americans given our lack of public transportation—and fewer cars means cleaner air. The Swiss are also leaders in recycling, waste management, and renewable energy. They harness the energy from all those glacial-fed rivers and collect their compost, from food to grass trimmings, turning it into biofuel. And don't even think about littering. You'll pay for every cigarette butt and dog turd that you get caught leaving on the ground. I couldn't help but think of India, where if every piece of litter carried a fine, not only could the country be cleaner, the government could use the fees to build schools, affordable housing, and public toilets. Switzerland's clean environment is a major reason why it's considered one of the happiest places on earth (and all this time I thought it was due to its high-quality chocolate). Also contributing to that happiness are the country's high wages, low unemployment, outstanding healthcare, and, something even better than chocolate: the avoidance of war. Switzerland, which is not a member of the European Union, has been committed to neutrality since 1515, and though it does have an army—military service is compulsory for men ages eighteen to thirty-four—it didn't fight in World War I or II. And it's the Swiss army we have to thank for giving us the best multi-tool, foldable pocketknife of all time.

I locked up my bike, jockeying it between the others—hoping I would be able to find it again—and set off on foot to wander around town. Halfway down Kramgasse, I came upon a crowd in front of a building where people were posing for selfies. I didn't see what was so special about the building, connected to nearly identical buildings standing in a row, until I read the sign above the doorway: "Einstein-Haus." Einstein's house.

Albert Einstein lived in Bern from 1903 to 1905, and it was in this very house that he developed the theory of relativity, $E = mc^2$, determining that mass has an equivalent energy (E) which can be calculated as mass (m) multiplied by the speed of light squared (c^2). I describe it like I know what it means, but even after reading *Physics for Dummies*, it's a concept I can't begin to grasp.

Einstein is also associated with the invention of the atomic bomb, which he said was the greatest mistake of his life. He did not actually create it, he merely signed a letter to President Roosevelt conveying that it was possible, and suggested the Americans create one before the Germans in order to dissuade the Nazis' use of it. Instead, to Einstein's horror, the U.S. used the nuclear weapon to obliterate Hiroshima and Nagasaki.

Einstein spent only half his life on atomic research; the other half was dedicated to his work for peace. I wondered if the people taking selfies in front of his house were aware of this side of him—the empathetic, pacifist one who said, "Peace cannot be kept by force; it can only be achieved by understanding." The one who agreed with Gandhi: "We should strive to do things in his spirit: not to use violence in fighting for our cause, but by non-participation in anything you believe is evil."

German historian Wolfram Wette, in an Institute for Advanced Study interview, said of Einstein, "Toward the end of his life when he was living in the United States, he dedicated many efforts to preventing the possibility of a third world war. He wanted a [unified] world government that would eliminate nationalism and the need for military aggression. He was absolutely opposed to nuclear weapons of any kind, and one of the final acts of his life was to sign what became known as the Russell-Einstein manifesto, calling for human beings to set aside their political differences in order to ensure world peace" and find peaceful means for the settlement of all disputes.

Eleven prominent scientists signed this manifesto, which stated, "There lies before us, if we choose, continual progress in happiness, knowledge, and wisdom. Shall we, instead, choose death, because we cannot forget our quarrels? We appeal as human beings to human beings: Remember your humanity, and forget the rest. If you can do so, the way lies open to a new Paradise; if you cannot, there lies before you the risk of universal death."

Why is this manifesto not drilled into the heads of every living human being? Because Einstein is surely right, that if there were a third world war, the fourth one would be fought with "stones and spears," such would be the resulting annihilation. He's also right that nuclear disarmament is the only answer to the question: *Do we want the human race to survive or not?*

Einstein, not just a peace activist but also a social justice warrior, spoke out against racism after the discrimination he observed in the U.S., and invited African Americans to his home. The fact that FBI Director J. Edgar Hoover kept him under surveillance for more than twenty years did not stop him. In *The World as I See It*, Einstein wrote, "Not until the creation and maintenance of decent conditions of life for all people are recognized and accepted as a common obligation of all people and all countries—not until then shall we, with a certain degree of justification, be able to speak of humankind as civilized."

While I do not share his aptitude for science—not even a subatomic particle's worth—my values are very much in line with his: that true religion is based on the natural and the spiritual, as opposed to dogma and theology, and that cruelty and hatred toward living beings is evil. I also wholeheartedly subscribe to his statement: "The best way to cheer yourself is to cheer somebody else up," as it's the very thing I always say about sharing pie.

In studying the timeline of his life, it was no wonder I felt so connected to Einstein—he was born on Pi Day, March 14, a day celebrated with pie! One could argue that his birthday would have also been fitting as the annual International Day of Peace (a.k.a. World Peace Day), but the United Nations General Assembly declared September 21 as that date, asking warring factions to observe twenty-four hours of nonviolence and ceasefire. It's not much, but twenty-four hours of peace is better than nothing. And not that Einstein would have minded, but the UN designated Gandhi's birthday, October 2, as the International Day of Non-Violence.

Einstein died on April 18, 1955, at the age of seventy-six, but learning of his death (from an abdominal aortic aneurysm, similar to how Marcus died) didn't leave me sobered—or sobbing— the way Gandhi's assassination did after visiting the museum in Mumbai. Though, like with Gandhi, reading about his stellar accomplishments—and his struggles to promote peace—left me, once again, humbled by how one man could have such a powerful and lasting impact. Standing there in the cosmic dust cloud of his legacy could have made me feel that my life was utterly insignificant, but I knew better than to belittle my own life in contrast to his. I held firmly to my dad's advice to not compare yourself to others, and instead took heart using Einstein's own advice: "Strive not to be a success, but rather to be of value."

Bern was surprisingly full of pie. I stopped at different cafés each day to drink a latte and write in my journal. Every place I went had pie, and in so many flavors. I had spent a lot of time in Switzerland over the years, but had never realized they liked pie so much. One take-out café near the Marzilibad Park had at least sixty mini pies lined up in rows. But unlike the hand pies of New Zealand where all you see is the crust, these were all open-faced tarts, their gorgeous fillings on full display in a Mardi Gras parade of colors atop a shortbread shell. The choices were plum, apricot, apple, black cherry, rhubarb, currant, pear, peach, cheese, and a raisin meringue. (Oddly, given the Swiss obsession with it, there was no chocolate.) The fruit on each tart was sliced and arranged to Martha Stewart perfection. I wanted to try some. I really did. More so, I wanted to ask if I could spend a day baking with them. But the line was so long—mostly swimmers in wet bathing suits, and a few office workers taking their lunch hour by the river, and I didn't want to wait. Besides, I was still being careful with my stomach and wasn't ready to test its limits.

On another day at another café, a contemporary place with sofas and lounge chairs in the shade of a canvas awning, I discovered a smorgasbord of large pies. They were artfully arranged on cake stands at varying heights laid out along the length of a black board. The name of each pie was written next to it in white marker: *Aprikose, Rhabarber, Apfel, Blaubeere, Birne.* It was a good way to practice German. Like pie flash cards—just match the word to the fruit, though the translations were pretty obvious based on the spellings, except for *Birne*, which means pear. I didn't have any pie here either. Would I ever get my appetite back for it? If I lost my taste for pie, who would I be? Me without pie would lead to an existential crisis—as if I wasn't already in the midst of one. I rationalized my disinclination to try the pies by telling myself I had lived in Europe and thus I already knew what, for example, a plum tart tasted like; the tangy fleshy fruit offset by the crunchy sweet crumble top, the butter cookie crust pleasantly disintegrating when biting down on it. I already knew how much I liked it, and how much I would like every single one of these pies. I also knew I would be back for a slice as soon as I fully recovered.

I wasn't entirely disconnected from pie. Back at Uschi's, on a Saturday afternoon, I made a banana cream pie. We were invited for Sunday lunch at Uschi's friend Monika's farm and I wanted to bring something special. Banana cream was special because when my parents were dating, my mom made my dad his favorite pie and he hadn't even finished his first slice when he said, "This is the best pie I've ever had. Will you marry me?" If not for that banana cream pie, I might never have been born.

Making this pie at Uschi's was a mixed bag of emotions, because it was in this very kitchen where I made my first pie for Marcus fourteen years earlier: apple with a lattice top. I carried it on the train from Bern to Stuttgart while it was still warm and, like a Pied Piper to the other passengers, it oozed the seductive scent of cinnamon. It was the first time I visited Marcus's home, and I'm convinced that pie prompted him to propose to me—though it took eighteen more months before we got engaged. Maybe banana cream worked faster. I had left Uschi's pie dish—a shallow metal tart pan—in Stuttgart, where it remained through the ups and downs of my marriage. I eventually returned it to her in Bern, where, six years after Marcus died, I was using it again. Not to seduce a man this time, but to simply bring a dessert to share over lunch.

As I stood at Uschi's stove, stirring the milk, sugar, and eggs to make the vanilla pudding, I became so hypnotized by the wooden spoon's rhythmic circles around the pan, I almost forgot I was in Bern. Part of me was still in Lebanon in the refugee camp, wrestling with the questions of how and why humanity keeps veering off course, how loyal citizens could be driven out of their own countries, how brutal dictators like Syria's Bashar al-Assad could remain in power, and why the desperation to hang onto that power resulted in corruption and crimes against humanity. Where were the Einsteins and Gandhis of our time? Even if we had them, how could their voices of reason be heard above the noise of the competitive fame-seekers and conspiracy theorists dominating the internet?

I didn't have answers for the past, or the present—I couldn't fix Lebanon or Syria or any other country's politics. But I was hoping to come up with a solution for the future—if only for the immediate future of my own life. I had three more weeks until my return to the U.S., but once I arrived at Uschi's, the pendulum of my trip's cuckoo clock seemed to stop, as if I had already reached its end. Maybe it was because Bern was so familiar, as if I were already home. Or maybe I was wishing to stall time because I was still wavering on my plans for Stuttgart. I dreaded going there. My old friends there had either moved away or were busy with new babies. Foong was in Germany for a month, but she was in Frankfurt with her husband. And while she had tried to help me set up a pie class with her women's group in Stuttgart, there were no takers as everyone was on summer holiday. Also on my agenda was Alpirsbach, the picturesque Black Forest village just south of Stuttgart, where Marcus and I got married. I planned to visit the cathedral where our wedding ceremony took place, to light a candle and say a prayer, and to teach a pie class at the inn where we had our reception. Finally, I was planning to visit his grave not far from there, near his parents' home, to say a final goodbye to the man I had loved—still love. I hoped that would give me the closure I had yet to find, as if closure is ever possible when a loved one dies unexpectedly. But even Uschi, who had seen me through every stage with Marcus—our courtship, our marriage, his funeral—questioned my plan. Echoing Barbara, she said, "Darling, are you sure that's a good idea? You should do things that make you happy, not add to your sadness."

I'm good at ignoring naysayers—like when I moved into and, four years later, out of the American Gothic House—but this time, even though I wasn't ready to admit it, I knew my friends were right. Salt, wound, obvious consequences. As they say in New Zealand, "Yeah, nah." Translation: I get why you'd want to, but don't.

With the banana cream pie packed into a shopping bag and dangling from the handlebars, Uschi and I rode bikes to the train station, where we boarded a train bound for someplace deep into the countryside. From our train stop, we boarded a bright yellow postal bus (Switzerland's rural transportation system run by the postal service) that took us—and the pie—even deeper and higher into the mountains.

At the exact scheduled time, because the Swiss excel at punctuality, Monika was there to pick up Uschi and me at the bus stop. A farmer with blond hair cut short and practical like a boy's, she had deep creases around her eyes that told of the seventeen years she had spent in the sun managing a vineyard in France. Her lean body and muscles spoke of her hard work, determination, and independence. We climbed into her Land Rover, and I held tight to the pie as we bounced up a dirt road through a forest to her farmstead. The dark alley of trees gave way to a sunny clearing where chickens scrambled to get out of our path. Dogs raced up to greet us, but the goats and sheep kept grazing, not bothering to look up from the grass. Off to the side was a chalet, an alpine-style farmhouse designed to withstand heavy snowfall, and from the looks of its thick beams, built to last generations longer than the classic, white Foursquare farmhouses like Doug's in Iowa.

Before we settled down to lunch, Monika gave us a tour of her property, starting in the barn. "I just taught myself to shear the sheep," she said, standing next to three round bags, each twice her size, overflowing with wool. "I still have to clean it," she added, pointing to the bits of straw mixed in with it. I noted the smell as well, pungent from the natural oils. "You can't wash it or you lose the oils that make it water repellant; you have to comb it to clean it. I'm going to spin it into yarn." Of course she was. And then she was going to knit sweaters and hats with it. Monika was like a Swiss Army Knife: she could do everything. But then the Swiss are born craftsmen and knitting is to them what baseball is to Americans—a national pastime. When I stayed with Uschi and Eve thirty-some years earlier, they taught me to knit. Instead of going to bars or dance clubs, their social lives consisted of inviting girlfriends over to knit. They'd sit in a circle around the coffee table, drinking tea, smoking cigarettes, and turning yarn into sweaters. I was better at knitting than smoking and made two cotton pullover vests that summer, but only because the women were there to fix my mistakes when I lost count of my stitches.

Leaving Monika in the barn, Uschi and I went outside to pet the sheep, running our hands over the warm thick velvet of their newly shorn bodies, the tactile sensation as satisfying as rubbing butter into pie dough. This feeling alone was worth the time and effort it took to get to the farm.

"I'll show you the turtles," Monika said, waving us over to a corral that was, apparently, not for horses.

"She has turtles, too? I asked Uschi, as we followed her. "How many animals does she have?"

"I counted twenty-three," she said.

"Twenty-four," Monika corrected her. Whatever the total, she had a big crew to keep track of—sheep, goats, chickens, rooster, cats, dogs—and, as we discovered, turtles. The five of them, leather footballs with legs, grazed alongside the chickens, protected by the fenced-in horse arena.

Monika's mom lives on the farm and joined us for lunch. An older though equally fit version of Monika, she had laid out a meal of salad and goat cheese on the picnic table. And, finally, dessert.

"I made an apple hazelnut cake," Monika said, as she set it down in front of us. "But I can't wait to try your pie."

Her cake, hearty and healthy enough to sustain you if you were, say, scaling the Matterhorn, was made with an abundance of apples and nuts, and only a little sugar. My banana cream pie more than made up for any sugar deficit in the cake. We ate way too much of each, but that's what hiking is for, so we set off from the farm, straight up a boulder-strewn riverbed.

"You have to be careful," Monika warned. "We're right at the base of the Alps and when it rains up higher, we get flash floods down here. Sometimes you can't see the rainclouds, so you don't know the water is coming."

The boulders we were climbing over had come from higher up, tossed down the mountain like flower petals, such was the force of the floods. I kept looking upstream, watching for the wall of water that could be descending upon us any minute, bringing half the mountain down with it. *Death by boulder crushing.* I had lost many things on this trip—my patience, my intestines, my tooth—but the one thing I hadn't lost was my morbid imagination.

"That is what I want," I told Uschi on the way back to Bern. "I want to live in the country like Monika. When I go to Iowa to pick up Jack, I'm going to look for a farmhouse there. I won't have mountains, but I want a creek and hiking trails. And maybe I'll get some goats."

Uschi smiled in her serene, big sisterly way, and patted me on the arm. "You should do that, darling."

I was already imagining the peaceful—and private—life I would create, a quiet version of the American Gothic House, where I would

write, instead of stressing myself out with a pie stand. The sudden
clarity made me want to get started on it immediately. I could skip
Germany and Hungary and fly back to the U.S. from Bern. I could—
but then I remembered my mantra. *Stay open. Stay in the present.* I
still had three weeks in Europe ahead of me and a lot could happen
in that time, something that might still alter, or at least inform, my
course. I held onto the idea, a dangling carrot of possibility, a shiny
object of hope.

One evening I went into town to meet Böbi, a childhood friend
of Uschi and Eve, with whom I had kept in touch since my first
trip to Bern. The annual Buskers Festival was taking place, with
jugglers, musicians, and acrobats performing on the streets, and Böbi
invited me to join her for one of the free outdoor concerts. We were
walking through the crowd when she saw an acquaintance of hers
named Susanne, who worked for the festival. Susanne wore Jackie
O sunglasses, a gold silk scarf, and turquoise chandelier earrings, the
look of someone who works in the arts. Böbi introduced me, telling
Susanne, "Beth is on a round-the-world trip."

"Oh, I did that," Susanne replied coolly, as if it had been nothing
more than a weekend holiday. "I did it for my seventieth birthday."

"Seventieth?" I gasped. "I thought you were around fifty! How
was it for you? Didn't you find it kind of grueling? I've been exhausted
since Thailand. I wish I had done the trip in my twenties or thirties,
not at fifty-three."

"I loved it," she replied. "I didn't find it difficult at all. And I
brought back such beautiful art and rugs."

*But did you go to India? What about Lebanon? And did you haul a
rolling pin around with you?*

I didn't ask her that. It wasn't a contest. Besides, I was too much
in awe to even think to ask—in awe because this meeting could
not have been a chance encounter. This was no random meeting of
friends in a crowd, or in a Beirut bar, or an Athens apartment. I was

convinced that whatever guardian angels were traveling with me had placed her in my path as an infusion of encouragement, a call to action, another message I needed to hear, delivered at exactly the time I needed to hear it. *You are never too old. It is never too late. You've had your Kur. Now get your ass back out there and keep going.*

I might not have needed Susanne's inspiration had I known the story of Nellie Bly before setting off on my trip.

Nearly a hundred and thirty years earlier, in 1889, journalist Nellie Bly traveled around the world solo as a single female during a time when it was believed women were not capable of such feats, delicate creatures that we are. Famous for her first-hand undercover reporting on a New York mental institution, where she pretended to be insane in order to get admitted, she was looking for her next story. Inspired by Jules Verne's *Around the World in Eighty Days*, she pitched her editor the idea of trying to break that record. (The book was fiction, but it was based on real-life adventurer George Francis Train, who made the first of his four round-the-world trips in 1870.) Bly wasn't seventy like Susanne, or fifty-three like me; she circumnavigated the world at the energetic and fearless age of twenty-five. Even more remarkable than her chutzpa was how light she traveled. Save for a few changes of underwear, a silk slip dress, a nightgown, and the specially tailored ankle-length wool coat she had made—in a gingham print, no less—she took no extra clothes for the seventy-two days it took her to successfully complete the journey. She fit everything, including toiletries, notebooks, and pencils, into a satchel the size of a large purse. Even with such scant baggage she still felt she had overpacked and complained about the jar of face cream that took up precious space in her handbag. Someone had suggested she also pack a revolver, a notion she readily dismissed. "I had such a strong belief in the world's greeting me as I greeted it, that I refused to arm myself," she wrote in her book *Around the World in Seventy-Two Days*, published in 1890. "I knew if my conduct was proper, I should always find men ready to protect me, let them be Americans, English, French, German or anything else." Her motto was as simple as the Golden Rule: Be kind and people will treat you with kindness in return. If she were alive today, it's clear where she would stand on the issue of gun control.

Bly wasn't the first woman to travel around the world solo. That record goes to Ida Pfeiffer, an Austrian travel writer, who rounded the planet twice before Bly's journey, once in 1848 and again in 1850. She was forty-five when she set off the first time. Knowing of the objections she would face, she didn't tell anyone of her goal; instead, she told everyone she was going to visit a friend in Constantinople (renamed Istanbul in 1930). Once she got there she kept going. When questioned about her motives, she claimed she was on a religious pilgrimage to keep the naysayers at bay. She merely wanted to follow her curiosity and explore the world the way a man could.

Men were always free to sail the seas, but women were previously forbidden from traveling on commercial sailing vessels, which is why the first woman to go around the world disguised herself as a man. That distinction goes to Jeanne Baret from France, who in 1766, chopped off her hair and wrapped her breasts to hide them so that she could join her lover as his assistant on a botanical expedition. Her lover died during the years-long journey, and given she was not trying to break any record for speed, she stayed in Mauritius for several years, finally completing the circle with her return to France in 1775.

Compared to these pioneering women and the conditions they must have endured, I had it easy. From this point forward, whenever I wanted to complain, or quit, I would ask myself, What would Nellie Bly do? or Ida? or Jeanne? I would try to be less wet matchbook, more flint and steel, like them.

Before leaving Switzerland there were a few more things I wanted to do. One was swim in the Aare River. It's a Swiss tradition in summer to float downstream in the rush of the clear glacial waters, though I don't know if the tradition goes back as far as Bern's medieval times. Uschi and I met at her friend Francesca's apartment, where we left our bags and walked several blocks in our bikinis and bare feet to the river. I often do unconventional, questionable things, but walking around a city in nothing but my bikini has never been one of them. While I was giddy with embarrassment, Uschi and Francesca carried on conversing as we walked, because for them, this was normal. Lack of modesty and vanity are two traits I admire about the Swiss culture, and when we got to the river, it was clear just how widespread these traits were. Women—and men—many much older and all much less self-conscious than me—strolled along the pathway that led upriver. We fell in line with the scantily clad pedestrians and once we had walked far enough, we launched ourselves off the concrete bank into the moving river that sped us downstream in a fire hose blast of force.

"Remember to hold your legs up," Uschi instructed me. "Otherwise your feet will scrape against the rocks."

First there was the shock of the cold water, followed by the terror of drowning in this untamed display of nature. "This is crazy! I can't believe you guys don't wear life jackets!" I yelled to Uschi. I didn't even see an inner tube. There were no lifeguards either. The antithesis of America, where litigation is one of the biggest contributors to its GDP, in Europe you are expected to take personal responsibility for your own safety. For example, when your friend tells you to keep your feet up, you should listen. I let my feet drop down for just a second and winced as my toes stubbed hard against the rocks. Millions of stones, worn round by the river, tumbled along the bottom. But any pain was overshadowed by the fascination of all that movement below—and the sound. To dip your head underwater was to hear the clattering of an endless rockslide.

After a five-minute joyride downstream, our bobbing bodies moving faster than the bicycles pedaling next to the river, we swam over to one of the many ladders spaced out at intervals along the bank. The ladders were to ensure you exited in time to avoid getting churned through the roller dam a little farther down. Seriously, these people are afraid of nothing. We climbed out, joined the procession of swimmers trekking back upstream, and repeated the launch-float-walk cycle four more times. Between the cold water and working to keep my head above it, it was such a calorie burner, it was no wonder I had seen all those swimmers waiting in line for pie earlier in the week—a thought that reminded me how much my health had improved since arriving and how much I'd been slacking on my pie mission.

The other thing I wanted to do before leaving was buy a thank you gift for Doug for dog sitting. I had been thinking about it ever since I left the U.S., but it wasn't until Uschi suggested a watch that I knew it was the perfect gift. A Swiss watch was solid and reliable, like Doug, and tough enough to withstand getting kicked by a cow or run over by a tractor. Also, like Doug, it was high quality and handsome, but not flashy. Most importantly, a watch was small enough to carry and light enough not to jeopardize my baggage limit. I rode the bike down to the city center, to the department store Uschi had recommended, and picked out a sturdy model with a white face (easy to read) and a silver band. It came in a black box embossed with the Swiss flag, red with a white cross. I'm not big on material gifts, but this was one I felt very good about buying. What didn't feel quite as good was Doug's latest text that included a picture of him kayaking with another woman. I didn't know he was dating. Doug and I were just friends, but seeing him with someone else made me wonder, *Am I feeling something more?* I shook my head, dismissing the thought. *No, we're just friends. He deserves to be with someone who doesn't want to keep flying off to other places.*

The Jura, a junior mountain range compared to the Alps, creates the Swiss-French border. High on a heavily forested ridge on the Swiss side, the Kamers have a cabin that has been in their family for generations. It has running water, though not for drinking, and they only recently had the place wired for electricity. I had been coming to the cabin with them since I met them—so long ago I had met their grandfather. But as time passes, so does life; the grandfather had been gone for decades, and now even their father was gone. Armin, the Ambassador, had died several years earlier of dementia.

We picked up Uschi's mother, Liselotte, at her apartment in Bern, and headed into the mountains, driving until the roads got narrower and windier, until finally coming to the grassy driveway that led to the cabin. A Little Red Riding Hood of an abode, it was made of timber and stone with a pitched roof covered in pine needles and brown shutters locked tight, with vines climbing up all around it. It looked a little lonely, and reminded me of the American Gothic House when I first saw it, and how my landlord said when I moved in, "Houses are happier with people living in them."

We unloaded our bags from the car, flung open all the doors and windows, and dragged a large table and chairs outside, where we set up our supplies for making pie. I had given Uschi a pie lesson years earlier when she visited Marcus and me in Portland, Oregon. She was due for a refresher. We each made a batch of dough, while her mom peeled apples—small yellow ones from Monika's farm.

"Eve really wanted to be here," Liselotte lamented. "But she had to work this weekend." Because she lived an hour outside of Bern, I had only seen Eve, Uschi's younger sister, once during my two weeks in Switzerland. She had let her hair go gray (because, remember, the Swiss are not vain), but was otherwise the same as when I first met her—relaxed and sure of herself, her laugh still light, even after raising two daughters.

"I wish she could have joined us," I replied.

Liselotte continued, "I have one apple left, and I see you have some scraps of dough. I can show you something to do with that." Normally as reserved as a librarian—and most often found with a book in her hand—Liselotte was suddenly animated, jumping into action. "I'm going to make an *Apfel im Schlafrock*." I tried to work out the translation in my head. Even after months of intensive courses, my German still sucked. Liselotte looked at me over the top of her spectacles and said dryly, "It means apple in a bathrobe."

I watched as she hollowed out the core of the peeled apple, which she then set on a circle of dough rolled to the size of a bread plate. I took photos as she worked, documenting each step.

"Normally you would fill the middle with sugar, butter, crushed almonds, and cream. We don't have the almonds, but it doesn't matter," she said as she sprinkled cinnamon and sugar into the hole. "And we don't have cream."

"We have coffee creamer," Uschi said.

"That's fine," she said. I liked how flexible she was, how her apple in a bathrobe didn't have to be perfect.

Liselotte poured a tablespoon or so of cream into the well, and then pulled the dough up around the apple to cover it in its namesake robe. She gathered the edges together at the top, folding them into pleats, and using her fingertips, pressed the dough to close any gaps. "And now, you bake it."

While the pie and the robed apple baked, we set the table for guests.

Uschi's Aunt Trix lived just down the mountain. She was Armin's sister, but things had been difficult around his death and the relatives hadn't spoken much since. Because I had known and liked Trix from years past, and because we had just baked two apple pies and an *Apfel im Schlafrock*, we had created the ideal excuse to invite her up to the cabin. She and her husband arrived right around the time Böbi and her boyfriend, who had been hiking in the area, came by.

Uschi brewed a pot of coffee while I cut slices of pie to pass to all the guests. "Liselotte," I said, "you'll have to show me how to serve the robe thing."

"Just cut it down the middle," she said.

I pushed the knife blade into it, revealing the softened fruit and the stripe of cinnamon in the center. I kept cutting, carving it into smaller bites so everyone could try it.

"Your pie was delicious," Trix said after taking a bite, "but there is something about this *Apfel im Schlafrock* that is particularly good."

Everyone at the table nodded in agreement.

I took a bite myself and she was right. There was something about it, a simplicity maybe, or the dough to fruit ratio leaning more heavily toward the dough that made it extra buttery. Surely it couldn't have been the coffee creamer. I posted a picture of it on my social media pages and people who hadn't even tasted it seemed to think there was something special about it, too, because, to my astonishment, out of all the pictures I posted throughout my entire round-the-world trip, the *Apfel im Schlafrock* got the most likes by far.

But my focus was on neither robe, nor pie; I was more interested in observing the family gathered around the table. I couldn't make out the conversations taking place—my comprehension of Swiss German was even worse than "regular" German—but I could feel the mood and it was as rich and warm as the coffee. It didn't take words to know that they loved each other, and that they were grateful to be together again.

This is what world peace looks like, I thought. *And it's how pie can play a role in promoting it.* Bearing witness to this gave me the fuel I needed to carry on. I needed the highest octane I could get, because my next stop, I was sure, would be my hardest.

I was finally going to Germany.

CHAPTER 11

Germany: Black Forest

Let us remember: One book, one pen, one child, and one teacher can change the world.
—**MALALA YOUSAFZAI**

The day I officially moved to Stuttgart, three months before we got married, Marcus drove me straight from the airport to a *Grillabend*—a barbecue—in the forest, where, over beer and spiral-shaped sausages, he introduced me to his friends. Among the group, I homed in on two women. One was Bibiana who, with her black hair pulled tight into a sleek ponytail and gold hoop earrings, could have passed for Salma Hayek's little sister. Like Foong, Bibiana is a global citizen. Mexican by birth, she was raised and schooled in Belgium. She went to architecture school in Germany, where she met her German husband Marc, also an architect. With her at the barbecue was Silke, one of Bibiana and Marc's classmates from architecture school. She was a petite, fair-skinned German with eyes as blue as the Caribbean Sea, a sprinkle of freckles, and an impish grin. Silke's husband, Matthias, worked with Marcus, which is how they were all connected.

During my three years in Stuttgart, Bibiana and Silke had each given birth to their first child, while my efforts to get pregnant were in vain. Marcus and I had a puppy instead: Jack. I wasn't so desperate to bear my own offspring as to seek intervention—the world was already populated enough—but after Marcus died, one of my first regrets (of many) was that we didn't have kids and that there would be no legacy of him. Eventually, I turned the regret into the fantastical notion that the universe, knowing he would die young, had been protecting me from the added challenge of single parenthood. As if life actually worked that way. As if my hyperthyroidism wasn't the real reason.

Thirteen years had passed since that *Grillabend*. Bibiana and Marc had since moved to Berlin and had another child. Silke, still in Stuttgart, also had a second child, but had recently divorced. Marcus, reduced to ashes, was buried forty-five minutes outside of the German city. And I was in Switzerland, in a quandary about where exactly I was going next.

Reasoning that instead of wallowing in grief in Germany, it would be better to go to Italy where I could research pie—a.k.a. pizza and calzone. I was one second away from hitting the purchase button for a train ticket from Bern to Rome, when I got a message from Bibiana. "We're on holiday in the Black Forest at Marc's family's cabin. Silke and her kids will be here for the weekend. Come join us." And just like that, my plans changed again.

The train, clinging to mountainsides and blasting through black tunnels, whisked me away from one fairy-tale land toward another. Gradually, as we sped along, the sharp granite of the Alps softened into steep hills covered in a tree canopy so dense in places even the sharpest blade of light couldn't pierce it. The resulting darkness earned the region its name—the Black Forest—though the forest was dark for other reasons. It had been a Nazi hideout during World War II and Hitler built a bunker hidden in the trees near the French border. The bunker was demolished in 1945, after Germany withdrew from the Western Front, but you can still see remains of the concrete. You can also see the crumbling straight lines of stone walls from a time two thousand years earlier during which the Teutons, the original tribes of Germania, fought off the Romans. It was Marcus who had educated me about this. He was well versed in his country's history and explained that the Romans, who had built the walls, had not anticipated that the Teutonic women, bare breasted no less, would be fighting alongside the men. They rushed out from behind the trees, screaming like banshees, and ambushed the soldiers, consequently ending the expansion of the Roman Empire.

This swath of land, almost one hundred miles long, is a protected nature park, the biggest in Germany. I was—as was just about everyone else in the Western world—familiar with this area, albeit unwittingly. How so? Because many of the Grimm's fairy tales are set in the Black Forest: "Snow White" and "Rapunzel," to name a few. I knew about Black Forest Cake, the chocolate-cherry cake layered with whipped cream, but had never associated the cake with an actual place. (The cake is named for *Kirschwasser*, the cherry schnapps distilled in the region.) It wasn't until the 1970s that I learned the Black Forest was an actual place, when the acid rain that fell there became international news. Caused partially by the air pollution from cars, acid infiltrated the soil and killed off half its trees. The forest recovered with the invention of lead-free gasoline and catalytic converters, introduced to Germany in 1985 (ten years after the U.S. adopted them). However, other perils continue to threaten the region, like logging. I could see patches that had been clear-cut, stripped naked by chainsaws and bulldozers, and, occasionally, places where tornadoes had leveled trees that lay tossed around like pick-up-sticks, strewn every which way. But what I mostly saw was endless shade and shadows.

The deeper into the forest we traveled the more I regressed, like Benjamin Button traveling backward in time a dozen years to when I rode through this same area on the back of Marcus's motorcycle. Wrapped in suits of protective leather, our heads inside full bubble helmets, dressed more for outer space than for the romantic country inn we were headed to, Marcus would reach back and rub my thigh to signal his happiness. My arms wrapped around his waist, I always replied with a light squeeze to let him know I, too, was happy. We would lean into the hairpin turns of the mountain roads, our bodies pressed together as a single unit to maintain balance as the engine hummed like music, the Ducati's melody a cello solo compared to the heavy-metal-band sound of a Harley. And the wind—oh, the wind—

that I could feel on my face even with the protective shield. This perfect union of man, woman, machine, and nature—that's what our love felt like.

I pressed my forehead against the glass, hard, trying to push the memory—and the longing—aside as the blur of green pines passed before my eyes.

I read the names of the tiny villages we passed—Kuppenheim, Oberndorf, Ottenau, Gernsbach, Weisenbach—tracking the map as we either stopped or sped through them. When we finally arrived at Forbach, I was already standing at the door, ready to jump off the train before it reached the station. The conductor had barely released the latch when I heaved my bag down the steps and onto the platform— and there was Bibiana, waiting for me like a life preserver to keep me from drowning in my memories. Dressed in an Izod shirtdress paired with espadrilles and gold hoop earrings, and her hair pulled back in her signature ponytail, she looked exactly as I remembered her from nine years earlier.

"Bibiana!"

"Beth! You made it! How was your trip?"

"Oh, well, it was . . ." I stopped myself from unloading my nostalgia on her. I wouldn't barrage her with the stories of my past, about Marcus's and my wedding in Alpirsbach, just a few valleys over from this one, and how our friends and family took over the entire hamlet. How Marcus, dressed in his black tuxedo, had waited at the altar, looking so handsome and so full of anticipation, as my dad walked me down the pink cobblestone aisle of the thousand-year-old church. And how, when we sat on our chairs facing the pastor, a ray of sun had beamed down through the stained glass onto Marcus and me, its spotlight anointing us with a sacred promise, while a cellist serenaded us with Bach. How we had recited our vows in both German and English, professing to love and honor each other. Forever. Till death do us part. Clueless that one of us would be dead in six years.

Bibiana called to a dark-haired girl farther down the platform, motioning for her to join us. "Kim, she's here."

"That's Kim?" I said. "Oh, Bibiana, she's beautiful, and so grown up. The last time I saw her she was in diapers." I turned to Kim. "I know you don't remember me, but I'm so happy to see you again."

"Nice to meet you," Kim replied sweetly in a British accent. If a voice could be a flavor, hers was peppermint, and it sounded just as sweet whether she was speaking Spanish, German, or English. She was already trilingual at the age of ten.

"I just need to get some bread, then we'll head to the cabin," Bibiana said as she led us inside the train station. There was no kiosk or bakery, only a vending machine. She fed a few coins into the slot, pushed a button, and out popped a round loaf of whole grain bread, as fresh as if there were elves baking inside the metal dispenser. I had seen the American cupcake trend become so crazy you could find cupcake vending machines in LA. And yet this was not Beverly Hills; it was the Black Forest, where the quality far surpassed the prices.

From the train station, we drove higher up a mountain and deeper into the woods. When the pavement ended, we kept going, climbing up a dirt road, until eventually, Bibiana pulled over on the shoulder and parked. "We're here," she said, though all I could see was forest, not a house in sight. We stepped out onto the plush carpet of pine needles and the three of us, each with a piece of my luggage, hiked down a gravel trail that led to a clearing in the trees. On the edge of the meadow was a log cabin with a peaked roof, green shutters, gingham curtains, and neatly stacked firewood. While the Kamer's cabin in Switzerland was Little Red Riding Hood, this one was pure Hansel and Gretel (another Brothers Grimm tale set in the region). It was so idyllic I could only laugh.

"It's adorable!" I said. "And I see you have a bathroom." Bibiana followed my gaze to the outhouse tucked off to the side.

"We have indoor plumbing now, but you can use that if you want," she joked.

"I will," I replied, not joking.

Marc, looking more handsome and fit than ever in his white T-shirt and jeans, came outside holding two cold beers. "Welcome, Beth. It's good to see you." His dimples deepened as he smiled and handed me a bottle. "Thought you might be ready for one of these after your trip."

I took the beer from him, immediately recognizing the green and white label with pine cones. "Hey! It's Tannenzäpfle Pils. This was Marcus's favorite beer."

"It's made nearby," Marc said, and then, shaking his head, he added, "I'm so sorry about him." Marc didn't have to say the word aloud for me to hear him thinking it: *Unfassbar*. I had heard it repeatedly at Marcus's German funeral. "Incomprehensible."

"Yeah. Thanks," I replied.

It was still *unfassbar* that Marcus was gone and that I was back in Germany without him, without any possibility of seeing him. I wouldn't see his parents either—they banished me from their lives the moment the funeral was over, looking for someone to blame over the loss of their only child. I understood this, because I also blamed myself, until months of therapy instilled the truth: the fault lay with the birth defect of a bicuspid aortic valve.

Nor would I see Marcus's grave. Visiting the burial site of his ashes had been one of my priorities for my journey. "I need closure," I insisted, ignoring the raised eyebrows of whomever I told.

I had done every possible thing I could do to climb out of the abyss and get back to living fully. I faithfully attended twice-weekly grief counseling sessions for nearly a year. I wrote about my grief ad nauseam, sharing to the point where people said my grief was over the top. I baked pies—hundreds, nay thousands of pies—to share with others suffering losses of their own. I moved into the American Gothic House and started the pie stand. I made new friends. I even dated a little, Doug being the most recent failed attempt. And I was taking this trip around the world. Visiting his grave, I reasoned, would hammer that final nail into the coffin to end my sadness once and for all. Like the Irish, I would scoop up a handful of soil from his burial site, sleep with it under my pillow, and be bestowed with a miracle. My emotional limbs severed by his death would grow back and I would feel whole again. The cabin was only a thirty-minute drive from the cemetery. I was so close. I could still get there.

But real miracles, I would learn, occur in the places you're not looking.

A little boy appeared by Bibiana's side. "Mama, what took you so long?" he demanded.

I looked down at him. "And who is this?"

"Oh, that's right. You haven't met Luc. He was born after you and Marcus moved to the States," Bibiana replied of her eight-year-old son.

"Hi, Luc," I said in English, unsure which language he preferred.

He studied me with his eyes—big, brown, shiny, and full of future. "Hello," he said tentatively. English was his preference. It was the language of the international school he attended, but he spoke a mix of three, including German and Spanish, and like Barbara in Lebanon, often in the same sentence.

"I have dinner ready," Marc announced. "We're having pasta and salad. Go ahead and sit." He motioned to the picnic table, a giant slab of wood that hugged the side of the cabin.

I took a seat on the bench, leaned my back against the wall, and looked out across the green meadow as I sipped on my beer—Marcus's beer.

Unfassbar. It was all so fucking incomprehensible. Even being here, in this enchanted forest, with caring friends, friends whose email arrived at the last possible moment before I bought a train ticket in a different direction.

In the morning, the kids and I climbed down the ladder of the sleeping loft to the kitchen where Marc was waiting, holding several large empty bowls. "Time to get breakfast," he said.

"Huh?" I said sleepily.

"You'll see," he replied.

"What about coffee?"

"Later," he said. "As soon as we get back."

I followed Marc, Bibiana, and their two kids down the dirt road. After a few minutes, they veered off into the bushes, spreading out the way search parties canvas a crime scene, but we weren't looking for bodies—we were hunting for wild blueberries. We foraged like a pack of bears, bending down to inspect each bush, pushing back the petite leaves to look in between and under them, picking the dark purple fruit while trying to avoid the bees buzzing around their hives buried in the ground. The berries were small, but plump and juicy, and perfectly ripe. For every cup I accumulated in my bowl, I ate the equivalent.

"Stop eating them!" Luc yelled from a few feet away.

"I'm not!" I yelled back, grinning at him.

"Let me see your tongue."

I stuck it out at him. Bibiana laughed and snapped a photo. She showed it to me and there was the proof: my tongue was as stained and purple as our fingers.

"They're so good, I can't help it," I teased Luc. "And there are plenty here."

"But we need enough for breakfast. And for pie." The way he looked at me with his Bambi eyes, so earnest and concerned, melted my heart and made me feel bad for teasing him.

"Don't worry," I assured him. "We'll have enough."

Back at the cabin, after eggs and toast—and, mercifully, coffee—Kim and I went outside to wash the blueberries under a spigot of spring water that flowed into a wooden trough made from a hollowed-out log. When the water was done dripping through our colanders, we returned inside to make pie. I had a work station already set up on the dining table for giving the kids a lesson.

Blueberry pie is one of the easiest pies to make. For the filling, all you have to do is toss the rinsed berries with some sugar and cornstarch, though there's still a matter of the crust. When it comes to making dough, kids don't have the same fear of failure that plagues adults. They don't take shortcuts and buy premade pie crust from the store. Kids don't worry about perfection; they just want to make stuff. They like tactile experiences. They like to dig in the dirt, and mixing dough is a little like playing with mud or like building a sandcastle.

After rolling the dough flat, Kim lifted it into the pie dish.

"That doesn't look nice," she said. The dough had torn as she pulled on it to adjust it in the plate.

"It looks fine," I assured her. "No one is going to see the bottom."

She accepted my reassurance with grace and moved on to the next task, rolling out the top crust. With a paring knife, she carefully scored it into strips, her face set with concentration. I recognized the look. She was "in the zone," that Zen-like place pie can take you, where you get so focused on your work that the rest of the world falls away. We were all transported to that place. Even Luc. Normally on the run, he hovered next to her, watching closely as she wove the strips into a lattice on top of the blueberries. Her hands, so delicate and small, moved deftly and confidently.

"That looks great, Kim. It's beautiful. I would hire you to work at my pie stand if I still had one."

When the pie was done, the kids got out paper and crayons. Without any prompting from me or their parents, they wrote out messages in German in a rainbow of colors. "*Willkommen*, Silke, Jule, and Jette," read Luc's in his childlike scrawl. Kim drew three stick figures in a car driving toward a pie with the caption, "*Wir haben selbst gemachter* pie!" (We made this pie ourselves!)

Silke and her two daughters, Jule and Jette, arrived in time for dinner. The girls, tow-headed and pale compared to Kim and Luc's Mexican complexions, had been shy throughout dinner, but they lit up when the pie was served.

"You made this?" Silke asked me.

"No. Kim and Luc did," I told her.

"It looks so good. And the welcome notes they wrote—it's so sweet."

Kim cut the pie, placing slices on our dessert plates. One of the slices slipped off the pie server and landed upside down on the plate. Kim, without missing a beat, looked at me and remarked, "Who says no one's going to see the bottom?"

Shocked by her quickness and how she busted me on what I told her during our pie lesson, I turned to Bibiana and laughed. "Wow! She's smart."

The next morning, when I climbed down from the loft, Marc was waiting at the bottom of the ladder with empty bowls for me and the kids. My feet had barely touched the ground when he handed one to me.

"This is like Blueberry Boot Camp," I groaned. "I normally never do anything—and I mean anything—before I have coffee."

He laughed. "Come on. This is fun."

It was fun. And in the way that life gives you what you need more than what you want, I needed fun more than I wanted coffee.

With the addition of our three new female members, our bear pack grew to eight, and with the extra hands it didn't take us long to gather enough berries to make more pie. But after breakfast—after coffee and before we started baking—we walked down to the lake, a sliver of blue-green water turned silver from the sun's reflection. While the kids played on the beach, Bibiana, Silke, and I sat on a rock outcrop. They were speaking in German at a pace too fast for me to keep up with so my attention wandered. I stared across the water, my eyes trying to focus on something unseeable—like the past.

During a pause in their conversation, I asked them, "What did you think about Marcus? How well did you know him?" I was hoping they could unlock a secret to him, even the smallest crumb of information that would break the spell he had on me.

"He was nice, handsome . . ." Silke started. "We always thought he was . . . I don't know the word in English . . . *unabhängig.*"

"Independent," Bibiana translated, nodding.

The insight wasn't helpful to my cause. I didn't learn anything new, but it was true. "He was definitely that," I agreed. "We both were." We were in our late thirties when we met, well established in our ways and our preferences. But why did it even matter what they thought of him or what they could tell me now? He was gone. I needed to move on, yet I was clinging to him as if he were alive, as if we were temporarily separated and could still get back together.

"At least I have Jack," I said, picking up a stick off the ground. "He would love it here. He'd be swimming in this lake right now." I threw the stick into the water.

"He's still alive?" Bibiana asked, surprised.

"Yeah, he's eleven. Almost the same age as Kim."

"Where is he now?" she asked.

"In Iowa. With my farmer friend, Doug," I replied.

"Farmer friend or . . .?" Bibiana inquired with a raised eyebrow. She smiled and looked at me—into me—like she knew something I didn't.

"He's just a friend," I insisted.

Silke changed the subject. "What kind of pie are we going to make this afternoon?" she asked. "I brought apples, peaches, and bananas. The girls are going to love baking with you. It will be a good distraction. The divorce has been so hard for them."

I had observed this as the younger one, Jette, who was six, had wet the bed the night before—a recent development, Silke confided, since Matthias had moved out.

We set up our pie-making workspace outside this time, on the big picnic table. I had taught a lot of pie classes, including many outdoors, but never in such a storybook setting—though the Swiss Jura comes close.

Under the blue sky, sheltered by the cabin, with the scent of hot pine-tree sap permeating the air, we created our confections. We made more blueberry pie, and progressed to peach. When we made banana cream, I assigned Jule to stand at the stove and stir the pudding, while Kim cracked eggs for the meringue. When we made apple pie, the younger ones, Luc and Jette, were entrusted with paring knives to peel the apples.

"You sure it's okay?" I asked Silke and Bibiana about the kids handling knives.

"Of course," they replied in unison. These were not helicopter parents and I wondered what else they would have said yes to. Would they let their first-graders swim in Bern's Aare River or drink sugarcane juice in an Indian slum? Probably. And I'm guessing the kids would be just fine.

Not only could the kids be trusted with the knives, they were such quick learners that little Jette removed a peel in one piece, holding up the long green spiral of skin for us to admire. It wasn't the unbroken peel that impressed me, however; it was her smile. Silke's girls had been so quiet when they first arrived, they bordered on sullen, but after all the pie making—as well as the berry picking, swimming in the lake, and lying on their backs under the night sky watching a meteor shower—they were animated and smiling all the time.

"How do we take away their screens and let them see what is inside themselves?" writes John Hunter in his book, *World Peace and Other 4th-Grade Achievements*. "How do we create something genuinely new? After all, our old ways of seeing and understanding and creating political relationships have manifestly failed to bring about world peace. Unleashing the creativity of the next generation may be our only hope."

It finally hit me. *This.* This was the reason I was meant to come here. The kids and their laughter, their generous hearts, their openness to learning new things, the way they cooperate and collaborate—they are our hope for the future. They are the ray of light that can reach through the dark forest, no matter how thick the trees.

Through these kids, multilingual and multicultural as they were, I had also witnessed one of Hunter's other assertions:

"If students remain solely within their own cultures, loyal only to their 'own kind,' they will put the planet at grave risk. But if they embrace a larger vision, they have the opportunity to heal the planet and create peace."

This little bunch was well on its way to becoming the healers and peacemakers of tomorrow. They were already working their magic in the present, because after spending four days with them in the wilderness, I let go of any remaining urge to visit Marcus's grave. They kept me from dwelling on the past and showed me that in order to move forward, I had to stop looking back. Forward is the direction I would go.

CHAPTER 12

Germany: Aachen

In the end, only three things matter:
how much you loved, how gently you lived,
and how gracefully you let go of
things not meant for you.
—BUDDHA

On the day Marcus died in 2009, I was in Terlingua, Texas, where I was spending the scalding-hot summer working on a memoir about trading my lucrative high-tech job for a simpler one as a pie maker. Six years later, on the anniversary of his passing, I was in Aachen, Germany, with Marcus's cousins, Claudia and Martina, sipping champagne from the souvenir flutes we had given to our wedding guests. Claudia still had a few, etched with our names and the date of our nuptials: September 20, 2003. If Marcus were still alive, we would have been married twelve years.

Forever. Till death do us part. *Unfassbar*.

I hadn't planned my visit to coincide with the anniversary of his death. I hadn't fully planned any of my European stops. I had an entire month on the continent to divvy up however I wanted. I hadn't planned on two weeks in Switzerland, nor had I planned on four days with friends and their kids in a Black Forest cabin. This unstructured approach had worked out well so far. In Europe, you can be spontaneous and jump on the next train to go anywhere. I had a rough idea that I would visit Marcus's family in northern Germany, and then head up to Hamburg to visit a journalist whom I'd met when she visited the American Gothic House. The journalist was away for the summer, but "The Cousins"—that's what we called them—welcomed me to come whenever it fit into my schedule.

I had always liked the cousins. They were healthy, fit, educated, open-minded, and family-oriented, but we grew apart after Marcus's death in the way coworkers do when taking a job with another company. You promise to stay in touch, but once you lose the physical connection, the friendship wilts like an unwatered plant. With this trip, I had an excuse to reconnect. And with pie, and offering to make it with them, I created an occasion to gather everyone together.

Aachen is the westernmost city in Germany, situated in the triangle where the border of Belgium and The Netherlands meet. The Siegfried Line, Germany's defensive front during World War II, ran past Aachen and, like the Roman walls in the Black Forest, remnants of it are still visible in the form of "Dragon's Teeth"— jagged rows of reinforced concrete blocks designed to ward off the advancing tanks of the Allied Forces. These reminders of war can be found everywhere in Germany as part of its *Erinnerungskultur*— Culture of Remembrance. Bombed out buildings, bunkers, and crumbling walls were intentionally left in place so that Germans will "never forget" and never repeat the past. Germans also recognize an annual day of mourning—*Volkstrauertag*—to commemorate armed forces, civilians who died in armed conflicts, and victims of violent oppression in all nations.

"Anniversaries provide self-reassurance. They offer a moment of respite to reflect on one's position in history," writes University of Konstanz professor Aleida Assmann on the *Deutschland.de* website. "Overcoming a traumatic past involves confronting it and gaining new direction from the memory of the crimes." She adds, "Memory cannot simply be kept alive; it must always be renewed." Aachen's concrete blocks, those sharp, menacing teeth protruding from the soil, aren't going to let anyone forget anytime soon.

Claudia, the eldest of Marcus's five cousins, lives with her husband Edgar and their three kids in Roetgen, a suburb of Aachen. Nestled in a quiet, immaculate neighborhood, their three-bedroom townhouse is modern and light, and filled with soccer balls, computers, laundry, books, sneakers piled by the door—all the things you'd expect to find in a busy family's home.

"Welcome. Come in. Let me help you with your bags." Seeing Edgar, and his high-beam smile, put me at ease, especially when he spoke to me in English instead of German. I still couldn't get comfortable with the language in spite of hearing it daily for the past three weeks, getting more practice, and even improving a little. "Claudia will be back soon. She's teaching an aerobics class," he said. "We got all the ingredients for the pies. The apples are out on the terrace."

I looked out through the French doors, where a huge orange cat sat next to a flat of homegrown apples, green and red tinged in color, marked by dark spots where worms may or may not have burrowed inside. I always appreciated backyard fruit for its organic qualities and freshness. As for the worms, discovering something alive and wiggling inside could liven up any pie lesson.

"I remember your cat. What's his name again?"

"That's Bilbao." We both watched the ginger tabby, a real-life Garfield turned sentry.

"He looks like he's guarding the apples."

One by one, family members arrived: Claudia; her sister Martina and brother Tobias; two out of three of Claudia and Edgar's teenage kids, Charlotte and Anton (their oldest, Leonie, was spending a year in Bolivia); two of Martina's kids, Jakob and Moritz; and Martina's husband, Johannes. Including me, we were a group of ten.

Everyone greeted me warmly enough, but I sensed a tension in the room as thick as Bilbao's girth. The awkwardness wasn't caused by any rift between us; I assumed the issue was with Marcus's parents. I never learned exactly why they didn't want me in their lives after their son died. We all deal with grief in our own way, and while I was going public with mine—blogging about it, no detail too personal— they had gone in the opposite direction and retreated into silence. I didn't need to reconcile with them or even understand them; I only needed to respect the space they created—a conclusion I reached only after months of therapy. But what did the cousins know? What had Marcus's parents told them about me? Nothing, as it turns out, because they had distanced themselves from the cousins as well.

The tension in the room, I determined, was merely the knowledge that we were bound by a terrible loss, and that this was the first time I had been to Aachen without Marcus.

"You've gotten so tall!" I said to Anton. In the place he lived in my mind, he was still a toddler, dressed in lederhosen and holding Jack's leash. "I still remember you fighting with your sister over whose turn it was to walk Jack when he was a puppy. And you couldn't pronounce his name; you called him Zeck." Anton smiled and dipped his head, as if to dodge the ball of embarrassment. "And look at you," I said to Charlotte his sister, older by several years. The shy, little blond girl I knew from previous visits had blossomed into a curvaceous young woman with a confident smile. "You're so grown up, and so pretty."

The last time I had seen the family was six years earlier, at Marcus's funeral, but the fog of grief that enshrouded me was so dense, I didn't remember seeing the kids. The only thing I remember is how Claudia came up behind me to fasten the buttons I had missed on the back of my dress. Her tenderness in that moment remains as crystal clear as an alpine sky.

"Okay, well, we might as well get started," I said. "You ready to make pie?"

Edgar brought the apples inside, Bilbao positioned himself in the center of the kitchen to keep us under surveillance.

We gathered around the dining room table in the center of the apartment's open floor plan. They lined up behind the individual work stations I had set up, discussing who would use which dish for their pie, as there were many to choose from. I had rummaged through Claudia's cupboards, collecting an assortment of baking dishes in round, square, and oval shapes, and a rectangle casserole dish that screamed lasagna. I also rounded up bowls, knives, and wine bottles that could double as rolling pins.

Claudia didn't bake with us. Instead, she circled the table taking photos, while Edgar uncorked a bottle of wine, something Spanish, white, and perfectly chilled for a hot August Sunday afternoon. I wished I could have plopped down in a chair to savor the glass he poured for me; instead, I forged ahead with the pie lesson, both hands covered in flour and in constant use. The wine would have to wait.

When I started in on the pie instruction, like always, I entered another realm where my surroundings fell away and all that mattered was the people around me, guiding them through the process so they would produce something they could be proud of.

The minute the pies were in the oven, I grabbed my glass of wine. As soon as the pies came out, the kids and parents all reconvened and circled around the table again. No longer tentative, they were a pack of wolves with pie as their prey!

"It's too hot to eat," I warned them.

"I have a solution for that," Anton retorted. He whipped around toward the kitchen and trotted back with a tub of vanilla ice cream.

What followed was a frenzy of slicing and scooping, eating and laughing. Claudia snapped more photos. Edgar poured more wine. Second helpings were served to all. In less than an hour, we were all sitting back in our chairs, relaxed, satisfied, reconnected, with our bellies bursting like boiled *Weisswurst*.

This is how wounds are healed. How grief is eased, though never fully erased. How estranged family members are brought back into the fold. You make pie together and sit down to eat it. This was better and more healing—and far more important—than any graveyard visit.

That night, while I slept in the safety of Claudia and Edgar's home, several time zones away, a young Uyghur man from China, wearing a yellow T-shirt and a backpack, walked the streets of Bangkok. He stopped at the Erawan Shrine, making his way through the crowd to pay a visit to the sacred golden Brahma. Instead of leaving marigolds on the altar, he left his backpack—with a pipe bomb inside it. I woke up to the news the next morning that the explosion killed 20 people and injured 125. It detonated at the shrine around 7 p.m.—the same time, seven weeks earlier, I had walked past it each evening, sometimes lingering to breathe in the incense and admire the sunburst of orange flowers after making pies at the Grand

Hyatt. I immediately started sending emails and checking Facebook to make certain my new friends at the Hyatt were okay. I didn't even think about getting coffee first.

"Some of the hotel's windows were broken and there was a lot of smoke," Samart wrote, "but we are all fine."

"I'm okay," Julia wrote. "And none of my coworkers were affected."

It was a relief to learn they were all right, but thoughts of the tragedy troubled me all day, along with the thought: *It could have been me.* But it wasn't me. I was still alive, still circumnavigating the world, still struggling to understand why peace was so out of reach.

Once they figured out the *who* came the question of *why*. Why did this happen?

I read every article I could find on the internet, including one in the *Bangkok Post* that pointed back to the "karma issue." It reiterated the reason the shrine was built in the first place—to put an end to the accidents that kept happening at the location while they were building the hotel. "Modernity and myth, politics and superstition, men and gods. All of these are intertwined inseparably at the site that has now become a place imbued with dark memories," the story surmised.

More explicitly, the article quoted Thai historian Siripoj Laomanacharoen, who said, "[When something bad happens] we often blame it on the 'dark forces' or on superstitious belief, when in fact we should look at what we have done wrong and what has brought about the tragic incident."

I had wondered the same thing after the American tragedy of 9/11. What if, instead of immediately saddling up his horse and fastening on his spurs, declaring we were going to "hunt them down," George W. first asked the questions, "What did we do to bring this on? What role did we play in this? And what do we need to do to address this and fix the problem to ensure peace?" Because, as we now know—what we should have already known from history—the solution wasn't to start a fucking war in Afghanistan and Iraq.

What happened in the Erawan bombing is that on July 9, just a few days after I left Bangkok for India, Thai authorities had forcibly deported over a hundred Uyghur men. Uyghurs are Turkic-speaking Muslims who live mostly in the Xinjiang region of western China, an area of unrest where hundreds of Uyghurs had been killed in an effort to exterminate them by yet another culture that believes it's superior to another. Large numbers of Uyghurs were fleeing, traveling by way of Thailand to seek asylum in Turkey. But instead of allowing them to continue on to Turkey, Thailand sent them back to China, where they would likely face persecution, abuse, and even death. In retaliation for the deportation, a couple of Uyghur extremists bombed the shrine. Instead of solving any problems, it only resulted in more animosity and more deaths.

Loss upon loss upon loss. It may not have affected me directly—and my friends in Thailand were okay—but the bombing was another tragedy added to my ever-growing list. How does one live with so much accumulated grief?

I knew of one thing, besides pie, that worked for me. Water.

"Salt water is the cure for anything: tears, sweat, a dip in the sea," Isak Dinesen famously remarked. A friend shared this quote with me about twenty years earlier and it has been one of my go-to forms of therapy ever since. I wasn't finicky about a place to dip; any body of water in which I could immerse myself would do. Anything to become buoyant. To have my ears underwater, to hear nothing but my blood pumping through my body, to blow air out my nose and watch the bubbles rise to the surface—this was my escape from life's pain. It allowed me to inhabit, even for the few seconds I could hold my breath, an alternate universe. Water was the healthy version, the one without the side effects of my other method: drinking wine.

The sixth anniversary of Marcus's death was two days away, a date I've dreaded every year since the medical examiner's call, and with its approach came the sledgehammer of remembrance.

Fuck *Erinnerungskultur*.

But luck was on my side, as just three blocks from Claudia and Edgar's house was the Roetgen *Therme*, a spa with natural mineral baths, saunas of varying temperatures, and steam rooms with aromatherapy choices of mint, eucalyptus, and orange.

I knew the drill; Marcus had taught me. We had spent many hours going in and out of cedar-lined sweat boxes and alternating between hot and ice-cold pools. He eased me into the co-ed nudity and how not to gawk at the full-frontal display of male anatomy, even if it was pierced. He explained how to use the electronic wristbands to open the lockers, schooled me in the German rule to sit only on your towel and not the bare wood, and showed me when to lift my arms to get the full effect of the masochistic heatwave when the *Saunameister* poured scented water on the coals.

Marcus and I had visited Roetgen several times, but had never been to its mineral baths. When I walked into the place, small and cozy and easy to navigate, the knife of grief twisted. We should have been here together. Marcus should still be alive.

I stripped, wrapped my towel around my naked body, and ventured outside to the heated saltwater pool, hidden from street view by the enclosed courtyard. The darkness of the rainy night was offset by the firefly twinkle of garden lights and the bioluminescent glow of the large pool. A handful of Germans lounged in the buff beneath umbrella tables, sipping beer, unconcerned with the rain or the nudity. I liked this part of the culture, the hardiness and immodesty, embracing nature rather than running from it, accepting the human body and all its imperfections without shame.

I lowered myself into the water and disappeared under the surface. Saltier and more effervescent than I expected, it was like bathing in warm Perrier. I took several breast strokes to swim deeper down into the silence. Except it wasn't silent; spa music played underwater turning the pool into a liquid sound bath. The surprise of it, combined with the rain, the steam, and the glowing of light, only added to the mystical atmosphere. I floated for a while, weightless and alone, suspended in a dreamlike state as drops of rain splashed on my face and salt seeped into my pores. Isak Dinesen was right.

Throughout my life, I've had glimpses of heaven, breaking the bounds of my earthly existence. Thinking back, it only happens when I'm in nature; that feeling of oneness with whatever realm lies beyond our limited comprehension, that absolute knowing that everything, no matter how painful or perturbing, is going to be okay. This was one of those moments. But my brush with nirvana was short-lived when I remembered—because I always remembered—what brought me here, causing me to inhale too quickly and choke on a mouthful of water. I swam over to the side of the pool and leaned my head on my arm, my tears adding to the mineral cocktail of pool water and rain. This round-the-world trip had been hard enough without battling my grief. But there was no avoiding it, because no matter where I went or what I did, the irrefutable fact remained: Marcus was gone and my life would be forever altered by his absence.

He didn't speak to me in the Roetgen pool like he did at the Bangkok one two months earlier. He didn't say, "It's time to let go, my love," in his breathy British voice. He didn't need to. He had already delivered the message. The rest was up to me. And there in that pool, steam rising as thick as it did at the hot springs in Rotorua, I drowned the vestiges of my sorrow, leaving them to disintegrate in the salt water.

After checking off "tears" and "a dip" from my Salt Water Cures Anything list, my next task was to sweat.

On the 19th of August, the day of dread, I borrowed Claudia's bicycle and spent the day alone, riding on the Vennbahn, Europe's longest rail-to-trail bike path. The 125-kilometer (78-mile) route starts in Aachen, passes through Roetgen—behind the *Therme*, where I got on—and heads east across Belgium into Luxembourg. The railway, originally used to transport coal from the mines in the north to steel factories in the south, traverses what was one of the biggest conflict zones in Europe during both World Wars. Today, its use is a peace-promoting and family-friendly pathway that encourages healthy activity, another example of how positive transformation is possible.

The weather was perfect for biking: sunny but cool enough not to sweat. I rode for several hours, crisscrossing the Belgium-Germany border several times as I pedaled along the meandering path through forests, fields, and rolling hills.

"Objective ambivalence" is the psychological term for experiencing simultaneous feelings that are in direct opposition to one another. Like how dark chocolate can be delicious in spite of its lack of sugar. I was in the full throes of this ambivalence, confused to be both happy and sad at once. Happy to be riding a bike and feeling the wind in my face; sad that Marcus was not around to share the adventure with. With this awareness in mind, I did what anyone invested in sanity and self-preservation would do: I just kept pedaling.

I stopped for lunch in Monschau, a touristy, historic village that survived the wars unscathed. The town square was lined with rows of traditional *Fachwerk* houses, an architectural style of exposed-timber beams set in angles, with white stucco filling the space in between. Marcus would have liked that I remembered the word *Fachwerk*. He also would have liked that I indulged in a full Italian meal of spaghetti carbonara and insalata caprese, and ended with a cappuccino.

He would have liked that Claudia and I went to the Aachen Cathedral the day before, lighting candles and paying homage to him rather than to Charlemagne (a.k.a. Charles the Great), the first emperor of the Roman empire who was entombed in 814 AD inside the church.

He would have liked that, after my bike ride, I went to the Roetgen *Therme* a second time. And how, when I got back to Claudia's that night, Claudia, Martina, and I drank a bottle of champagne. We made a silent toast: *To Marcus, who left us far too soon. The light of the world is dimmer without your fiery spark.* We then clinked our glasses, said, "*Zum Wohl. Prost.* Cheers," aloud, and swallowed the bubbles, delicate and light enough to lift our spirits.

He would have liked that I treated Claudia and the family to lunch a few days earlier at Vapiano, a favorite contemporary Italian café of ours ever since its first location opened in Frankfurt—and the last place we ate together in Stuttgart.

He would have liked that I used his frequent flyer miles to travel around the world in the first place, to make pie, to spread a message of peace and love and community-building. He would have liked that I went to Germany, immersing myself in his country, teaching his cousins and their kids how to make apple pie, spending time with his family, and looking through our wedding photos together. He would have liked that all of us were there, sharing memories and making new ones, because of him.

When I set off on my trip, I was determined to go to Germany and visit his grave, convinced it would be a panacea for closure. But Marcus is not in that grave. He is in the stars. He is in the candlelight in the cathedral. He is in the sun and wind on the bike path, in the strength of the *Fachwerk* houses, in the flavor of the carbonara, the froth of the cappuccino, the bubbles of the champagne. He is in the heat and saltwater of the mineral baths. He is and always will be in my heart, a heart that is still beating, and still capable of love.

I opened my journal later and, for the hundredth time, read the Tibetan Buddhist tantra I had taped inside the cover:

> *As a bee seeks nectar from all kinds of flowers, seek teachings everywhere. Like a deer that finds a quiet place to graze, seek seclusion to digest all that you have gathered. Like a mad one, beyond all limits, go where you please and live like a lion, completely free of all fear.*

I had pushed my limits to make it this far, but I was not fearless. Even if I had the fortitude of a lion, you'd be hard pressed to find a lion without scars. My scars from losing Marcus were as permanent as the oven burns on my arms, but it's the scars that make us who we are. The scars are reminders of how fully, how courageously we have lived, despite the pain.

CHAPTER 13

Hungary

> Hope is being able to see that there is
> light despite all of the darkness.
> —**DESMOND TUTU**

Including Germany, I had been to eight countries in almost three months—New Zealand, Australia, Thailand, India, Lebanon, Greece, and Switzerland. Ten if you counted touching down in Egypt and crossing into Belgium on my bike ride. I baked and shared pie with hundreds of people. I survived India without getting sick, Lebanon without getting in a car accident, and Greece without landing in a hospital or getting mugged. I reunited with Marcus's family and tightened my grief belt by another notch. I had faced and overcome my greatest fears: loneliness, death, and losing loved ones while traveling. By this point I was operating in hovercraft mode, my body still physically in Europe but my mind airborne, already in flight back to the U.S.

I could have ended my trip after Aachen. It would have made the perfect narrative: Go around the world, make pie and promote goodwill, and end with the ultimate resolution of my love story with Marcus. But life doesn't fit into tidy, fairy-tale endings. It's full of plot twists and reversals of fortune, and, if you're lucky, the story continues. My story continued in Hungary.

Still, I had fought the temptation to skip this last stop, arguing with myself: *What more could I possibly learn or accomplish?* A lot, as it would turn out. Just as the heart has an infinite capacity to love, the mind and soul possess endless room to learn and grow. There is always something new to discover just around the corner as long as we remain open to it.

Stay open. Stay in the present. Stay curious.

To save time, I opted to fly to Budapest instead of taking the train, but I first had to take a train from Aachen to Dusseldorf, the closest airport.

Before boarding my flight bound for the eastern edge of the European Union, I went to the ladies' room for what Marcus called "a tactical pee," to preempt a later stop. While washing my hands, I noticed a woman on the floor rummaging through her open suitcase. On top of her pile of clothes were several bags of Trader Joe's pecans. I smiled, assuming she was going to use the nuts to make pie. I made this assumption because on my many trips to Stuttgart, I had filled my own suitcase with pecans. Pecans are not exotic to Americans, but the nuts are a novelty in Europe since pecan trees don't grow there. Ditto for cranberries, which I had hauled over to Germany for the American-style Thanksgiving dinners I made for Marcus's parents, and, one year, for the Kamers in Bern. They do celebrate a kind of Thanksgiving in Europe. In the German-speaking countries, it's called *Erntedankfest*. It's held in early October to honor the harvest, marked by parades, music, and dancing rather than football games, gluttony, and Black Friday. I wanted to strike up a conversation with the woman and inquire about her pirate's booty, but my flight was boarding, so I left her to her repacking.

Hungary, a member of the European Union, feels more Eastern European than Central, given its neighbors are Ukraine, Romania, Slovakia, Slovenia, Croatia, and Austria. Before World War II, Hungary was not a country, rather a kingdom, and had been one for 1,000 years, even after the Ottoman Empire's 150-year occupation ended. A desire to reclaim territory lost after World War I drew it into the Axis powers, and onto the wrong side of the Hitler's war. After surrendering to the Allies, the monarchy dissolved in 1946, and the country became part of the Soviet Union's Eastern Bloc, but it wasn't until 1989 that communism gave way to democracy.

Long before Hitler came along, however, Hungary was occupied by an equally evil thug, Attila the Hun. Unlike Hitler, he did not suffer from a Napoleon complex as he was built like the Hulk, but he, too, was a war-mongering murderer, plunderer of other lands, and destroyer of cities. At the height of his terror, circa 434 AD, he was known as the "Scourge of God" and considered public enemy number one of the Roman Empire. He made peace pacts only to break them, and was so blood thirsty and heartless he killed his own brother. When he died—ironically from choking on his own blood on his wedding night—his empire died with him.

Like a Marvel comic book villain, Attila the Hun's legend as the world's most notorious terrorist lives on, as does Hungary's poor choice to side with the Nazis, but a pendulum eventually swings to the other side—Bruce Banner always overcame his Hulk alter ego only to change back again—and apart from the uprising of a failed revolution in 1956, the country has been peaceful ever since the end of the war. At the time of my trip, Hungary ranked twenty-second on the Global Peace Index, a number considered "very high," as opposed to just "high." Pendulums, however, can be easily propelled and in the coming days that I was there and for weeks afterward, Hungary's peace standing would be called into question.

Budapest is the capital of Hungary. The one city is actually two—Buda and Pest (three if you include Óbuda or "Old Buda" on the western side)—divided by the Danube River. The Danube's source lies in Germany's Black Forest, where I'd been only a week earlier; just one more example of how every place and person is connected like one long thread in the weaving loom of life.

Upon landing in Budapest, I took a taxi to the home of my hosts, Ron and Ryan. Ron is an old family friend from Southeast Iowa. He used to be a Catholic priest, but after moving to San Francisco, he fell in love with a woman and left the priesthood to marry her. The marriage was lonely, he said, and they eventually divorced. Several years later he got remarried. To a man. Ryan.

When Ron learned I was setting off on a round-the-world trip, he extended an invitation to Budapest where he and Ryan ran their BudaBaB bed and breakfast out of their three-bedroom apartment. He also offered his kitchen and said he would organize a group of his friends for a pie class. I had never been to Hungary and I admit it wasn't high on my priority list of countries I wanted to visit—I was more interested in exploring Asia and Africa—but as I had insisted from the beginning, World Piece was not about the places; it was about the people. And Ron and Ryan's story fit with my cultural acceptance crusade, especially in the wake of the U.S. Supreme Court's approval of gay marriage as a civil right. Also fitting was Ron's connection to Iowa, to my family, and to my childhood.

I hadn't seen Ron since I was in seventh grade. Back then, he was one of those progressive 1970s priests who wore bell bottoms when he wasn't presiding over his guitar-music masses. He was still the lanky, soft-spoken man I remembered—minus his black shirt and clerical collar. Now he dressed more like a backpacker in baggy cargo pants, Birkenstocks, and a floppy hat, with a bike messenger bag slung across his shoulder. His hair, no longer brown but gray, was clipped short, as was his beard. What hadn't changed was his kindness, and when I stepped through the doorway of his apartment building, he welcomed me as warmly as if I were entering his church.

From the outside, Ron and Ryan's building was a fortress, its outer stone walls blackened by city soot. Inside, it was like a setting from a Stephen King novel, as we walked through a dark and cavernous foyer that could have passed for a torture chamber. When we reached the elevator, an ancient contraption of a thing, I told Ron, "I would be happy to take the stairs." He nodded toward my giant suitcase. "I mean, if not for this."

Imprisoned behind the bars of the metal cage, we could see the floors passing as we traveled higher, my morbid imagination spurred by the sound of cables creaking, grinding, and screeching as they strained against our weight. I had worried about death so much before my journey started. I had felt its cold whisper a few times during my travels. That mobile home barreling down in our lane on a New Zealand highway. The knife and stick fight in the Syrian refugee camp. The food poisoning—or whatever it was—in Greece. And now, on my last stop, my ninth country, here was a new one I hadn't anticipated: *Death by broken elevator cable.*

The instant the cage door opened wide enough to drag my luggage through, I leaped out onto terra firma. Ron slid around me to lead the way. All of the apartment entrances faced an open-air courtyard, accessible by a narrow wraparound walkway, barely passable without knocking over a few of the neighbor's potted plants, some of which I bumped before finally reaching Ron's apartment.

Ron's husband, Ryan, opened the door for us. I was dazzled by his good looks—white teeth, blue eyes, brown hair graying at the temples, and a gray goatee. Fourteen years Ron's junior, he could pass for Malibu Ken with an AARP membership. "Welcome," he said. "Let me show you your room. We'll let you get settled before we take the tram to the city center."

Although Hungary is a painter's landscape of rolling green beauty, Budapest isn't known for ample parks or green space. Its towering rows of sunlight-blocking buildings turn the streets into narrow, dark alleys, made darker still by the physical scars of war and neglect from its communist years. Relief from this claustrophobia comes in the form of the wide, blue swath of the Danube River, where steady traffic of tour boats flows in both directions. On the far sides of the banks, cornice-topped palaces span entire city blocks, interrupted only by cathedral domes and spires. It's the kind of Gothic architecture that inspires great art. Not in the way the rustic, little American Gothic House was the muse for Grant Wood's painting, but in a louder, more dramatic way as this stoic city has given birth to world-class composers. Looking across the water where ghosts of the past hovered in the evening air, I could almost hear a symphony accompanying the scene, though not the cheerful "Blue Danube Waltz," more like Bartók's soundtrack for *The Shining*.

I arrived when the country was celebrating its biggest, most important holiday: Saint Stephen's Day, named for the founder of the country—a kingdom then—a thousand years earlier. Festivals were taking place all over the city, including one called the Street of Hungarian Flavours.

Food stalls lined the Buda side of the Danube River with vendors hawking their traditional specialties. We made our way down the street, passing oil-filled woks big enough to contain an entire cow, with hunks of meat sizzling in the fat, heaping platters of sausages and grilled chicken legs, ham hocks hanging from tent poles, whole pigs roasting on a spit, and silver trays loaded with chocolate-dipped marzipan balls. A wooden trailer made to look like a cabin stood out among the makeshift folding tables of other vendors. The cooks inside were all men, dressed alike in Romanian red headscarves and black T-shirts that showed off their muscles. The sign above the window read "Királyi Kürtőskalács." *Kürtőskalács* (pronounced kurtos kalacs) are chimney cakes, made from yeasty dough wrapped around metal rods that spin over hot coals. The dough is basted with butter and sprinkled with sugar as it cooks. These chimney cakes, referred to as cones but shaped more like tubes, have been around since the 1600s, though are said to have originated in Transylvania in the twelfth century. If you ever wondered what Dracula devoured besides human blood, now you know.

We didn't feel like eating anything sweet, so we moved on to another booth serving *lapcsánka*—potato pancakes. The potatoes are grated, mixed with flour, egg, and garlic, then fried in an oil-filled skillet. Greasier and tastier than your basic hash browns, these were served on a waxed-paper-lined plate and smothered in sour cream.

We took our plates to a picnic table and as I watched the oil leak out from all sides of the pancake and pool on the paper, I must have furrowed my brow, because Ryan remarked, "Hungary is not good for your cholesterol."

I picked up my fork anyway, but Ron cautioned, "They're still a little hot."

Artery-clogging qualities aside, the potato pancakes had the same comfort-food effect as mac and cheese. I would have happily eaten more, but this was just a quick snack on our walking tour. Oddly, we would forego sampling the many other local specialties within reach only to dine on burritos at a Mexican restaurant later.

Leaving the food festival, we walked through the Castle Garden Bazaar where elephantine statues of World War I soldiers towered above us; several of the soldiers held the limp bodies of fallen comrades. Tourists posed for selfies with them, smiling at the camera, while the dead men, forever frozen in position, had nothing to smile about at all. The juxtaposition prompted one of those perplexing questions that kept cropping up in my travels: What message is this art supposed to convey and for what purpose? It's part of the Culture of Remembrance, yes, but once you're a few generations removed from the history it represents, does public art educate? Does it stir empathy and understanding? Or does it simply become reduced to a superficial snapshot in an endless scroll of Instagram posts?

We continued across the Chain Bridge, the first permanent bridge across the Danube, flanked by massive stone lions guarding the entrances on both shores. And that is how, like every other pedestrian crossing the bridge since its construction in 1849, we made our way from Buda to Pest.

On the Pest side, after dining on Mexican burritos, we boarded one of the yellow cars on tramline number 2—voted one of the most scenic tram rides in the world by *National Geographic*—for the return ride to Ron and Ryan's. I held onto the hanging strap and looked out the window, trying to take in every detail of the city as we slithered through it in the dusk. As the sky changed like a Renaissance painting in progress from shades of blue to pink, with brush strokes of lavender, my impression of Budapest changed along with it. What I initially saw as a cold, hard city became more beautiful by the minute, and the glow of streetlamps and lit storefronts only added more warmth and detail to the canvas.

A bend in the track took us close to the river, where the tram slowed just long enough to get a glimpse of another art installation. Lined up right at the edge of the river bank were multiple pairs of shoes. As usual, given my lack of education in world events, let alone art history, I didn't know what I was looking at—or its significance. In the fading light, what I saw wasn't entirely clear and I had seen it mostly out of my peripheral vision from a moving tram going twenty miles per hour. Maybe I had only imagined it. Once I learned more, I wished I had only imagined it.

Ryan, a medical social worker and college professor, explained. "It's called 'The Shoes on the Danube.' It's a memorial to the Jews who were made to take off their shoes at gunpoint before being shot and pushed into the river." As if that wasn't brutal enough he added, "They were all tied together so no one could escape."

And there it was again, the whiplash of war and peace, good and evil, right and incomprehensibly wrong.

Conceived by filmmaker Can Togay and sculpted by Gyula Pauer, the artist crafted sixty pairs of shoes out of iron in the styles of the mid-1940s, to commemorate the victims of the heinous acts carried out by the Arrow Cross Party. Women's high heels, men's loafers, work boots, and children's shoes represented the range of those killed; these sickos didn't discriminate against whom they targeted. They murdered 3,500 Hungarians, 800 of them Jews, keeping their shoes because they were of great value late in the war. The Arrow Cross Party didn't stop at the river; during its five short months in power, they killed an estimated 10,000 civilians and force-marched 80,000 innocents to concentration camps in Austria.

This story of cruelty was proof that public art could indeed stir empathy, so much so I felt sick to my stomach.

As we rolled on, away from the city center and the war memorials, I tried to focus on other things, like the street names and shop signs. I couldn't understand a word of Hungarian. Its spelling, with the double acute accents and umlauts going every which way over its letters, including fourteen vowels, didn't resemble any other language I had studied. And with consonants made up of multiple letters like dzs, cs, and sz, the alphabet was as intimidating as calculus. Hungarian, I was certain, would be even harder to learn than German. Even Ron and Ryan spoke only a few polite words of it. But to hear the woman's voice announcing each stop over the tram speakers, the way she delicately slurred the words and how she could make a "k" sound so soft and turn an "s-h" into white noise, was as soothing as an NPR newscast. But even the announcer's voice couldn't dredge my heart out of the river where it had plunged along with all those lost lives.

Back at the apartment, Ron and Ryan introduced me to their nightly routine, temporarily restoring my emotional balance. Starting in the kitchen, Ron scooped Neapolitan ice cream into big bowls. Then, in the living room, we settled onto the leather sofas to binge-watch *Good Witch* via bootleg access to the Hallmark Channel. I had never seen the show, but I became an instant fan of its positive message. The witch, Cassie Nightingale, runs a bed and breakfast, though in an old stone New England mansion, not in a pre-war-era apartment in post-communist Hungary like Ron and Ryan's B&B. Her guests always arrived in some state of crisis or discontent, but by the end of each episode, Cassie had solved everyone's problems using her intuitive magical powers, the bulk of which was kindness.

Would my own troubles be resolved by the time I left Hungary? Time was running out. It was the end of my first day out of only four that I would spend in Budapest, and less than a week before flying back to California. Would I get my Hollywood ending, where everything I had set out to answer was tied up with a happily-ever-after bow? Could I return to the U.S. with a heart that was no longer hurting? Would I have moved the needle even a nanometer toward a more peaceful world?

The answer was clearly no. Because I could not stop thinking about *those shoes*.

Luckily, I had pie, that simple combination of fruit, flour, butter, and sugar, to rescue me from my melancholy.

"All right, Bethie," Ron announced the next morning. "You ready to go shopping for your pie ingredients?" His shopping bags and wheelie cart were already parked by the door.

"Sure. Just give me one sec."

I chugged down the rest of my coffee and washed out the mug that read "Iowa: The end of the rainbow." Earlier, I had snapped a photo of a postcard on the refrigerator with the cheeky quote, "Iowa: Actually, we're just outside the middle of nowhere." The assortment of other Iowa memorabilia displayed on the fridge included black and white pictures—one of Ron as a young boy wearing overalls and bottle feeding a sheep; another of his family's farmhouse in snow—all fastened by a Jackson Pollock splatter of decorative magnets bearing slogans like "Iowa: A Place to Grow" and "We Love Quilts. Kalona, Iowa."

It could have been Doug's refrigerator door, though Doug's was so overloaded with photos and magnets you could barely find the door handle. I emailed the photo to Doug and he replied, "It looks like an Iowa refrigerator door." His was a dry humor and the brevity of his remark made me laugh.

Seeing these Iowa souvenirs in Hungary, on my last stop of my round-the-world journey was like a scene straight out of *Good Witch*. Was it a sign? Did Iowa hold a place in my future? I had to go back to pick up Jack—I couldn't wait to see that little rascal—but after that, I didn't know what my next move would be. After the day on Monika's farm in Switzerland, I talked of renting a farmhouse of my own, but I didn't really know, and the unknown is an uncomfortable place to inhabit. I had been too busy trying to save the world to think about it, but the end of my Summer of Suspended Disbelief was nearing. I felt a surge of angst, so I fished my mantra out of my psychological tool kit to control it.

Stay open. Stay in the present. Breathe. Buy pie ingredients.

The Great Hall Market is Budapest's biggest market. From the outside, with its Gothic architecture and colorful ceramic tile roof of green and orange, it looks like a smaller version of Mumbai's CST train station. Inside, it's a carnival of food stalls and souvenir shops.

"Jesus, Ron!" I blurted out as we entered. "Oh, sorry. I didn't mean to swear, but good god, this place is enormous! I would be lost here without you."

He laughed it off and said, "Come on. I want to take you to a special place."

I followed him and his wheelie cart as we pressed through the mass of fellow cart-toting shoppers. Sunlight filtered down through the third-story windows. Above the windows, orange canvas stretched like a circus tent across the ceiling. Stalls were jam-packed with paprika, Hungary's most prevalent cooking spice, the bright red flakes packaged in everything from plastic bags and jars to designer souvenir tins. Hanging above the paprika were the dried chili peppers the paprika spice comes from. Ristras—fat bundles of the red pods tied to string—dangled in numbers too many to count.

Hungary is famous for its paprika, but the plant (and spice) originated in Central Mexico. It was another one of those garam masala stories I'd been learning along the way, how we can't accuse others of cultural appropriation when the origins of everything—pretty much every single thing—are connected to another place.

As overwhelming as the market was, food and wares were grouped together by type to make shopping relatively easy. Besides paprika and peppers, the bulk of vendors were selling cheese, sausages and salami, breads, noodles, pots and pans, and, the thing we had come for: produce. Pyramids of grapes, blackberries, watermelons, cherries, apricots, peaches, and apples filled the horizon with an edible rainbow, their combined scents pervading the hall with a sweet, earthy, pleasant pungency. But as we came upon the endless summer of fruit, Ron kept walking—all the way to the strudel section. In other words, pie!

Rétes is the Hungarian name for this renowned pie-like pastry with filling wrapped burrito-style inside a thin, flaky crust.

"My favorite is cherry," Ron said. "What would you like?"

"It's hard to decide," I replied. This was the Baskin-Robbins of strudel shops with too many choices: curd cheese, dill-curd cheese, apricot, sour cherry, pumpkin-poppy seed, apple, apple-cinnamon, plum, cabbage, potatoes, and various combinations of them all. I scanned the miles of strudel lined up end-to-end in rows.

"I'll go with apple," I finally said. Apple was my baseline for pie tasting and I was always surprised at the many ways it could vary.

Like paprika—and Indian samosas coming from Iran, and American pie being born in Egypt—strudel's origin is not native to Hungary. Since early versions of *rétes* resembled baklava, it's likely it came from the Turks when Hungary was ruled by the Ottoman Empire. Previously made with layers of dough, baked in a sheet pan, and served in slices, it was not the familiar tube-shaped pastry we know today.

Hungary isn't only famous for strudel. It's also a cake-lover's paradise. Its many pastry shops display cakes too pretty to eat. Later that afternoon we would sample a few—because being in Budapest and not eating cake would be like going to Napa Valley and not drinking wine. It would feel like we had taken a time machine back to the Belle Époque, sitting at a café beneath chandeliers and gold-flake wallpaper, where we would share cakes six layers high, creamy, marzipan-filled wedges iced to within an inch of their lives. *Death by frosting.* While impressive in their artistry—Samart in Bangkok would certainly admire them—the cakes had a style over substance issue. Using my criteria for judging pie contests, which comes down to the inability to stop myself from taking another bite, I wouldn't give the Hungarian cakes blue ribbons.

The strudel at the Great Market Hall, however, was what my friend Jane calls "WTC"—worth the calories. Laced with raisins, walnuts, and cinnamon, the apple filling was more complex and spicier than my version of apple pie, and I was used to a thicker crust, but did I want more? Yes. Yes, I did.

When we finished our strudel and our shopping, we dragged Ron's wheelie bag, heavy with apples and peaches, onto the streetcar and back to the apartment, again risking our lives by taking the elevator.

The next day, I led the pie class for Ron and Ryan's friends. The first to arrive was Kat, a young American woman with a job in finance. Then came Sandra and Larry, an American couple transplanted from New York City. I was introduced to the rest as they filtered in: Marguerite, a red-headed American woman who worked for philanthropist George Soros; Marguerite's friend Andras, who was half Canadian, half Hungarian; Philip from England; and Philip's Irish friend Siobhan. It wasn't a group of local Hungarians, a concession to my goal of total cultural immersion in each country, but pie is pie and people are people, no matter where they're from and what language they speak. And had I not been reminded in every place I'd been how every culture is really a blend of cultures, and how every blood line can be traced to common ancestors? So, in fact, this mixed group did fit with my peace mission, and the variety of nationalities counteracted Prime Minister Viktor Orbán's nationalistic desire "to preserve a Hungarian Hungary." Plus, I figured since Marguerite worked for Soros—whose Open Society Foundations promotes freedom of expression, accountable government, and societies that promote justice and equality—that had to count for something.

With the blinds closed to keep the summer's butter-melting heat at bay, we proceeded to make a mess out of the BudaBaB kitchen. Flour dust floated in the air, sugar turned the tabletop into a white sand beach, and slimy peach and apple peels landed on the floor next to Marguerite's Shih Tzu who, uninterested in the free snacks, slept under a chair. Ron and his friends lined a ragtag collection of pie plates, casserole dishes, and ramekins with dough and constructed an art gallery's worth of pies, while Ryan circled the room taking photos. It was another successful pie class for the books—the last one of my trip—but I was too busy supervising to feel anything other than fully engaged in the present. For once I didn't need a mantra to stay there.

"Bethie," Ron called over to me. "Let's get a picture of this to send to your mom and dad." He pulled his pie out of the oven and held it up, grinning at me and my camera, his joy radiating out like the steam off the pie.

While everyone else had used my angel cookie cutter to decorate their pie, I noticed that Ron had carved a pitchfork in his as a nod to my pie stand. "Oh, Ron, I love it!" His hand-carved tribute to me— and my life of pie—spoke louder than words.

Inside BudaBaB, there was lively chatter and laughter, but outside the thick walls, just over one hundred miles away on Hungary's border, something decidedly less joyful was brewing. My journey had coincided with the European migrant crisis of 2015. Europe was seeing its largest flow of asylum seekers in decades. Numbers would eventually peak at 1.3 million, with about half of them coming from Afghanistan, Iraq, and—no surprise—Syria, where conflicts old and new created circumstances so dire, people were willing to gamble their lives in leaky boats, in airless freight trucks, or on foot because anything was safer than staying put. But the safer places, including countries like Hungary, didn't want them—at least Viktor Orbán didn't want them. Two days after I left Hungary, Orbán would close its train stations to keep migrants from passing through on their way to Germany. It would seal its borders with Serbia and Croatia, and spend over a hundred million euros on razor-wire fencing. Amnesty International would later call on the EU to hold Hungary accountable for violating international law and for its failure to protect human rights. And yet, surprisingly, Hungary's ranking on the Global Peace Index remained unchanged, which is why the true definition of world peace is not limited to the absence of war, rather the wellbeing of all people—all of them.

I followed news of the exploding crisis closely, increasingly frustrated by my inability to do a damn thing about it, but Saint Ron saved me from getting sucked into a vortex of despair. "Bethie," he said, "I know what you need. I'm taking you to the waters."

"You mean like Lourdes?"

"You'll see," he said, his eyes twinkling with mischief.

Water is as great a healer as pie, and thanks to Ron, a soak in Budapest's famed Széchenyi (pronounced say-chay-nee) Thermal Bath, the largest medicinal spa in Europe, awaited. Unlike Germany's mineral baths where nudity is the norm, swimsuits are required at Széchenyi, thankfully, given I was with the former priest I've known since I was eight.

The bathhouse, a hundred years old in age, is palatial in size, and goldenrod in color. With fifteen indoor and outdoor pools, plus a variety of steam rooms, saunas, and icy plunge pools, it's an aquatic Disneyland with the crowds to match. The pools were packed with bobbing heads, and the chaises, hundreds of them, were occupied by sunbathers.

We started in the hottest of the big outdoor pools, where I floated around trying to count how many different languages I heard spoken: French, German, English, Hungarian, Hebrew, Korean, Japanese, Spanish, and a few I couldn't identify. I came up with more than ten—certain that the term "melting pot" originated in a hot pool like this one. Our bodies may have been a variety of colors, shapes, and sizes, but together we were a commonwealth of sugar cubes, our individual appearances, differences, opinions, and issues dissolving in the warm liquid. The solution to world peace was right here, within reach of my pruned fingertips: Get world leaders and warlords to hold their negotiations in these United Nations of steaming mineral waters—and serve them pie afterward. Forget titles and money, material acquisitions and land grabs, it's nature that nurtures us. To achieve peace, we just need to relax, to take time to feel good in our bodies so that the mind and spirit can follow.

As for me, after a few hours at the spa, I felt refreshed enough to do another circle around the planet—almost.

I should have gone back for another soak the next day to be spared another heart-wrenching history tour. Instead, on my last day in Budapest, Ron, Ryan, and I ventured farther into their neighborhood, the Jewish Quarter, threading our way through its brick streets and war memorials. Plaques on the sides of buildings declared "People used to live here," leaving off the self-evident second half of the sentence: *until Nazis killed them.* Square blocks of concrete with brass plates on top were embedded in the sidewalks. The plates were engraved with the names of even more victims—people who had no relatives to keep their memories alive, acknowledged and immortalized only by these name tags, which also listed their birthdate, year of deportation, and cause of death: eugenics, euthanasia, concentration camp, or extermination camp. *Stolpersteine,* they're called—stumbling stones (a project of German artist Gunter Demnig)—and there are thousands of them dotting Budapest's pavement.

We stopped at the Jewish Ghetto Memorial Wall, filled with peepholes. I pressed my forehead against the stone wall and peered through the tiny openings, surprised to see 3-D vintage photos of people who had once inhabited this neighborhood before being sent to their deaths.

I didn't know how much more of this *Weltschmerz* I could take before my heart was damaged beyond repair. It's said that humans have equal capacity for kindness and cruelty, that in each one of us there is an angel and a demon. But where are the checks and balances? And how do we keep the balance tipped in favor of the good? Aren't we smart enough, and evolved enough, to stop ourselves from following some psychopathic despot's orders to torture or kill our own friends and neighbors? Why don't we pause and say, "Hey, wait a minute. This is not right," instead of acting like blind and barbaric sheep? And it's still happening long after World War II. I often think of Rwanda and still don't understand how it could have happened, or how it keeps happening in Myanmar, Cambodia, Bosnia, Darfur, Iraq, and more. Of all the perplexing questions on my journey, these were by far the most troubling.

Among the sobering relics of a grisly past, a sunnier trend called "ruin bars" has sprung from the ashes. As the name suggests, these are bars, more like hipster cafés, operating in the remains of the buildings that bombs didn't completely obliterate.

I followed Ron and Ryan into Szimpla Kert, the first and one of the most popular ruin bars in Budapest. Remaining true to the ruins theme, the establishment had no roof for its broken walls to hold up. Once inside, an onslaught of color and whimsy distracted from the history that surrounds it. Christmas lights glowed and mirrored disco balls sparkled. Geometric-patterned flags and pennants, strung across the sky, flapped overhead. A mosaic mermaid made from flattened bottle caps marked the women's bathroom door. The shell of an old East German Trabant car was outfitted with a table and chairs. Gnomes on swings hung from crossbeams. And, of course, there were people drinking beer. It was another world, somewhere between Willy Wonka's Chocolate Factory and a Grateful Dead concert.

Deeper in the menagerie, a potted tree caught my eye, its tall and skinny trunk held up by a bamboo pole with white paper tags tied to its delicate branches. I went over to get a closer look while Ron and Ryan searched for a place to sit. At the base of the tree a laminated sign read "Wish Tree for Peace."

> *Make a wish. Write it down on a card or on a piece of paper. Tie around a branch of a wish tree. Ask your friends to do the same. Keep wishing until the branches are covered with wishes.*
> —*YOKO 2014*

The idea for the tree came from Yoko Ono's IMAGINE PEACE project with the hope that our collective consciousness will work its magic. Like the TM meditators in Fairfield, Iowa believe: Put the positive energy out there, focus on it hard enough, and you will manifest it.

The tree was sponsored by Discover Peace in Europe, a project that established "peace trails" in seven European cities, including one in Budapest. The routes, outlined on a map connecting the sites to visit, are designed to draw awareness to human rights, democracy, and peace and the stories of people, past and present, who have made an impact. While the mission is to emphasize peacemaking efforts rather than memorialize the destructive effects of war—think positive reinforcement instead of negative—Budapest's Peace Trail includes a stop at The Shoes on the Danube.

Those shoes. I would never forget them. No one should ever forget them. No one should ever commit such evil crimes against humanity again. We can't change the past, but we can choose our future actions. We always have a choice. We can (and should) choose peace. Why is that so hard for us?

I didn't tie my own wish for peace onto the branches—I was living and breathing and baking my wish for it every day—but I did post a few pictures of the tree on social media. About a week later, I got a message from a woman in Wisconsin, Deb Nies of Waunakee.

She had seen my photo, she said, and it had given her an idea. A pear tree in her yard had been struck by lightning and suffered a lot of damage. She had contemplated cutting it down. Instead, she found a new purpose for it—as a wishing tree.

"I put up a sign and set out a bucket of tags and markers for passersby," she wrote. "The next thing I knew the tree was filling up with wishes. I read them and they were so meaningful. 'I wish for my mom to get cured of cancer.' 'I wish for my husband to come home safe from the Middle East.' And 'I wish to never get bullied again.' My wounded pear tree has become a beacon of hope."

The tree and Deb's effort grew so popular the local news did a feature story and it even got its own Facebook page.

On the way back to Ron and Ryan's—for one last evening of ice cream and an episode of *Good Witch*—I saw a promotion for TOMS Shoes plastered on the window of a store. In another one of those well-timed messages from whatever spirit guides were traveling with me, the ad read, "See the world. Change the world. What if the simple acts you choose today could profoundly shape the future of someone you've never met? The world is up to us. This is your summer. Make it matter."

This was my summer. In my own small way, I made it matter.

CHAPTER 14

The Homecoming

What can you do to promote world peace?
Go home and love your family.
— **MOTHER TERESA**

AUGUST 27: FRANKFURT AIRPORT

After 3 months, 30,000 miles, 10 countries, and 211 pies, I was finally heading back to the United States. The world is round, like a pie, and having nearly completed a full circle around the globe, I was counting the hours and minutes until my flight departed for Los Angeles and the Great Homecoming.

"Life's a voyage that's homeward bound," wrote Herman Melville.

But where is home? I asked myself as I lugged my bags through the Frankfurt *Flughafen* and browsed the duty-free shops, sniffing bottles of perfume to kill time. *Where am I going to live?*

When I finally boarded the plane and fastened my seatbelt, I was a twelve-hour flight away from completing my circumnavigation. I had stuck it out to my end date; I didn't give up and had given it my all. I should have been elated. So why was I so confused? so numb? so hungry? I would have given anything for a cheeseburger.

To escape my busy mind and avoid falling asleep on the shoulder of the woman next to me, I started in on my queue of films. Out of the hundreds of choices on Lufthansa's menu, I ended up with *Eat, Pray, Love*; *Wild*; and *Under the Tuscan Sun*. All three films, I realized, were about independent, single women—all privileged white women, I acknowledge—traveling into the unknown, not unlike me. We'd all had our pain, our suffering, our quests to move past it, our miles traveled, our obstacles encountered along the way, our resilience. We were heroines on similar but different journeys.

We are all, each and every one of us—regardless of color or privilege—the heroes of our own stories. Some of us travel farther or take bigger risks. Some of us go to ashrams and eat pasta. Some of us hike trails. Some of us renovate houses. Some of us bake pie. But I know not to compare my story, my dreams, my actions, my decisions, my accomplishments, or my failures to anyone else's. As my sister reminded me that day I was by the pool in Thailand, we are all on our own paths, on our own uniquely personal journeys. And mine, at least this part of it, was about to come to an end. To every ending there's a new beginning, but what the hell was I going to do next? The question that had niggled me the entire trip around the planet continued to recirculate in my mind like the air on the plane.

In between films, I checked the flight map, tracking our progress as we followed the earth's arc—Greenland, Newfoundland, Medicine Hat, Montana, Las Vegas—covering the 5,771 miles (9,288 kilometers) in a matter of hours, as compared to early travelers who spent months at sea. I sometimes wonder if I would have been one of those intrepid explorers, though with my predisposition to seasickness where the mere thought of being on a ship makes me nauseous, maybe not.

Just before we landed, when the in-flight entertainment ended and before the U.S. immigration instructions began, an advertisement came on. In a deep baritone, its narrator boomed, "Home can be a house, a town, a country, or the whole world. It's up to you." It was as if the universe wanted to validate my nagging question. But through a Warsteiner beer commercial? Really?

We were so close to LAX, I could make out the San Gabriel Mountains, the Hollywood Park racetrack, the specks of blue swimming pools dotting the brown landscape. I was so impatient to land I wanted to jump out the window, so I played some music to quell my restlessness. I pushed my earbuds in as deep as they would go and pressed play, only to find that the self-help hotline to the

universe was still connected when Sarah McLachlan started singing
"Drifting." I was sure she was talking to me when I listened to her
words.

"You have been drifting for so long," trying to fill up your
emptiness with the company of strangers, she crooned. *Maybe I had
been.* But, she continued, there are people below "who love you and
they're ready for you to come home."

People below—on the ground that I could almost touch. *Can't
this plane land any faster?*

At last, engines thrusting, rubber burning black streaks on the
tarmac, and passengers clapping, we coasted along the LAX runway.
My heart thumped louder than the Jack Johnson song blasting in my
ears as we taxied toward the gate—and the same terminal I departed
from three months earlier. When I left, I had the trepidation of an
eight-year-old going off to camp; coming back, I was eighteen again
with the giddiness I felt upon returning from college after living away
from my family for the first time. There was more to these emotions
than the obvious discomfort of setting off into the unknown, versus
the relief of returning to the comfort and safety of what's familiar.
I am lucky to have been born to nurturing parents who gave me
both the foundation of security and the freedom to fly. Parents who
trusted me, who encouraged me every time I left, and welcomed me
back to their nest whenever I needed. No matter how far I went or
for how long, I always looked forward to returning to them.

I put my earbuds away and switched my phone out of airplane
mode. Once I got a signal, my phone dinged so many times, other
passengers turned to look. It was the sound of hitting the jackpot
on a slot machine, except that the prize was a message—multiple
messages—from my mom telling me she and my dad were waiting
in baggage claim. My parents, over whom I had bawled my eyes out
when they dropped me off three months earlier, were there to pick
me up upon my return. They hadn't died. No one had died. Then
again, even if I had been given a crystal-ball guarantee that everyone
would be okay in my absence, it wouldn't have changed anything. I
still would have cried when I left.

I zipped through immigration—nothing to declare—and rolled my suitcase past customs for the last time. God, I would not miss dragging that thing around! Popping out through the security doors, I scanned the hundreds of faces lined up along the barricade and spotted my mom. She looked so petite among the mass of tightly packed bodies and tall chauffeurs holding name signs. Her hair, dark and short, had been cut into a spunky new style. Her outfit, a yellow jumpsuit, flats, and a flowered shoulder bag all matched. Yep, that was my mom.

Once we found each other, we locked on with the lunar force of a tide. The recognition of a mother and her offspring isn't just visual—it's visceral. I saw my mom's brown eyes change from expectant to shining to misty, and we both teared up with relief, releasing the underlying anxiety we had each been holding onto for the past fifteen weeks.

Thank god, you are home safely! she said without words.

You're still alive and you're okay! I conveyed through my tears.

Our silent-film moment dissolved, replaced by the full volume of airport noise that nearly drowned out my mom's voice when she said, "Come on. Dad is over here."

My dad pushed through the crowd as he saw us approach, his blue eyes sparkling from beneath his seaman's cap, his smile bright enough to light up the entire Tom Bradley terminal. Without any regard for the people trying to get around us, he grabbed me in a bear hug. "Welcome back, Boo!"

Whatever stress, sadness, and sickness I had endured throughout my journey, the power of this reunion—and this love—made every bit of it worthwhile.

Before leaving the airport, we took a few selfies—like the "victory shots" I always did for my pie classes. I studied the photos later. My parents looked the same: healthy, happy, and vibrant. Which was a tremendous relief given their skin cancer surgeries over the summer. Their scars were already healing, their prognoses positive, and neither looked worse for the wear. In fact, they looked better than I remembered.

Did I look the same? My hair was a little longer. I had lost maybe a pound or two, though that could have been wishful thinking, and my face looked tired, though that could have been from the dehydration of the flight.

The bigger question was, Was I the same person as I was when I left? A young woman I met during my travels insisted, "This must be a life-changing trip for you." I paid lip service to her by nodding in agreement, but inside I shook my head at her naiveté. No, this trip wasn't the stuff that changes lives. It is not life changing to spend a summer getting on and off airplanes, staying in people's homes and a few nice hotels, and making pies with some really nice people. Life changing is when your husband drops dead at forty-three. Life changing is when you have to bury your angelic terrier's body, ripped open and half-eaten by a coyote. Life changing, even if less tragic, is having to move out of the tourist-attraction home you so dearly loved after you inadvertently became the attraction. (Never mind there were snakes living in it.)

I can think of many adjectives for my World Piece mission: interesting, informative, enlightening, educational, exhausting. But did it really change me? The more important question was, Did it change the world?

Paul Paynter, from the Yummy Fruit Company in New Zealand, had emailed me a few weeks earlier, while I was in Germany, and weighed in with his own insights to this. "I thought from the start that you had this trip 'arse about face' as we'd crudely say in NZ. That is, it was never going to be about what you could teach the world so much as what the world could teach you."

He was right. I had learned so much, but how was I going to make sense of all that I'd gathered? What did it all mean? What difference did it make?

My questions were partly answered in a comment left on one of my blog posts. "The reward for effort is sometimes not realized until long after the work is done," Bill Jabas wrote. "Like a farmer, you've sown a seed and somewhere it's growing."

I stayed with my parents in Redondo Beach for three days, basking in their love and in their hot tub, dining on my mom's homemade meals of creamed tuna on biscuits, and drinking my dad's three-olive martinis. I was in LA. With my parents. I was home. Sort of. But not really.

Jack was still back in Iowa on Doug's farm. My trip wouldn't be complete until I was reunited with my dog. Restlessness, anticipation, and jet lag gnawed at me until I was once again airborne—headed for the Midwest.

I passed the hours of my flight staring out the window, watching the landscape change. Flying across the Mojave Desert, I was in Lebanon. The Rocky Mountains took me back to the Swiss Alps. And when we were above Iowa, a green and yellow patchwork of circles, squares, and stripes, with towers of cumulus standing in for snow-capped mountains, I was in New Zealand. There is no place on the earth that is as foreign as we think.

The Quad Cities International Airport was no LAX so it was easy to spot Doug who was waiting behind the TSA checkpoint. He stood over to the side to avoid blocking the path of passengers, such were his good manners. I instantly recognized him by his smile and plaid short-sleeve shirt. As I moved toward him, his face, freckled from a lifetime of sun and a heritage of German-Irish blood, turned as red as his hair, which was neatly combed and parted on the side. His muscles, built by baling hay, strained the seams of his sleeves. He really was Opie Taylor, but with bigger biceps.

He stepped toward me and we hugged like a pair of seventh graders; awkward, self-conscious, and brief—and interrupted by my carry-on swinging around, slugging him in the ribs.

"Sorry," I said, stepping back.

He reached for the strap of my bag and said, "Let me get that for you," lifting it like it weighed no more than a soy bean and slinging it over his recently repaired rotator cuff.

"Is Jack in the car?" I asked.

"No. I wanted to video tape your reunion," Doug said. "Better to do that at the farm where you have more room."

"Oh . . . okay," I said, calculating the two-hour drive back to his place.

In the car, a bouquet of wildflowers—delicate lavender petals and slender green stems—sat in a canning jar in the cup holder. Propped up next to it was a "Welcome Home" card with a gift certificate for a massage inside.

"I thought you might need it," he said at the exact same time I said, "That's exactly what I need!"

We stopped for milkshakes and talked the entire two hours back to his house, about his crops, about the countries I'd been to, and about the weekend plans. My return coincided with Doug's annual pig roast, a three-day gathering of family dinners, a canoe outing, and, the main event, a party for two hundred people with live music, potluck dishes, and pork. I had attended it the previous year and it was as much a cultural experience as any I'd experienced in the past months of international travel. I may have grown up in Iowa, but I had always lived in cities. Even after living in the American Gothic House, which was surrounded by corn fields, farm life was still foreign to me.

When we turned off the highway onto Doug's road, the lull of smooth pavement gave way to the loud crunch of tires on gravel, a change of tune that always excited Jack and Daisy when we visited the farm during those months Doug and I had briefly dated. I would roll down the windows for them, laughing at how their noses twitched from the fragrance of natural fertilizer spread on the fields. Farmers have a name for this pig stench: the smell of money.

A mile down the gravel, Doug pulled into his driveway, passing under the canopy of maple trees, their leaves the size of dinner plates, their trunks a hundred rings thick. Mali, Doug's spaniel mix, raced alongside the car. We left my bags in the back of the SUV and I petted Mali's belly when she offered it to me, while Doug went to open the door for my terrier who was lunging at the glass, barking to be let out.

Jack ran up to me, but paused for a moment, taking stock of the situation. Three months was by far the longest we'd ever been apart. Surely, he hadn't forgotten who I was. Once he got reoriented to the fact that, yes, it was his mom who was squealing and crying and cooing, he returned the sentiments, licking my face, batting me with his tail, and whimpering with emotion. I scooped him up and buried my face in his fur, leaving it pressed against him, my lines of tension dissolving like the contrails in the sky above. This is what I had been waiting for, this reunion, like the one with my parents in LA, only this time I was the mother and Jack was my child. He wriggled out of my arms and tore around the yard in circles—the Ferrari of dogs— shedding the happy energy that couldn't be contained in his fifteen-pound body, while I kept laughing and crying and wiping my nose on my arm. Doug captured it all on camera.

Inside, Doug's house smelled of the nineteenth century. The combination of faded wallpaper, crown molding, and uneven, creaky wood floors made it every bit as quirky and charming as the American Gothic House, but without the tourists. But what I first noticed, besides the grandmotherly scent, was how clean it was. There was not a speck of dust or cat hair in sight. And the tile around the bathtub had been freshly caulked. The last time I had seen it, the cracks were as wide as the Grand Canyon and black with mold. The kitchen floors had been scrubbed free of coffee stains and paw prints. But more noticeable than the bachelor pad's sanitation, was the apple pie on the table.

"You made that?" I asked.

"You taught me well."

I looked closer at the decoration made with extra dough on top. His original design had melted during baking, but it appeared to be three-quarters of a circle with a missing piece. "Is that my World Piece logo?"

"Yes, ma'am. I thought we could have it for dessert. I'm making cheeseburgers for supper."

"Cheeseburgers? I've been craving one since somewhere over Greenland."

A few days after arriving on the farm, the festivities began. The weekend kicked off with a Friday night fish fry. Guests began arriving from Wisconsin, Oklahoma, Kansas, and Chicago, filling up the guest rooms, setting up tents in the yard, and hooking up their RVs to the electrical shed next to the barn.

One of the RVs belonged to my friend Don, my former neighbor at the American Gothic House. A Korean War vet, he was in his eighties, widowed, and arthritic with an Archie Bunker mindset, but underneath his cloak of bigotry was a heart of gold. He had come to my aid too many times to count, clearing my sidewalks after a snowstorm, towing my Mini Cooper out of the mud, tilling my garden, and protecting me from my toxic neighbors, dubbed The Binoculars for all their spying on the activity at my house—activity that was as constant as their calls to the sheriff. Don was integral to my well-being in Eldon, and when he and his wife moved to their son's house an hour south, my sense of security went with him.

"You're coming on the river with us, Don," I insisted.

"No, Hon," he argued. "I can't with these old hips."

"We can go in a canoe together. All you have to do is sit in the front and I'll paddle."

"You gonna toss me overboard?"

"Very funny. Just come."

"Oh, all right. I suppose I could."

There were more than twenty of us on the outing, all suited up in life jackets and sunhats. We brought sandwiches and cookies and pop, though some, like myself, would call it soda.

"You should put your feet in the water, Don," I said as soon as we launched. "Just roll up your pant legs."

I was pretty good at talking him into things, and as I watched him take off his shoes and hike up the cuffs of his striped bib overalls I smiled with the satisfaction of winning another round.

"You should put on some sunscreen," I urged when I saw his skin. His feet were size-ten vampires; they hadn't seen daylight in years.

"I don't need none of that," he said. "I survived all these years without it."

"Don . . ."

He waved me off.

I let it go, because as soon as he dipped his feet in the river, dangling them over the sides of the canoe into the current, I could see his body relax. Even with his back to me, I could tell he was happy, the happiest I had seen him since his wife, Shirley, died two years earlier. To take off his shoes was to shed a thousand pounds of grief. I kept paddling, leaving him to enjoy his catfish-filled foot spa.

The Des Moines River was no glacier-fed Aare like in Switzerland. Instead of a pristine, light-blue gusher, it is murky brown and lumbers along more slowly than a tractor. There were no people worshipping in its shallows like on the sacred Ganges in India, and no barges or tour boats cruising up and down it like on the Danube in Hungary. Humble and deserted as this rural Iowa river may be, it flows into the Mississippi, which travels down to the Gulf of Mexico to the Caribbean Sea, which connects to the Atlantic Ocean, which is a part of all oceans and where all the rivers of the planet merge. It was another reminder of our interconnectedness. You can be canoeing through the cornfields of Lee County and simultaneously be conjoined with the entire world through a network of waterways.

We were on the water for four hours, with Doug pointing out every tree, plant, bird, and cloud formation along the way. "There's a bald eagle's nest," he said, pointing to a pile of sticks high in a tree. "That's a cottonwood tree," he added. He pointed to a bluff. "That's where the vultures roost," he said.

We stopped only once on a sand bar to stretch our legs, hunt for arrowheads, and swim. Don, too stiff to get out, stayed in the canoe drinking the Budweiser someone brought over to him.

Don and I were the last ones to reach the take-out where Doug's canoe trailer was parked, so we held onto a half-sunken tree limb as we waited for our turn. The second we pulled up to the boat ramp, a pitstop crew of friends descended on us, grabbing our bow and dragging us far enough out of the water to step on dry land. I jumped out, but Don could barely move. A Tin Man with a heart but no oil, he turned his rusty body slowly, and used his arms to pull his legs out of the canoe. He must have been aching terribly, but he didn't complain.

"Let me help you," I said. "Hand me your shoes."

I kneeled on the ground and took one of his feet, pruned and pink. I didn't tease him about his sunburn like I normally would. I just focused on the task and tried not to cringe at his long toenails.

I didn't hear Doug approach, but there he was, kneeling by my side and reaching for Don's other shoe. "You did great out there, Don," he said. Then, with his rough farmer's hands, he slid the black leather orthopedic sneaker onto Don's craggy, sunburnt foot as gracefully as if it were Cinderella's slipper. It took my breath away.

Doug wasn't Opie Taylor; he was Prince Charming!

How did I not see it before? He had always been kind to me and shown up for me, but to see him display the same care and compassion for my friend, an old man with unkempt toenails? It opened my eyes. And my heart.

Doug turned to me and smiled—as if he could see inside me, all the way into the wounded, troubled parts of me. He didn't have to say the words; I could feel them. "I'm here. I've always been here for you."

Grant Wood once said, "I had to go to France to appreciate Iowa." But me? I had to go all the way around the world only to find, like in Paulo Coelho's *The Alchemist*, that the treasure was always right there, in the place where I started. I just needed to "see the pyramids of Egypt" first. (If Cairo hadn't been so hazy when I changed planes there, I actually would have seen them.) But I couldn't have learned any of that from an artist's quote or a novel. I had to set forth on my own journey and clear some obstacles. I had been holding onto the psychic baggage of my past wounds so long it had become part of my identity. Until Marcus showed up in Bangkok and whispered in my ear. Until I visited Marcus's homeland of Germany and said my final goodbyes to him in that Roetgen pool. Until I made it back to LA and made sure my parents were in "good order," as my dad liked to say. Only then was I ready and able to open up to new love and a new life.

Doug, who has the patience and faith of a farmer, had never given up on me. I was just lucky that he was waiting for me, and that he welcomed me back into his life, into his home, into his bed.

So yes, my trip was life-changing after all. Just not in the way I expected.

The sun disappeared behind a thousand acres of corn stalks, leaving a pink dusk to settle over the farm. At last, the long, late-summer day relented and the sky turned black, giving the stars and constellations their chance to shine. The heat lingered and the air was so thick with humidity you could lean on it. Fireflies hovered above the grass, blinking like the candles that flickered on the picnic tables. Cows mooed in the distance. Bats swooped down on mosquito patrol. The younger kids swung in the hammock, while the older ones played cornhole. Beer flowed from the kegs set up next to the hay wagon where people sat on hay bales. Neighbors and friends from near and far waited in line to fill their plates with potato salad, macaroni salad, bean salad, marshmallow salad, and cabbage salad, along with juicy slabs of roasted pork cut straight off the pig that had been smoking since dawn.

But upstaging all of this was the pie.

I had offered to give a pie class to Doug's relatives and houseguests. Although it added a fun bonus activity to the weekend festivities, the ulterior motive was to get help making pies for the pig party. I had expected three or four people to show up, but so many more wanted to participate, we ended up with twenty pies—strawberry rhubarb, apple, apple crumble, peach, peach crumble, key lime, and chess—the same ones I made in the American Gothic House. Without realizing it, I had recreated the Pitchfork Pie Stand for the party. In Doug's granary, I set up a table in front of his rock-climbing wall, next to his buckets, shovels and pitchforks—pitchforks used for straw, not for posing in front of a little white house with a Gothic-style window. The best part of the effort—and it was a lot of effort—was that I wasn't selling the pies; everything was free.

I thought my World Piece trip had ended in LA, or with my reunion with Jack, but here I was, sharing homemade pie and its of message of kindness, generosity, and love. I studied the faces of all the people eating it—farmers, bankers, mechanics, schoolteachers, physical therapists, college students, young moms, grandparents. All around me, everyone was smiling and nodding. Some of them came back for seconds, even thirds.

"This is really good," I heard again and again. "Thank you for making it."

"It wasn't just me," I insisted. "It was a community effort." And it was.

When I wasn't serving pie—or checking on Don who could barely walk after the canoe outing—I was holding hands with Doug, greeting guests as if we had always been a couple. We were a team, seamlessly transitioning into a pair of old work boots that had been reunited after one went missing. We were sturdy and comfortable, the leather of our lives softened by wear.

I settled into a lawn chair next to Doug to eat and listen to the music. The band, using the porch as a stage, strummed their fiddles and guitars, ignoring the hooting owls and barking dogs as they launched into a folksy cover of "Stand by Me."

I looked over at Doug, his foot tapping to the beat, his eyes glistening brighter than the string of garden lights. He looked back at me with a grin. "This is our song," he said.

I smiled back at him before digging my fork into my slice of peach crumble. "And this is our pie."

As I took a bite, I closed my eyes to savor the sweetness, not just of the peaches and brown sugar, but of everything—everyone, every experience, and every pie—that brought me to this place. I sat back in my lawn chair and, finally—after all those months, all those miles, all those pies, all the effort, all the confusion, coincidences, disappointment, joy, frustrations, and happy surprises—I exhaled.

EPILOGUE

> He is happiest, be he king or peasant,
> who finds peace in his home.
> —JOHANN WOLFGANG VON GOETHE

As soon as I settled in at Doug's farmhouse, I started working on this book, but life—and death—interrupted me.

A year and a half after the surgeries my dad had while I was in India and Greece, his melanoma metastasized. The cancer spread into every organ, bone, and lymph node of his body, everywhere except for his brain. He was given his terminal diagnosis while I was in Washington, DC, marching in my pink pussyhat along with four million other people in protest over a newly elected leader whose rhetoric and behavior ran counter to my peace mission.

Upon my return from the Women's March, Doug once again took over Jack's care so I could fly from Iowa to LA and spend the last three weeks of my dad's life with him. I made him banana cream pie. I rubbed his feet and played his favorite song, "Clair de Lune," in repeat mode on my phone. I bathed him, wearing my jog bra and shorts so I could support him in the shower. I emptied his bed pan and even wiped his butt. I sat by his bedside listening to him breathe—raspy, intermittent, and labored breaths—until the final one. One day shortly before he died, my mom found me crying in the bathroom and said, "You will never regret this time." She was right. Shattered heart notwithstanding, it was a privilege to be there, to help the man who brought me into this world leave it with grace.

"Keep writing," he told me right before he died. "Write about me."

"I will, Dad," I promised. "I will."

Three months after my dad died, Jack was diagnosed with diabetes and congestive heart failure. It was another death sentence, drawn out over two years. I administered insulin shots twice a day, cooked him special meals, made countless trips to the vet, and said my "last goodbye" to him at least three times, but he always managed to come back from the brink, such was his remarkable strength and resilience. A year after his diagnosis, he went blind and was thus robbed of his favorite activities—swimming in the pond, fetching sticks, and herding the cows—but it was when he stopped eating and could barely walk that we reached the point of no return. The one thing he could still enjoy was the wind in his face, so I took him for rides on the side-by-side (think off-road golf cart) so he could—so we both could—feel that firehose blast of life-affirming air. He would hold his face up to the sky and his nose would twitch, breathing in as much of this earthly existence as he still could, and I could tell it made him happy. On the last day of his life—one of the worst days of mine—we went for an extra-long ride around the farm and then I said farewell to my little warrior. He was fifteen and a half years old and to my astonishment, after all his near-death experiences, he had not only lived a full life but exceeded his breed's life expectancy. Of all my accomplishments, keeping him alive through all our adventures and mishaps—coyote attacks, near drownings, and the occasional heart-stopping motorcycle chase—is something I should be proud of. Yet the grief sticks with me like California beach tar, my tears always quick to break through the surface. When they come, I brace myself and let the waves of sadness wash over me, knowing they will pass.

My biggest fears, the ones that had nearly kept me from going on my pie journey, had been realized. My dad and Jack are gone. My mom, however, is doing fine, still driving and working full-time at eighty-five, even with progressive macular degeneration. One day she couldn't read anything on her computer monitor and thought she had lost her vision for good. Turns out a switch on her monitor had gotten bumped and once she adjusted it, she could see again. If only there were a control button like that for life.

When I first decided to stay with Doug, I realized he had plenty of room to house not just Jack and me, but the four goats I used to visit when I lived in the American Gothic House. Their owner, I had learned, had suffered a stroke and could no longer care for them. After a little persuading from me, Doug agreed to adopt them, and gave them a new barn and pasture twenty times bigger than what they'd had before. Goats are like dogs with hooves—they're feisty, affectionate, and funny, and not destructive like people assume. They love to be petted and brushed and given treats, like the apple peelings from my pies. We named them Cinnamon (for her color), Mr. Friendly (for his gregarious nature), Chaps (for the thick hair on his back legs), and Mamacita (because she was Chaps's mom). It wasn't until after they came to live with us that I realized I had manifested everything I had visualized for my future that day on Monika's farm in Switzerland: a life in the country, a farmhouse, goats, and, as an unexpected bonus, a new partner.

Not everyone was convinced that this new life I had established was viable. A friend asked me, "How is that going to work? A nomad like you and a farmer like Doug who is tied to his land?" Well, we've been together seven years and counting, so it's working just fine. And it's not like we don't go anywhere. One of our trips was to Chile, using the last of Marcus's frequent flyer miles. We stayed with my artist friend Vanessa high in the Andes, in the village of Pisco Elqui. She runs a café so we made pie—because I can't go anywhere without making pie—and I taught her how to make key lime. Along with the limes from her trees, we added the local drink of pisco (a type of high-proof brandy) as an ingredient, and it has been a regular item on her menu ever since.

I've stayed in touch with many of the people from my World Piece journey. Barbara Abdeni Massaad traveled from Beirut to stay with us on the farm. We held a soup and pie supper fundraiser and Barbara took the proceeds directly back to the refugees in the Beqaa Valley. Uschi Kamer from Switzerland visited us in Iowa as well. As I do with all my guests, I took Barbara and Uschi to the American Gothic House, a fifty-minute drive from Doug's, to pose for pictures.

No matter how many times I stop by, I get pangs of nostalgia for those four magical years I lived there, a feeling exacerbated by seeing the house empty. The house seems lonely to be so void of life without a harried pie maker living in it. Though as far as I know, the snakes are still there.

My connection to New Zealand lives on in unexpected ways, like when I buy apples at the grocery store and find the varieties that Paul Paynter introduced me to, like Jazz and Sweet Tango. I always read the stickers on the skin, hoping one day I'll come across one from the Yummy Fruit Company. Regrettably, I've never been able to repair my friendship with Charity. Once in a while I check her social media feed to see how she's doing. From what I can glean, she is well, still knitting and connecting with authors—and she got a cute new haircut. I can't shake my disappointment over how we left things—and my shame for what I contributed to that—but I've also learned from it. If I catch myself being impatient or pushy, I try to be more mindful of my fear of running out of time and money. I turn to the mantra that got me through my journey and add, *Slow down and be generous with money*.

In Sydney, Kate continues to thrive and tells me her mom's dementia is holding steady. Foong, the global citizen, had her wings clipped for several years by Australia's strict pandemic lockdown, unable to travel, though last we were in touch she and her husband were staying at their apartment in Germany. Lynne and Edgar are still living on their Brownlow Hill farm, but with some new additions: all three of their children (now adults) have moved onto the property—one son has taken over the farming operations from his dad, and another has moved into the "American Gothic House" cottage I had fantasized about renting. Their brood of pets now includes a flock of peacocks and, happily, Kate tells me that Skippy is still hanging around.

In Bangkok, Samart took a job with another hotel, and Julia left for a job in Riyadh, Saudi Arabia. The pandemic ended that gig, so she is now semi-retired and living in LA. Because I spend a lot of time in California, I've been able to see her and finally give her a pie lesson in her new home to make up for missing her in Bangkok.

I fulfilled the promise I made in Mumbai and went to Nikhil Merchant's Indian restaurant, Imli, in Los Angeles. At the time, it was being run out of a temporary food-court space as construction on the bigger kitchen was delayed. Nikhil's butter chicken, just spicy enough to shoot sparks across your tongue and creamy enough to worry about the calorie-count, made it well worth the drive to Whittier, twelve miles southeast of Downtown LA. I brought him a cherry pie, which we shared over a cup of chai. On my next visit, when his new location finally opens, he is going to make me his favorite street food dish he told me about in Mumbai, *sev puri*. Deepa Krishnan is still running Mumbai Magic Tours. Razak still works as a guide, but mainly on weekends as he has another job during the week. Deepa assures me she has a crew of equally bright and engaging college students to give tours. After all, employing students and nurturing their skills to go on to other jobs is the mission of her program.

In Lebanon, a bomb blast at Beirut's port in 2020 that killed 218 people, wounded 7,000, and left tens of thousands of people homeless, was followed by an economic collapse that left families in dire need of food. So Barbara did what she does best and published another cookbook, *Forever Beirut*, this time with proceeds going to the Lebanese Food Bank. Meanwhile, the war in Syria goes on, now in its twelfth year. Wissam Alghati, the Syrian refugee I met in Lebanon's Beqaa Valley, is now living in Istanbul, though the rest of his family still lives in the apartment next to the refugee camp. And the sick baby whose formula Barbara was paying for is healthy and thriving—and still living in a tent at the camp. I often wonder how that young boy who threw my pie in the ditch is doing. I worry about him and all the other kids everywhere who are victims of war.

Uschi moved to Burundi for her job with the Swiss Agency for Development and Cooperation (SDC). I knew Burundi was in Africa, but I had to find it—and its capital city of Bujumbura where Uschi is living—on the map. (It's between Rwanda, Tanzania, and the Congo.) I plan to visit Uschi there and make pie, especially as

Burundi's ranking on the 2022 Global Peace Index was 131 out of 163 countries, but with the U.S. shamefully and inexcusably ranking only two spots higher than Burundi, any World Piece efforts are needed more in my own country.

The Overlack Family—Bibiana, Marc, Kim, and Luc—recently moved from Berlin to Munich and love it there. "The Cousins" in Aachen are all well, with Charlotte spending a college semester in Tennessee. It's a two-day drive from Iowa, so unfortunately when Claudia, Edgar, and Anton came to the U.S. to visit her, we couldn't make the logistics work to see each other. I've promised them to return to Germany for a visit.

Ron and Ryan attempted their own round-the-world journey, but the pandemic ended their trip midway, stranding them in New Jersey for three months. When they finally got back to Budapest, the grime on their stone building had been sandblasted back to a beautiful shade of white. In spite of the improvement, they sold the bed and breakfast and moved to Cuenca, Ecuador, where they got a French bulldog with a big personality. Fittingly, they named him Jack, and though naming him after my terrier was unintentional, I like to think of their Jack carrying on the legacy of mine. We trade emails about our time together and I talk of visiting them in South America. Until then, I continue to eat ice cream and watch *Good Witch* reruns on my own.

In more recent news, my old neighbor and friend, Don—the one whose need for help with his shoes after canoeing led to my realization that Doug was The One—survived COVID, but passed away soon after from cancer. Uschi's mom, Liselotte, whose Apple in a Bathrobe was the most-liked social media post on my trip, also lost her battle with cancer. She was like a second mom to me and I can still hear her calling me "Bettli" in her heavily accented sing-song voice. I miss them both.

I also miss the goats, badly. When we adopted them, they were of various, indeterminate ages—the youngest was at least ten—and over the past seven years, one by one, we've lost them, each loss another crack in my heart.

One thing I have yet to learn in life is how to accept death. I'm forever paranoid of more loss—inevitable and unavoidable as it may be. I hold my breath when I get phone calls from my siblings. I inspect our pets daily for any changes or signs of illness. And I worry every time Doug leaves the house, even when he's doing things less risky than farming. As my own expiration date inches closer, I remind myself of what a privilege it is to have lived even this long. If I ever take longevity and good health for granted—mine or others'—or find myself feeling ungrateful for all that I am blessed with, all I have to do is think of those shoes lined up along the Danube River.

Time doesn't stand still, so we keep moving forward, staying open to whatever new surprises life has in store. We keep the faith that the hardships we've suffered will be balanced out by happiness, and that loss creates space for something new—like getting another dog. At the start of the pandemic, Doug and I became the proud parents of a Chihuahua. I volunteered to foster this tiny thing that the animal shelter had named Peanut. Fostering seemed like a good idea as I wasn't ready for a new dog so soon after losing Jack, but less than twenty-four hours after bringing her home, I knew there was no turning back. This unintentional adoption is what's affectionately called a "foster fail," and I've never been happier to fail at something. A Chihuahua may be an unlikely breed for a farm, but Peanut is a lot like Jack: tough and fearless—but not as reckless. She can be found every evening on Doug's lap as he reads *The Economist* or *The New Yorker* in his rocking chair and every morning burrowed under the covers next to me.

World peace has been in a slight but steady decline over the past fifteen years, and Russia's 2022 invasion of Ukraine has accelerated its deterioration. With all the ongoing global issues—the pandemic, climate crisis, and political unrest—I won't be repeating my round-the-world trip as I had hoped. There will be no do-over—no traveling to India outside of monsoon season, no continuing the search for the stone-tablet pie recipe in Greece, no experiencing New Zealand during its glorious summer—at least not linked in a continuous circle. But writing this book has allowed me to take the original trip all over again, and to take my time this time, to dig deeper into the history of each place, to savor the details, to hear the conversations in my head, to reconnect with the people I met, and to travel lightly with no luggage or rolling pin to haul around.

It took me three months to make my way around the world, but it has taken me seven years to write the story about it. The writing journey has been as epic as the trip, because as I wrote about each country, I experienced the same roller coaster of emotions I had when I was there. This was especially true for India. While I still don't understand that country, I continue to be intrigued by it. My Netflix viewing history proves it, as I gravitate toward anything filmed in India, Bollywood or otherwise.

I will never know the impact I had on others, but I do know the impact others had on me. I still remember the woman in Greece who carried my heavy suitcase down into the depths of the metro station and made sure I got on the right train. To this day she reminds me that the world can still surprise you with random acts of kindness from strangers. "Holiness is always tied to little gestures," Pope Francis said a few weeks after my return. There are little gestures of holiness happening all around us if we take the time to recognize and appreciate them, which is easier to do when you turn off the news. And whether it's the use of a turn signal or letting someone with fewer items go ahead of you in the grocery line, there are countless ways to be kind. Enough acts of kindness could one day add up to world peace.

When I dwell too much on the past, I think of the little Mexican-German kids I made pie with in the Black Forest and I'm reminded that the future is sure to be brighter because of them. My lifelong friends in Switzerland, the Kamers, assure me that family will always be there for me, even when not related by blood.

When I get discouraged about the lack of manners and civility in our society, I think of the cleaning woman at the apartment complex in Bangkok who smiled and bowed with her hands in prayer every time I saw her, sometimes with only one hand while she held a broom in the other. Picturing her gentle display of grace restores my faith.

When I despair about the ongoing plight of refugees all over the world, I go back and watch Wissam Alghati's short film, finding hope in those young children, displaced, traumatized, and living in tents, yet confidently declaring their desire for—and belief in—peace.

And when I fear that people are becoming too selfish, I imagine Charity Nelson in her New Zealand Christmas Cottage, surrounded by her mountains of books and shopping bags and teacups, her knitting needles moving at ninety miles per hour, whipping colorful strands of yarn into her next prayer shawl, and know that her gift will touch someone's heart.

I'm still making pie and finding my inner peace in the baking process, while appreciating my cozy, rural, home life with Doug and all our animals—but I'm also still trying to make sense of the human condition and all its complexities, especially as the world has become more divided and less peaceful than when I made my trip. Pie enhances lives and spreads joy, but it has not stopped the rise of autocratic governments or kept the future of democracy from teetering on the edge of a cliff, globally and at home. I can't sit back and watch the world burn, but what else can I do to help? The answer that keeps coming up is this: Write about your World Piece experience. Tell your story. Share your insights and convey what you learned. Inspire others to be part of the solution. Offer examples of what's possible.

Not everyone can travel around the world to explore its myriad cultures. But I can bring the world—and a message of hope—to you. This book is my contribution to society, my responsibility to give back, and my prayer for a better and more peaceful world.

RECIPES

USA: Apple Pie

This is the recipe I learned from my pie mentor, Mary Spellman, in Malibu, California several decades ago. It's the recipe I used for my Pitchfork Pie Stand and in every country I've traveled to. As I suggest to all my my pie students: don't worry about perfection; improvise if you need to; keep a light touch; and just relax!

BASIC PIE CRUST

2-1/2 cups all-purpose flour
1/2 cup butter, chilled
1/2 cup Crisco (or instead of shortening, use lard or butter)
1/2 tsp salt
Ice water (fill 1 cup but use only enough to moisten dough)

FILLING

7 large (or about 10 medium) Granny Smith apples, peeled

(NOTE: The number of apples will depend on size of apple and size of pie dish. The general amount is about 3 pounds per 9-inch pie. You can use any kind of tart apples, and can combine varieties. Try Braeburn, Jonathan, and Gala. Avoid Fuji as they're too watery, and Delicious as they're too bland.)

1 cup sugar (I usually use less, about 3/4 cup)
4 Tbsp flour (to thicken the filling)
1/2 tsp salt (you'll sprinkle this on so don't worry about precise amount)
1 to 2 tsp cinnamon (I don't measure. Use however much you like!)
1 Tbsp butter (you'll dot the top with it before putting on the top crust)
1 beaten egg (you won't use all of it, just enough
to brush on pie before baking)

INSTRUCTIONS

In a deep bowl, use your fingertips to massage the butter and shortening into the flour until you have lumps of butter the size of mixed nuts. Drizzle in ice water a little at a time and use your hand to toss it with the flour to moisten it. Continue adding water until the dough is moist enough to hold together.

(Don't try to force the dough to bind; let the water do the work.) Do a little squeeze test; if it crumbles, add more water.

Now divide the dough in two and form each half into a disk shape. (To avoid the stickiness, rub flour on your hands before handling it.) Sprinkle flour on your rolling surface, place a disk of dough on it, and sprinkle flour on top of it. Roll it thin (until you can almost see through it) and wide enough in diameter to fit your pie dish plus some overhang. (If the dough is sticky, sprinkle more flour on it. If it's getting too warm to work with refrigerate the dough until it's chilled.) Trim excess dough with scissors (don't tear it!) so there's an overhang of about 1 inch from the dish edge.

(NOTE: I don't normally refrigerate my dough before rolling, unless the kitchen is so hot it makes the butter melt. I do, however, refrigerate the dough after I've rolled it out to keep it cold while I'm peeling the apples.)

If you've already peeled your apples in advance, preheat the oven to 425°F (220°C). If not, peel the apples now and preheat the oven when you're done.

(NOTE: I assemble the filling in two layers as described below, but you may find it easier to toss the apple slices with the sugar, spices, and flour in a large bowl.)

For layer one: Place half of the peeled and sliced apples into the pie dish (I slice the apples directly into the dish), arranging and pressing down gently to remove extra space between slices. Fill the dish with enough slices so you don't see through to the bottom crust. Cover with half of your other dry ingredients (salt, cinnamon, sugar, flour), then add the remaining apples and sprinkle with second half of dry ingredients. Dot with 1 tablespoon butter and cover with the top crust. Trim the top crust so the overhang is even with the bottom crust.

Working your way around the dish (turning your dish and not your body as you go), roll the top and bottom crusts together to sit like a rope along the rim of the pie dish. This seals in the filling. You can make it decorative by crimping it with your fingers or just press down the edge with a fork, and also cut out shapes or letters with any leftover dough to place on top.

Brush with beaten egg. Poke vent holes in the top (get creative here with a pattern).

Bake at 425°F (220°) for 10 to 15 minutes until crust starts to brown. Turn oven down to 375°F (190°C) and bake for another 30 to 40 minutes, until juice bubbles and thickens. If it gets too brown while baking, turn down the temperature. To be sure it's done, poke a knife into the vent holes to make sure apples have softened. Do not overbake or the apples will turn mushy.

Share the pie with a friend or someone in need.

New Zealand: Mince and Cheddar Hand Pies

I went straight to the source and asked Mr. Z for a hand-pie recipe, but the one he sent me was a little too exotic for my taste. (Chicken and oyster pie? Um, no thanks.) So I scoured the internet for "traditional New Zealand hand pies" and found this one on the *Recipes by Carina* website. I tested the recipe and these pies were #$@!% delicious! Better than anything I tasted in New Zealand. Now I want to try Carina's other recipes, and there are many! Check out her website for more: www.recipesbycarina.com.

CRUST

2 Sheets Frozen Butter Puff Pastry

FILLING

2 garlic cloves, crushed
1 tsp cooking oil
1 lb ground beef (in NZ they call it "mince")
1 cup mushrooms, sliced and cut small enough for a
hand pie (I added these and was glad I did!)
3 tsp Dijon mustard
1 Tbsp Worcestershire sauce
1 Tbsp soy sauce
1 tsp ground black pepper
1/3 cup flour
2 cups beef stock
1/4 cup cheddar cheese, grated
1/4 cup mozzarella cheese, grated (I use all cheddar
or whatever cheeses I have on hand)

INSTRUCTIONS

Place a large cast iron skillet (or fry pan) on the stove and turn on the heat to medium. While the pan is heating up, add the oil and crushed garlic. Cook for a few minutes. Turn the heat to high and add in the beef. Use a wooden spoon to break up the meat and stir continuously until browned. Stir in the mushrooms, if using. (These are not part of Carina's recipe, but it's pie—you can put anything you want in it!) Turn the heat down to low and add the mustard, Worcestershire sauce, soy sauce, and pepper, stirring to combine.

Sprinkle the flour over the beef and cook for a few minutes, stirring constantly. (It will be thick.)

Slowly stir in half of the beef stock (I used beef broth). Once combined, pour in the second half.

Reduce the heat to low and simmer the beef filling for about 30 minutes or until thickened, stirring occasionally.

Cool the filling fully before putting it in the pies. (It can be made a few days ahead of time and kept in the fridge.)

When you're ready to make the pies, remove the puff pastry sheets from the freezer and thaw at room temperature. Roll the sheets to make them a little thinner and cut out 4 circles from each sheet to fit your 5-inch pie tins. (If you don't have this size pie tin, you can use a muffin tin to make smaller pies. You can also make one large 9-inch pie.)

Place a cut-out of pastry in each of the pie dishes, pressing down lightly to push out any gaps. Fill the pastry shells with the meat mixture and sprinkle grated cheese on top. Cover with a circle of puff pastry, and fold the overhanging bottom pastry over the top to seal in the filling.

Cut vent holes into the top of each pie to allow the steam to escape. Refrigerate for at least 30 minutes before baking. (I always skip this step and they still turn out.)

Bake at 400° F (200° C) for about 20 to 25 minutes or until the pies are golden brown.

Cool in the pan for 5 to10 minutes before serving.

NOTE: You can freeze both the filling and the pies. The pies can be frozen baked or unbaked. Do not thaw the pie before baking (or reheating if already baked.)

Australia: Cornish Pasty

This is a recipe for the traditional Cornish pasty, with few ingredients and simple instructions. For a good tutorial on making these, watch Cousin Jacks Pasty Company's video on YouTube. These make an excellent meal, or snack. You can add other spices or veggies to this, but this is the original style. If you're ever in Sydney, head over to Cousin Jacks and try some of their other varieties. Also check out Pie Face and Harry's Café de Wheels while you're Down Under.

SHORT CRUST PASTRY

3 cups all-purpose flour
1 cup butter
1 tsp salt
Ice water (approx. 1/3 to 1/2 cup)
Egg (to brush on top before baking)

FILLING

1/2 lb skirt steak, chopped (use more if you like)
1 small potato, peeled, sliced very thin, and cut into pieces
1/2 large turnip or swede (a.k.a. rutabaga), diced
1 small onion, finely chopped (equals about 1/2 cup)
1/2 cup fresh parsley, chopped
Salt
Pepper

INSTRUCTIONS

In a large bowl, use your fingertips to blend together flour, butter, and salt until it resembles coarse meal. Drizzle in ice water a little at a time until the dough holds together. Gather the dough into ball, wrap it in plastic wrap or seal in an airtight container, and refrigerate.

Preheat oven to 425°F (220°C).

Chop up the skirt steak and set aside. Peel and slice potato into very thin slices, then cut into smaller pieces. Dice the onion. Peel and dice the turnip (or rutabaga). Chop up the fresh parsley. In a large bowl, mix the ingredients together and season with salt and pepper.

Roll out the dough on a floured surface to about 1/8- to-1/4-inch thickness. Using an 8-inch plate as a guide, trace the edge of the plate with a knife to cut circles out of the dough. (You should get about 8 to 10 pasties.) Wad the scraps into a ball, roll out, and repeat. (NOTE: Alter the diameter of your circles to make smaller snack-size pasties or larger meal-size ones.)

Place a scoop of the meat mixture in the center of each circle. Fold the dough over the filling to make a half-moon shape. Pinch the edges together to seal, then flute the edges by using your fingertips to fold and twist. Place on greased cookie sheet and lightly brush pastries with beaten egg.

Bake at 425°F (220°C) for 10 to 15 minutes or until crust starts to brown, then turn the oven temperature down to 350°F (176°C). Bake for another 20 to 25 minutes to ensure filling is fully cooked. They should be lightly browned.

Serve hot or at room temperature.

Thailand: Rainbow Cake

Sadly, I lost the original recipe that Samart gave me in Bangkok. He sent me a replacement, but it was a handwritten copy that I couldn't quite decipher. So I hunted down other rainbow cake recipes—there are many out there—and cross-referenced several to come up with this one. I hope Samart approves. Even if he doesn't, this tastes great, especially with that hint of lemon. But the best part is that it's guaranteed to make people smile. A special thanks to the pastry crew at the Grand Hyatt Erawan in Bangkok for this happy memory.

CAKE

3 cups all-purpose flour
4 tsp baking powder
1/2 tsp salt
1 cup unsalted butter, softened
1-1/2 cups sugar (white)
5 egg whites
1-1/2 cups milk (add more if the batter is too thick)
1 tsp vanilla extract
1 tsp lemon extract
Food coloring, preferably gel type (You can mix drops to create
the 6 colors: purple, blue, green, yellow, orange, red)

FROSTING

2-1/2 cups heavy whipping cream (must be very cold)
3/4 cup powdered sugar
16 oz mascarpone cheese
1 tsp vanilla

INSTRUCTIONS

You will need 6 small bowls for the batter and 6 round 9-inch cake pans. (If you don't have 6 pans, just bake in batches.) Line the bottom of the pans with a cut-out circle of parchment paper. (You can grease the pans instead, but the paper is a good insurance policy.)

Preheat the oven to 350°F (180°C).

In a large bowl, whisk the flour, baking powder, and salt together and set aside. In a mixing bowl, cream the butter and sugar, then add the egg whites and beat until blended. Add the vanilla and lemon extract, then slowly add the milk and flour, alternating between the two.

Divide the cake batter evenly between 6 bowls. (Samart would weigh the batter, of course, but you can use a measuring cup or just eyeball it like I do.) Add drops of food coloring to each of the bowls to get the desired colors and stir. Keep adding drops until you get the intensity of color you want. (It takes a lot more than you'd expect.)

Bake each cake at 350°F (180°C) for about 15 minutes. Test for doneness by inserting a toothpick in the center; when it comes out clean, it's done.

Make sure the cake is completely cooled before frosting!

Using an electric mixer, mix the chilled heavy cream, mascarpone, powdered sugar, and vanilla. Do not overwhip or it will start to curdle.

Dust off any loose crumbs from the cakes. Spread frosting on each layer starting with purple on the bottom, then blue, green, yellow, orange, and red (or magenta) on top, stacking one on top of the other as you go. Use the remaining frosting to cover the top and sides. Refrigerate for at least an hour before serving, and store any leftover in the refrigerator. This is a cake you will serve with pride. Especially one that is as vibrant and fun as this.

India: Vegetable Samosa

I've kept in touch with the food blogger and restaurateur I met in Mumbai, Nikhil Merchant. He shared his personal "homestyle" samosa recipe. But the best part about this recipe is having a woman in New Jersey test it for me. She said, "I could have ordered the spices online, but I would have missed out on the wonderful adventure of shopping at the Delight Big Bazaar in Parsippany. It was like being transported to Mumbai. Many women shopping there were in lovely saris. Instead of the usual pop elevator music, the background music was soothing ragas." She added, "The experience of making the samosas really makes me appreciate how much goes into those we order out, and the chefs behind the scenes working their magic for the delight of my taste buds." Her story makes me feel my "World Piece" story has made a difference in someone's life. I hope to hear many more stories like this one.

Makes about a dozen medium-sized samosas

DOUGH

2 cups all-purpose flour
1/4 cup melted ghee
1/4 cup water (may need a little more or less)
1 tsp salt
2 tsp whole carom seeds (a.k.a. ajwain, and not
to be confused with cardamom)

FILLING

2 large potatoes (about 1 lb), boiled and skinned
2 tsp fresh ginger root, diced
2 tsp green chili paste
2 tsp canola oil + the oil you will need for frying (enough to cover samosas
in a deep pot)
1 tsp whole cumin seed
1 tsp whole fennel seed
1 small onion, finely chopped

1 tsp paprika (for a spicier samosa, use red chili powder—not American chili powder)
1 tsp coriander powder
1/2 tsp turmeric
1 tsp dried mango powder
1/2 tsp garam masala powder
1/2 cup green peas (frozen are okay)
1/4 cup fresh cilantro, finely chopped
Squeeze of lime
Salt to taste
1 to 2 Tbsp flour (to make slurry)

INSTRUCTIONS

Boil the potatoes. While the potatoes are cooking, prepare the dough. Mix together all ingredients except water and rub well with your fingers to make a coarse, fat-infused flour. Start adding lukewarm water one tablespoon at a time until you get a stiff dough. (You don't want it too supple, but you do need it moist enough to hold together and roll out easily.) Divide the dough into 6 balls, cover with a damp cloth, and set aside for 1/2 hour to rest.

For the filling, blend the diced ginger and chili paste together, and set aside. Heat oil in a pan and crackle cumin and fennel seeds. Add diced onion and cook until tender. Turn the heat down to low and add the ginger-chili paste and the other spices. Cook briefly. (If it's too hot, add a teaspoon or so of water to keep the spices from burning.)

In a large bowl, crumble the potatoes into a chunky texture. Add the onion-spice mixture and blend until the potatoes are coated with it. Add the cilantro and peas, mix in a squeeze of lime, and salt to taste. Set aside to cool.

To form the samosas: In a small bowl, mix 2 tablespoons flour with water to make a slurry. Take ball of dough and roll it out into a thin, oval disk between 6 and 8 inches in diameter. (Try to make the shape symmetrical and roll the dough a little thinner than a tortilla.) Cut the oval in half and, taking one half, rub a thin slurry of flour and water on the straight side. Lift the half disk and use your fingers to shape it into a cone, sealing the straight, slurry-rubbed side. Fill the cone with the potato mix, gently pressing it down to fill the corner of the pocket. Using more slurry, seal the open edge to make a triangular pastry. Set on a tray or work space. Repeat this for the rest of the dough, until you have 12 samosas.

Fill a deep, heavy-bottom pot (I use a Dutch oven) with enough canola oil to cover the samosas and turn stove on high setting to heat. When the oil is almost "smoking hot," turn the stove heat down to medium and drop a small ball of dough into the oil to test the temperature. The dough should rise. (NOTE: It did not rise when I tested the recipe, but the dough was definitely frying, so I moved forward and it was fine. Also, when I tested, I heated the oil before I formed my filled samosas, but it might have been more sensible to wait until I had all 12 of them ready to fry.)

To fry, add 2 to 3 samosas at a time so they are not crowded. Use a ladle to douse them with hot oil to ensure the samosas are covered. Gently fry on medium until golden brown.

Once they're browned, remove the samosas with a slotted ladle (or slotted spoon), and place onto paper towels to drain.

Serve with ketchup, chutney, sweet date chutney, or dipping sauce of your choice.

Lebanon: Apricot Pie

In Beirut, I tasted some delicious Lebanese pies (a.k.a. man'oushé or flatbread), as well as several Armenian ones, and was torn about which of them to include in this book. I left the choice up to Barbara Abdeni Massaad, my host in Lebanon who without hesitation surprised me by answering, "Apricot!" When I made it in her kitchen with her homegrown apricots, I was winging it, but for the book, my friend Kathleen Beebout offered her award-wining recipe.

For recipes unique to Lebanon, pie or otherwise, I highly recommend getting Barbara's cookbooks *Man'oushé: Inside the Lebanese Street Corner Bakery*, and her newest one, *Forever Beirut: Recipes and Stories from the Heart of Lebanon*.

BASIC PIE CRUST

2-1/2 cups all-purpose flour
1/2 cup butter, chilled
1/2 cup Crisco
1/2 tsp salt
Ice water (fill 1 cup but use only enough to moisten dough)

FILLING

5 cups apricots, cut in half with pits removed
3/4 cup sugar
1/2 tsp almond extract
1 tsp orange zest (optional)
1/4 cup cornstarch
4 Tbsp butter, cut into chunks
2 Tbsp coarse sugar (a.k.a. sanding sugar)

INSTRUCTIONS

In a deep bowl, mix the flour and salt. Then, using your fingertips, massage the butter and shortening into the flour until you have lumps of butter the size of peanuts and almonds. Drizzle in ice water a little at a time and toss the water around in the flour to moisten it. When the dough holds together on its own (from the water, not by force!), do a "squeeze test." If it crumbles, add more water. Divide the dough in two and form each half into a disk shape. (Rub flour on your hands to take out the stickiness of handling it.) Sprinkle flour on your rolling surface and roll thin (so you can almost see through it) and big enough to fit your pie dish with extra for overhang. With scissors, trim overhanging dough to about 1 inch from the dish edge.

Combine all ingredients and pour into pie shell. Dot with 4 tablespoons butter. Cover with top crust and seal and flute the edges. Brush with Half & Half (or heavy cream) and sprinkle with 2 tablespoons coarse sugar. Bake at 425°F (220°C) for 20 minutes. Turn oven down to 375°F (190°C) and bake another 30 to 35 minutes until golden brown.

Greece: Honey Goat Cheese Pie

I never did find the stone tablet in Greece, the one with the first-ever recorded pie recipe. But it must exist, or have existed at some point, because an internet search shows that others have talked about it and tried to replicate the ancient recipe. For help with this, I turned to Georgia Kofinas, the Greek-American cookbook author I met in Athens, whom I credit for the delicious filling. The crust is my own version of several others that didn't turn out. You can also just use my regular pie crust recipe for this.

Makes one 9-inch pie

CRUST

2 cups flour (try a mix of all-purpose and whole wheat)
1/2 tsp baking soda
1/2 tsp salt
1/4 cup olive oil
3 Tbsp honey
Ice water (about 1/4 cup, enough to bind the dough)

FILLING

16 oz goat cheese
3/4 cup honey
3 large eggs
1 tsp vanilla extract
1/2 cup all-purpose flour
1 tsp baking soda
1 Tbsp fresh orange or lemon zest (optional)

INSTRUCTIONS

For the crust, use a large bowl and whisk the flour, baking soda, and salt together. Stir in the olive oil and honey, then add water a little at a time until the dough holds together. Form into a ball, cover in plastic or in an airtight container, and refrigerate for 30 minutes while you make the filling.

(NOTE: One of the recipes I saw called for finely chopped pistachio nuts in the crust, which sounds very tasty!)

For the filling, combine the goat cheese, eggs, honey, and vanilla, and orange or lemon zest (if you're using), and blend well. Add the flour and baking soda. Filling should be the consistency of a thick batter, not runny.

On a floured surface, roll the dough into a circle, about 1/4 inch thick or thinner. (Because this is a free-form galette, it needs to be thick enough to hold the filling with the support of a pie dish.) Place the dough on a parchment-paper-lined or greased baking sheet. (To move the dough without breaking it, use a pastry scraper to lift it off the surface, fold it half, then unfold it onto the baking sheet.)

Spoon the filling into the center of the dough circle, spreading it out until it's a few inches from the edges. Lift the edges up all the way around to contain (but not cover) the filling, making folds in the dough around the perimeter, as freeform or as decorative as you like.

Bake at 400° F (200° C) for about 35 to 40 minutes. (If the crust gets too dark, turn the temperature down.) Filling should be firm, not jiggly, and golden in color.

Let cool. Serve with a drizzle of honey. Store in the refrigerator.

Switzerland: Apfel im Schlafrock (Apple in a Bathrobe)

Of all the social media posts during my trip, the one about the Apple in a Bathrobe was the most popular. (My posts about Jack's adventures on Doug's farm came in a close second.) Liselotte Kamer, my "Swiss mom" who taught me how to make this, passed away in 2022, but including this recipe keeps her spirit alive. That said, it's not a definitive recipe as we improvised on the ingredients when we made it—and so can you.

Below, the dough recipe is for 4 medium apples, but I list the spices for a single apple because you will likely be making just one using leftover dough scraps. If making more, simply multiply the amount of spices. But remember, you don't have to follow a recipe for this at all.

BASIC PIE CRUST

(amount for single crust, makes enough "robes" for 4 medium apples)

1-1/4 cups all-purpose flour
1/4 cup butter, chilled
1/4 cup Crisco (you can use lard or butter instead of shortening)
1/4 tsp salt
Ice water (fill 1/2 cup but use only enough to moisten dough)

FILLING

(amounts are for **one** apple)

1 apple (Granny Smith or tart apples of your choice)
2 tsp butter
1 or 2 tsp sugar (white, but it's probably good with brown sugar too)
1/2 tsp cinnamon
1 tsp almond meal (or any finely chopped nuts)
1 Tbsp heavy whipping cream
1 egg, beaten (to brush on dough)

INSTRUCTIONS

To make the crust, use a deep bowl, add the flour, salt, butter, and shortening. Massage the fat into the flour with your fingertips only until the texture is chunky, with pieces of butter the size of mixed nuts. Add ice water a little at a time (I drizzle it in instead of using tablespoons), lightly tossing it to mix with the flour. Keep adding water until the dough holds together without force. (Do not overwork the dough, and do not knead it.)

Form the dough into 4 disks and refrigerate while you peel and core the apples using a coring tool or a paring knife. Create a well and leave the apple whole (do not slice). Discard the stem and seeds.

In a small bowl, mix the sugar, spices, and ground nuts. Set aside. (Or, just do what Liselotte did and fill the cored apple with the various ingredients, adding one at a time.)

Flour your rolling surface and place a small disk of dough on it. Sprinkle flour on top of the disk and roll out large enough in diameter to completely encase the size of the apple. (Don't worry about the shape being a perfect circle.)

Place an apple in the center of the rolled-out dough, fill the apple's hollowed-out center with the sugar-spice-nut mixture, and pour in a tablespoon of cream. Top with 2 teaspoons of butter. Pull the dough up to surround the apple (like a robe!) and seal edges either by folding them over the top or gathering them into pleats, then pinch to close. You can also decorate the top with a small cut-out shape of dough. (My angel cookie cutter from Newtown, CT, is perfect for this.) Poke a vent hole in the top.

Place on baking sheet (ungreased is fine) and brush with beaten egg.

Bake at 425°F (220°C) for about 10 minutes to set and brown the crust, then turn the oven down to 375°F (190°C) and bake for another 30 to 40 minutes or more, until apple has softened. (The bigger the apple, the longer the baking time.)

Invite friends (and estranged family members) over and serve with a good cup of coffee. Vanilla ice cream with this would be good too.

Germany: Blueberry Pie

BASIC PIE CRUST

2-1/2 cups all-purpose flour
1/2 cup butter, chilled
1/2 cup Crisco
1/2 tsp salt
Ice water (fill 1 cup but use only enough to moisten dough)

FILLING

3 pints blueberries (I pile them high!)
1 cup sugar (I tend to use less)
1/4 cup cornstarch
1 Tbsp butter
1 egg, beaten (to brush on top)

INSTRUCTIONS

In a deep bowl, mix the flour and salt. Then, using your fingertips, massage the butter and shortening into the flour until you have lumps of butter the size of peanuts and almonds. Drizzle in ice water a little at a time and toss the water around in the flour to moisten it. When the dough holds together on its own (from the water, not by force!), do a "squeeze test." If it crumbles, add more water. Divide the dough in two and form each half into a disk shape. (Rub flour on your hands to take out the stickiness of handling it.) Sprinkle flour on your rolling surface and roll thin (so you can almost see through it) and big enough to fit your pie dish with extra for overhang. With scissors, trim overhanging dough to about 1 inch from the dish edge.

Rinse and drain blueberries. While the berries are still damp, place in a large bowl and mix with the sugar and cornstarch, tossing the berries around until they are coated with the dry ingredients. Pour into pie shell, add the pat of butter, and cover with the top crust. Trim and crimp edges, brush with beaten egg, poke vent holes, then bake at 425°F (220°C) for 15 to 20 minutes.

Turn the oven down to 375°F (190°C) and bake for another 20 to 30 minutes, until berry filling is bubbling and thickened. (Allow at least 10 minutes after it begins to bubble to let juice really thicken.)

SIDE NOTE: Blueberries make an ideal filling for mini pies or pies in a jar.

Hungary: Cseresznyés Rétes (Cherry Strudel)

When I was in Budapest, I had the apple strudel, which I loved, but I wanted to include the recipe for my host Ron's favorite: cherry. Just writing down the recipe—inspired by *Zsuzsa is in the Kitchen* blog—made my mouth water. This uses frozen phyllo dough instead of homemade. I know I preach that it's better to bake from scratch, but every recipe I read cautioned that making phyllo is very complicated.

This recipe calls for sweet cherries (like Bing), finely ground almonds, and vanilla. But you can use tart (sour) cherries and walnuts, and spice up the recipe with cinnamon, lemon zest, and anything else you can think of. Remember, the rétes menu at the Great Hall Market was a mile long! The possible fillings are endless, so use your leftover phyllo dough to try some others.

CRUST

4 to 6 sheets frozen phyllo pastry (buy in frozen-food section)

FILLING

1/3 cup melted butter
2 cups sweet cherries, pitted (like Bing variety),
(approx. 1-1/2 lbs fresh, unpitted)
1 cup sugar (more or less, based on your taste and
flavor of cherries) + 1 Tbsp to sprinkle on top
1 tsp vanilla
1 to 2 tsp fresh lemon zest (optional)
3/4 cup finely ground almonds (can be raw, but roasted will add flavor)
1/4 tsp cinnamon (optional)
1 egg, beaten
Powdered sugar for dusting

INSTRUCTIONS

Thaw the frozen phyllo dough in the refrigerator for several hours.

Wash the cherries and remove the stems and pits. If your cherries are large, you may want to slice or even chop them. Combine cherries with the sugar, vanilla, and lemon zest (optional), and set aside for an hour. After an hour, if there is any excess juice, use a strainer, pressing lightly on the cherries to drain. Set the cherries aside.

(NOTE: I hate wasting the juice and sugar. To avoid this, you can skip the macerating step and wait until you're ready to add the fruit to the phyllo before adding the sugar—in which case you might want to cut the sugar back to 1/2 cup. Alternatively, cook the filling first by mixing the cherries and sugar with 3 tablespoons cornstarch and heat on the stove for about 10 minutes to thicken. Cool before spooning onto phyllo.)

In a small bowl, mix the cinnamon (if using it) with the ground almonds.

To prepare the pastry, lay a clean, dry tea towel on a clean surface and place 4 sheets of phyllo on it. (Use 6 sheets for a thicker pastry.) Cover with a damp tea towel or damp paper towel to keep the phyllo from drying out and cracking. (Seal any unused phyllo in an airtight plastic bag and return to the freezer or store in the refrigerator.)

Lay another clean, dry tea towel on your work surface and place 1 sheet of phyllo on it. Using a pastry brush, lightly brush the entire sheet with melted butter, taking care not to tear it. (These sheets are more fragile than tissue paper!) Sprinkle with 1 tablespoon of ground almond. Place the next sheet on top the buttered one. Brush with butter and sprinkle more ground almond. Repeat this for each sheet of pastry. (If the pastry tears, make sure the torn areas are not lined up on top of one another.)

After the last sheet is buttered, spoon the remaining ground almonds along the long edge of the phyllo. Gently arrange the cherries on top of the almonds. (Leave about 2 inches on each end free of cherries and almonds as the ends will get tucked under to hold in the filling.)

Using the edge of the towel, lift the phyllo on the long edge to flip it over the filling. Keep rolling by lifting the towel until you've created a long roll.

Gently lift the roll onto a parchment-lined baking sheet. Tuck the ends under, then brush the top, first with butter, then with the beaten egg. Sprinkle 1 tablespoon of sugar on top.

In a preheated oven, bake at 375°F (190°C) until golden brown, about 25 to 30 minutes. Strudel will be crispy on the outside and you will be drooling over it, dying to eat it.

After the strudel has cooled to room temperature, dust with powdered sugar and cut into slices.

Cover any leftover strudel with a clean tea towel and store at room temperature for up to 3 days.

ACKNOWLEDGMENTS

There are so many people that helped make this trip—and this book—possible. And there were so many, many beautiful souls who hosted me, fed me, guided me, supported me, and made pie with me along the way. I'm sure I'm missing some names in the list below, but here are a few:

First, I have to thank Marcus Iken, my late husband, for giving me the wings to fly with his frequent flyer miles.

NEW ZEALAND: Paul Paynter, Terrence Skelly, and the staff at Yummy Fruit Company; Grace Bower, Brett Zimmerman, Louise Watts, Annette Nelson; and, above all, I offer my thanks (and apologies) to Charity Nelson.

AUSTRALIA: Kate Hayward, Foong Broecker, The Sydney Women's International Club, Sam Cawthorn, Pip and Chris Bundey, Ali and Bill Hayward, Lynne and Edgar Downes, and Skippy the baby wallaby.

THAILAND: Julia Gajcak; Saul Mercado and the U.S. Embassy; the Grand Hyatt Erawan and the kitchen staff who made space for me—Samart Boonta, Supaporn Nueng Sagurnvong, Chatkawew (Lhin) Sahawat, Jean-Marc Breney, Ryan Dunn; the Pacific City Club staff—Marcel Jacquat, Ellie Dixon, and Daniel Hayward; and the lovely woman who stopped sweeping to greet me with her gracious bow.

INDIA: Deepa Krishnan and her three generations of family; Lavanya Shanbhogue; Nikhil Merchant; the Four Seasons Hotel and the welcoming staff there including Vikram Reddy, Niharika Tandon, Neetika the adorable concierge, Prajakta my baking assistant, and Andrew Harrison; Sushmita Biswas; Anne Geenen; and last but not least, Razak my slum—er, *neighborhood*—tour guide.

LEBANON: Barbara Abdeni Massaad and her beautiful family—Serge, Albert, Mia, Sarah, Belle, Pepito, Tchu Tchu and Chicamoo; and the Alghati family, in particular, Wissam Alghati for his peace efforts.

GREECE: Georgia Kofinas and Fr. Stavros Kofinas; Christina Panteleimonitis and Lauren Wadowsky; Viki Papagiannopoulou; and Christopher Bakken who started the chain reaction of Greek connections; my Airbnb hosts on Drakou Street who cared for me while I was ill; and the stranger who helped me with my luggage in the metro station. I will never know your name but I will always remember your kindness.

SWITZERLAND: My Swiss Family—Ursula, Eva, and Liselotte Kamer; Böbi Luthi; and Monika Krebs. I send you all a Matterhorn of love.

GERMANY: Bibiana, Mark, Kim, and Luc Overlack; Claudia, Edgar, Charlotte, and Anton Ziller (and Leonie for use of her room while she was away); Martina, Tobias, and Juergen Schnakenberg; Johannes Blum; Jakob and Moritz Assman; Silke, Jule, and Jette Wagner. I'm so thankful we reconnected. You made my time in Germany both healing and fun. And Silvia Tyburski, sorry to miss you while I was there, but I appreciated your support from afar.

HUNGARY: Ron Schmitz and Ryan James. Your hospitality went above and beyond!

UNITED STATES: A giant slice of gratitude goes to the rest of my team back on American soil, starting with my parents, Tom and Marie Howard, and my siblings Anne, Tim, Mike, and Patrick. Thank you to Nan Schmid, Kathy Eldon, Sue Finn, Libby Gill, Patti Durflinger, Kathy Knapp, Vicki Chelst Turner, Jim Keppler, Maggie Galloway, Susanne Flother, Paula McLain, Pamela Redmond, Patti Callahan Henry, Ron Block, Carol Barnett, Janice Molinari, Jane Windsor, Alison Hutchens, Kathleen Beebout, Deb Nies, Angela Hynes, Charity Nebbe, Steve Boss, Lisa O. Stearns, Jenn DePersis, Debbie Griffle, Chris Chambers, Molly Moser, Matt Michael, and so many, many others that the list would be longer than this book! Whether you encouraged me before I left, cheered me on during my travels, welcomed me back upon my return, read all or parts of my manuscript, or provided moral support throughout the writing process, I appreciate you! I also appreciate those who tested the pie recipes at the eleventh hour: Connie Sherman, Kay Compton, Marlyn Hoksbergen, Judith Evnen, Carolyn Solomon, Hattie Peck, Vernita Salinas, Kim Losen, and Sarah Hardin. You turned a task that I was dreading into a joyful, community-building event—reinforcing the spirit of pie!

ALL AROUND THE WORLD: Thank you to the friends and followers on social media. I may have a love-hate relationship with Facebook, but without it, I would never have made some of the global connections I did. The interactions I had with all of you on the site—your comments, "likes," invitations, encouragement, tips, and suggestions—made me feel less alone during my travels.

For generously contributing to my travel fund: Dianne Patterson, Al Soltow, Joseph Pietras, Robert Volland, Linda Hanson, Benjamin Davis, Jean Luadzers, Carla Dudeck, Douglas Arenberg, Doris Elkins, and everyone who bought World Piece T-shirts and aprons. (World Piece merchandise is still available through my website.)

Alice Martell is the loveliest of literary agents. Thank you for believing in this book and its message. For the invaluable editing help, as well as meaningful friendship: Kee Kee Buckley, Jeanne Ambrose, and Mike Lord—and Emily Sandack, who is the best copy editor ever. I can't bear to think of how this book might have looked without all of you! Dave Pittman, I'm still using your charming hand-drawn pie logo. And a special shout-out to Kris Verdeck for the "Finish the Fucking Book" plaque that hung above my desk until I made it to the last page. I sent it on to another writer with instructions that when she's done, she has to pass it on to yet another writer.

Lastly, my gratitude and love for Doug Seyb is beyond measure. I couldn't have done any part of this without you.

ABOUT THE AUTHOR

Beth M. Howard is the author of four books, including *Making Piece: A Memoir of Love, Loss, and Pie* and the cookbook, *Ms. American Pie*. She has written for *The New York Times*, *Real Simple*, and *Country Living*, among many other publications. She is a regular commentator for Tri States Public Radio in Macomb, Illinois, and has given a TEDx Talk on the healing powers of pie.

From 2010 to 2014, she lived in the iconic American Gothic House in Eldon, Iowa, where she ran the Pitchfork Pie Stand. Her story has been featured on CBS *This Morning*, CNN's *Anderson Cooper 360°*, BBC, NPR, the Hallmark Channel, the History Channel, in the *Los Angeles Times*, *Better Homes & Gardens*, and more. She divides her time between Iowa and Los Angeles, and continues to write, bake pie, and advocate for peace.

Her website is www.theworldneedsmorepie.com.

Made in USA - North Chelmsford, MA
1356694_9781732672567
01.31.2023 1618